China's Econ
and the
Maoist Strategy

China's Economy and the Maoist Strategy

John G. Gurley

Monthly Review Press
New York and London

Library of Congress Cataloging in Publication Data
Gurley, John G
    China's economy and the Maoist strategy.
    Bibliography: p.
    1. China—Economic conditions—Addresses, essays,
lecures. 2. China—Economic policy—Addresses, essays,
lectures. 3. Mao, Tse-tung, 1893- 4. Capitalism—
Addresses, essays, lectures. I. Title.
HC427.9.G87   330.9′51′05   ′76-26314
ISBN 0-85345-395-0

Monthly Review Press
62 West 14th Street, New York, N.Y. 10011
47 Red Lion Street, London WC1R 4PF

Manufactured in the United States of America

10 9 8 7 6 5 4 3 2 1

Contents

v

Preface

These essays may interest both China experts and professional economists. But most of them were not written with those two groups foremost in mind. Instead, I have tried to address myself primarily to people who, while not pretending to such expertise, still want to know something about the extent of economic progress in China and the reasons for it. I would be especially pleased if this book were read by people in underdeveloped countries who may be able to improve their own lives one of these days partly through knowledge about China's dramatic transformation. Nevertheless, I have written the essays as an economist, using critical economic reasoning, which is expressed, I hope, in something resembling the English language.

The first essay was published in E. Friedman and M. Selden, eds., *America's Asia* (New York: Pantheon, 1969); in *The Center Magazine*, May 1970; and subsequently in several other places, including the *Monthly Review*, February 1971. It is included here because it presents an overall view of Mao's strategy and aims in developing the economy of China, and because it contrasts Mao's economics with our own bourgeois theory. Accordingly, it serves as a readable introduction to the topic of the book.

The second essay, on the formation of Mao's economic strategy, was written during the summers of 1973 and 1974 and was published in the *Monthly Review*, July-August 1975. Its purpose is to describe and explain the formation of Mao's views on economic development prior to 1949—how those views were fashioned from both theory and practice. The first two essays should provide a good introduction to the potentially fruitful ways in which Mao and his followers perceive the processes of economic development.

The third essay surveys China's economy from 1840 to the present through the medium of book reviews. It was originally written in 1966–1967, when I was a fellow at the Center for Advanced Study in the Behavioral Sciences. After having been put aside for seven years, it has finally been resuscitated with extensive revisions, additions, and deletions. While several of the book reviews have been published previously, the essay as a whole appears here for the first time.

The next piece is the bulk of a chapter from my recent book *Challengers to Capitalism: Marx, Lenin, and Mao* (San Francisco: San Francisco Book Co., 1976). Instead of the grand sweep and the fine detail of the previous essay, this offering provides in relatively few pages the outstanding features of the major economic programs of the Chinese Communists from 1949 to 1974. Readers who are in a hurry to find out what actually happened after 1949 might turn to this essay first.

The fifth essay was written for a Ford Foundation conference held in Ibadan, Nigeria, in April 1973. In it I set forth what the Chinese had accomplished in rural development since 1949 and explained how their achievements and failures might be helpful to the efforts of other underdeveloped countries. The essay was published in Edgar O. Edwards, ed., *Employment in Developing Nations* (New York: Columbia University Press, 1974), and in *World Development*, July-August 1975.

In the following essay I use what I know about financial theory to analyze the various roles of China's financial institutions and practices, both before and after liberation. Some of the analysis is based on what I learned during a visit to China in August 1972, when the group I was with had an opportunity to interview officials of the Ministry of Commerce in Peking and of the People's Bank of China in Canton.

In the next essay, I explain Mao's views of economists (not flattering!) and the Maoist position on such things as bourgeois markets, prices, and profit motives. This piece may appear more fun than instructive, but I believe it contains many of the most serious objections that Maoists have to capitalism. Neither this nor the previous essay has been published before.

Finally, I ask the question, Is the Chinese model diffusible? My answer is mostly negative—until, that is, oppressed peoples elsewhere carry out their own revolutions and so put themselves in a position to learn from China's development experiences and to implement whatever aspects of those experiences they consider suitable for their own countries.

Altogether, these essays should give the reader a reasonable account of the progress of the Chinese economy from 1840 to the present, especially from 1949 onward, and an understanding of Mao's economic strategy and the ways it has been translated into policies. They do not cover everything, but the large gaps will become obvious to readers, who can fill them in by reading some of the books they mention and discuss.

Yvette Gurley spent many hours attempting to enhance the lucidity of these essays and to impart some grace to them. If readers detect those qualities, they now know their benefactor.

1

Maoist Economic Development: The New "Man" in the New China

While capitalist and Maoist processes of economic development have several elements in common, the differences between the two approaches are nevertheless many and profound. It is certainly not evident that one approach or the other is always superior, either in means or ends. What is evident, however, is that most studies by American economists of Chinese economic development are based on the assumption of capitalist superiority, and so China has been dealt with as though it were simply an underdeveloped United States—an economy that "should" develop along capitalist lines and that "should" forget all that foolishness about Marxism, Mao's thought, great leaps, and cultural revolutions, and get on with the job of investing its savings efficiently. This unthinking acceptance by American economists of the view that there is no development like capitalist development has resulted in studies of China that lack insight.

The practice of capitalism has not, of course, met the ideal specification for it as theorized by Adam Smith. In general, the theory holds that an economy can develop most rapidly if every person, whether as entrepreneur, worker, or consumer, is able to pursue his own self-interest in competitive markets without undue interference from government. Progress is best promoted, not by government, but by entrepreneurs owning the material means of production, whose activities, guided by the profit motive, reflect consumers' demands for various goods and services. Labor productivity is enhanced by material incentives and the division of labor (specialization); economic progress is made within an environment of law and order, harmony of interests, and stability. It is by these means that economic development, according to the theory, can best be attained, and its attainment can best be measured by the national output.

In practice, many markets have been more monopolistic than competitive, government has interfered in numerous and extensive ways in competitive market processes in pursuit of greater equity in income distribution, higher employment of labor, and better allocation of economic resources. Capitalism of the individualist, competitive type has to some extent given way in most parts of the industrial-capitalist world to a state welfare capitalism, in which government plays a larger role and private entrepreneurs and consumers somewhat smaller ones than those envisaged by Adam Smith and his disciples. Despite these departures from the ideal model of capitalism, however, it is fair to say that the main driving force of the capitalist system remains private entrepreneurs who own the means of production, and that competition among them is still widespread and worldwide.

There is no doubt that capitalist development, whatever importance its departures from the Smithian model have had, has been highly successful in raising living standards for large numbers of people. It has been relatively efficient in using factors of production in ways best designed to provide all the goods that consumers by and large have demanded. It has also encouraged new ways of doing things—innovative activity and technological advances.

At the same time, however, there is a heavy emphasis in capitalist development—as there now is throughout most of the world—on raising the national output, on producing "things" in ever-increasing amounts. Implicit is the view that human beings are merely an input, a factor of production, a means to an end. Moreover, capitalist development has almost always been uneven in several crucial ways—in its alternating periods of boom and bust; in enriching some people thousands of times more than others; in developing production facilities with much more care than it has devoted to the welfare of human beings and their environment; in fostering lopsided development, both in terms of geographic location within a country and, especially in low-income countries, in terms of a narrow range of outputs, such as in one- or two-crop economies. The lopsided character of capitalist development has been evident historically in those nations that today have advanced industrial economies, but it is especially evident in the underdeveloped countries (with their mixture of feudal and capitalist features) that are tied in to the international capitalist system—those countries that, by being receptive to free enterprise and foreign capital, regardless of whether they are also receptive to freedom, are in the "free world."

This lopsidedness shows itself most markedly, of course, in the matter of trade. As satellites to the advanced capitalist countries, the underdeveloped regions supply raw materials, agricultural products, minerals, and oil, and receive in return manufactured and processed goods as well as basic food items. Much more trade takes place between the underdeveloped and the advanced capitalist countries than among the underdeveloped countries themselves. One consequence of this is the poor transportation within South America and Africa—while there are good highways or railroads running from mines, plantations, and oil fields to the seaports, it remains difficult to travel from one part of the continent to another.

The economic development of these poor capitalist countries is lopsided in many other ways, too. A few cities in each of these countries, with their airports, hotels, nightclubs, and light industries, are often built up to the point where they resemble the most modern metropolis in advanced industrial countries—but the rural areas, comprising most of the country and containing most of the people, are largely untouched by modernization. Industry, culture, entertainment, education, and wealth are highly concentrated in urban centers; a traveler to most of the poor "free world" countries, by flying to the main cities, can land in the middle of the twentieth century, but by going thirty miles out into the country in any direction he will find himself back in the Middle Ages. Education is usually for the elite and stresses the superiority of the educated over the uneducated, the superiority of urban over rural life, of mental over manual labor. The burden of economic development, which is essentially a restraint on consumption, is shared most inequitably among the people; the differences between rich and poor are staggering—they are nothing less than the differences between unbelievable luxury and starvation.

While some of these characteristics are not peculiar to the poor countries tied to the international capitalist system (they can be found in the Soviet socialist bloc, too), and while some are related more to feudalism than to capitalism, much of the lopsided development is intimately connected with the profit motive. The key link between the two is the fact that it is almost always most profitable, from a private-business point of view, to build on the best. Thus a firm locates a new factory in an urban center near existing ones, rather than out in the hinterlands, in order to gain access to supplies, a skilled labor force, and high-income consumers; to maximize profits, it hires the best, most qualified workers; a bank extends loans to those who are already successful; an educational system devotes its best efforts to the superior students, and universities, imbued with the private-business ethic of "efficiency," offer education to those best prepared and most able; promoters locate cultural centers for those best able to appreciate and afford them; in the interests of efficiency and comparative advantage, businesses are induced to specialize (in cocoa or peanuts or coffee)—to build on what they have always done best.

This pursuit of efficiency and private profits through building on the best has led in some areas to impressive aggregate growth rates, but almost everywhere in the international capitalist world it has favored only a relative few at the expense of the many, and in poor capitalist countries it has left most in stagnant backwaters. Capitalist development, even when most successful, is always a trickle-down development.

The Maoists' disagreement with the capitalist view of economic development is profound. Their emphases, values, and aspirations are quite different from those of capitalist economists. Maoist economic development occurs within the context of central planning, public ownership of industries, and agricultural cooperatives or communes. While decision-making is decentralized to some extent, decisions regarding investment versus consumption, foreign trade, allocation of material inputs and the labor supply, prices of various commodities—these and more are essentially in the hands of the state. The profit motive is officially discouraged from assuming an important role in the allocation of resources, and material incentives, while still prevalent, are downgraded.

Perhaps the most striking difference between the capitalist and Maoist views concerns goals. Maoists believe that while a principal aim of nations should be to raise the level of material welfare of the population, this should be done only within the context of the development of human beings, encouraging them to realize fully their manifold creative powers. And it should be done only on an egalitarian basis—that is, on the basis that development is not worth much unless everyone rises together: no one is to be left behind, either economically or culturally. Indeed, Maoists believe that rapid economic development is not likely to occur *unless* everyone rises together. Development as a trickle-down process is therefore rejected by Maoists, and so they reject any strong emphasis on profit motives and efficiency criteria that lead to lopsided growth.

In Maoist eyes, economic development can best be attained by giving prominence to people rather than "things."

Recently, capitalist economists have begun to stress the importance for economic growth of "investment in human capital"— that is, investment in general education, job training, and better health. It has been claimed that expenditures in these directions have had a large "payoff" in terms of output growth. Although this might seem to represent a basic change in their concept of workers in the development process, actually it does not. "Investment in human capital" means that economic resources are invested for the purpose of raising the skill and the educational and health levels of labor, not as an end in itself but as a means of increasing productivity. These economists are concerned with the "payoff" to investment in human capital, this payoff being the profit that can be made from such an expenditure. Indeed, the very term *human capital* indicates what they have in mind:

people are another capital good, an input in the productive engine that grinds out commodities; if one invests in people, they may become more productive and return a handsome profit to the investor—whether the investor is the state, a private capitalist, or the laborers themselves. Thus the preoccupation of capitalist economists is still with people as a means and not as an end.

The Maoists' emphasis, however, is quite different. First of all, while they recognize the role played by education and health in the production process, they place heavy emphasis on the transformation of ideas, the making of the communist human being. Ideology, of course, may be considered as part of education in the broadest sense, but it is surely not the part that capitalist economists have in mind when they evaluate education's contribution to economic growth. Moreover, ideological training does not include the acquisition of particular skills or the training of specialists—as education and job training in capitalist countries tend to do. The Maoists believe that economic development can best be promoted by breaking down specialization, by dismantling bureaucracies, and by undermining the other centralizing and divisive tendencies that give rise to experts, technicians, authorities, and bureaucrats remote from or manipulating "the masses." Finally, the Maoists seem perfectly willing to pursue the goal of transforming people even though it is temporarily at the expense of some economic growth. Indeed, it is clear that Maoists will not accept economic development, however rapid, if it is based on the capitalist principles of sharp division of labor and sharp (meaning unsavory or selfish) practices.

The proletarian world view, which Maoists believe must replace that of the bourgeoisie, stresses that only through struggle can progress be made; that selflessness and unity of purpose will release a huge reservoir of enthusiasm, energy, and creativeness; that active participation by "the masses" in decision-making will provide them with the knowledge to channel their energy most productively; and that the elimination of specialization will not only increase workers' and peasants' willingness to work hard for the various goals of society but will also increase their ability to do this by adding to their knowledge and awareness of the world around them.

It is an essential part of Maoist thinking that progress is not made by peace and quietude, by letting things drift and playing safe, or, in the words of Mao Tse-tung, by standing for "unprincipled peace, thus giving rise to a decadent, philistine attitude." Progress is made through struggle, when new talents emerge and knowledge advances in leaps. Only through continuous struggle is the level of consciousness of people raised, and in the process they gain not only understanding but happiness.

Mao sees individuals as engaged in a fierce class struggle—the bourgeoisie against the proletariat—the outcome of which, at least in the short run, is far from certain. The proletarian world outlook can win only if it enters tremendous ideological class struggles.

Maoists believe that each person should be devoted to "the masses" rather than to his own pots and pans, and should serve the world proletariat rather than, as the *Peking Review* has put it, reaching out with "grasping hands everywhere to seek fame, material gain, power, position, and limelight." They think that if a person is selfish he or she will resist criticisms and suggestions, tend to become bureaucratic and elitist, and will not work as hard for community or national goals as for narrow, selfish ones. In any case, a selfish person is not an admirable person. Thus Maoists de-emphasize material incentives, for these are the very manifestation of a selfish, bourgeois society. While selflessness is necessary to imbue people with energy and the willingness to work hard, Maoists believe that this is not sufficient; they must also have the ability as well. And such ability comes from active participation—from seeing and doing. To gain knowledge, people must be awakened from their half slumber, encouraged to mobilize themselves and to take conscious action to elevate and liberate themselves. When they actively participate in decision-making, when they take an interest in state affairs, when they dare to do new things, when they become good at presenting facts and reasoning things out, when they criticize and test and experiment scientifically—having discarded myths and superstitions—when they are aroused, then, says the *Peking Review*, "the socialist initiative latent in the masses [will] burst out with volcanic force and a rapid change [will take] place in production."

Finally, if people become "selfless," there will be discipline and unity of will, for these "cannot be achieved if relations among comrades stem from selfish interests and personal likes and dislikes." If people become "active," then along with extensive democracy they will gain true consciousness and ultimately freedom, in the Marxian sense of intelligent action. Together, selflessness and active participation will achieve ideal combinations of opposites: "a vigorous and lively political situation . . . is taking shape throughout our country, in which there is both centralism and democracy, both discipline and freedom, both unity of will and personal ease of mind."

Maoists believe that workers and peasants will accept Marxism-Leninism, for it is the ideological reflection of the reality of the proletariat. The feudal and bourgeois classes, on the other hand, will not readily accept it, and hence protracted struggles against them will be necessary. Within the framework of Marxism-Leninism, individuals are involved in a dynamic process of gaining freedom, in the sense of becoming fully aware of the world around them, responding rationally to it, and engaging in active decision-making in regard to their own lives. Outside of the framework, individuals are subjected to the dictatorship of the proletariat and, it is hoped, will in time be transformed into proletarians. Mao's thought, built on Marxism-Leninism, is meant to lead to true freedom and to unity of will based on a proletarian viewpoint.

For Marx, specialization and bureaucratization were the very antithesis of communism. People could not be free or truly human until these manifestations of alienation were eliminated, allowing them to become all-around communist beings. Maoists, too, have been intensely concerned with this goal, specifying it in terms of eliminating the distinction between town and countryside, mental and manual labor, and workers and peasants. The realization of the universal being is not automatically achieved by altering the forces of production, by the socialist revolution.

Rather, it can be achieved only after the most intense and unrelenting ideological efforts to raise the consciousness of the masses through the creative study and creative use of Mao's thought. Old ideas, customs, and habits hang on long after the material base of the economy has been radically changed, and it takes one mighty effort after another to wipe out the bourgeois superstructure and replace it with the proletarian world outlook. This transformation of the "subjective world" will then have a tremendous impact on the "objective world."

In many ways, Maoist ideology rejects the capitalist principle of building on the best, even though the principle cannot help but be followed to some extent in any effort at economic development. However, the Maoist departures from the principle are the important thing. While capitalism, in their view, strives one-sidedly for efficiency in producing goods, Maoism, while also seeking some high degree of efficiency, at the same time and in numerous ways builds on "the worst": experts are pushed aside in favor of decision-making by "the masses"; new industries are established in rural areas; the educational system favors the disadvantaged; expertise (and hence work proficiency in a narrow sense) is discouraged; new products are domestically produced rather than being imported "more efficiently"; the growth of cities as centers of industrial and cultural life is discouraged; steel, for a time, is made by "everyone" instead of by only the much more efficient steel industry.

Of course, Maoists build on "the worst" not because they take great delight in lowering economic efficiency; rather, their stated aims are to involve everyone in the development process, to pursue development without leaving a single person behind, to achieve a balanced growth rather than a lopsided one. Yet if Maoism were only that, we could simply state that, while Maoist development may be much more equitable than capitalist efforts, it is surely less efficient and thus less rapid; efficiency is being sacrificed to some extent for equity. But that would miss the more important aspects of Maoist ideology, which holds that the resources devoted to bringing everyone into the socialist development process—the effort spent on building on "the worst"—will eventually pay off not only in economic ways by enormously raising labor productivity but, more important, by creating a society of truly free human beings who respond intelligently to the world around them, and who are happy.

The sharp contrast between the economic-development views of capitalist economists and those of the Chinese Communists cannot be denied; their two worlds are quite different. The difference is not mainly between being Chinese and being American, although that is surely part of it, but between being Maoists in a Marxist-Leninist tradition and being present-day followers of the economics first fashioned by Adam Smith and later reformed by John Maynard Keynes. Whatever the ignorance and misunderstanding on the Chinese side regarding the doctrines of capitalist economics, it is clear that many Western economic experts on China have shown little interest in, and almost no understanding of, Maoist economic development. Most of the economic researchers have approached China as though it were little more than a series of tables in a yearbook which could be analyzed by Western economic methods and judged by capitalist values. The result has been a series of unilluminating studies, largely statistical or institutional in method, and lacking analysis of the really distinctive and interesting features of Maoist development.

Like seagulls following the wake of a ship, economists pursue numbers. The main concentration of numbers pertaining to the economy of Communist China is in *Ten Great Years*, which was published in September 1959 by the State Statistical Bureau. This volume contains a wealth of data on almost all phases of economic activity, and so it has become one of the main sources for much of the empirical work on Chinese economic development. But throughout the 1950s economic data were published in hundreds of other sources—in official reports, statistical handbooks, economics books, and articles—so that altogether massive information, of varying degrees of reliability, became available on the first decade or so of China's development efforts. After 1958, however, the release of aggregate data just about came to a halt, so little research on the 1960s has been done by economists outside of China. The data of the 1950s continue to be worked over, adjusted, and refined, though there is no longer much more that can be said about them.

Much of this research has been concerned in one way or another with China's national output—its absolute size; its rates of growth; its components, such as agricultural and industrial output, or consumption and investment goods; the extent to which national output has been affected by international trade and Soviet aid; and the planning methods utilized in its production.

There are, of course, scores of studies, though mostly of an empirical nature, on specialized aspects of the economic process. A few Western economists have actually visited China in recent years and have returned with much information, but mainly of a qualitative nature.

Economic research on China suffers from an ailment common to most of economics—a narrow empiricism. Thus most of the research studies of the Chinese economy deal with very small segments of the development process, and within these tiny areas the researchers busy themselves with data series—adding up the numbers, adjusting them in numerous ways, deflating them for price changes, and doing a lot of other fussy statistical work. Each economist tills a small plot intensively, gaining highly specialized knowledge in the process, finally ending up an expert in very cramped quarters. There are not many economists in the China field who try to see Chinese economic development as a whole, as "the comprehensive totality of the historical process." If the truth is the whole, as Hegel claimed, most economic experts on China must be so far from the truth that it is hardly worthwhile listening to them.

Moreover, it is often painful. Even a casual reader of the economic research on Communist China cannot help but notice that many of the researchers are not happy—to say the least— with the object of their investigation. This is immediately noticeable because it is so very unusual in economics. Ordinarily, economists are utterly fascinated and almost infatuated with their special areas of study—even with such an esoteric one as "Game Theory Applied to Nonlinear Development." But not so our China experts. Indeed, it is quite apparent that many of them consider China to be, not the Beloved, but the Enemy. And in dealing with the Enemy, their research often reveals very strong, and undisguised, biases against China.

These biases show up in a variety of ways, from such trivial things as changing Peking to Peiping (à la Dean Rusk), which reveals a wish that the Communists weren't there; to the frequent use of emotive words (the Communists are not dedicated but "obsessed"; leaders are "bosses"; a decision not to release data is described as "a sullen statistical silence"; the extension of the statistical system becomes "an extention of its tentacles further into the economy"); to the attribution of rather sinister motives to ordinary economic and cultural policies (education and literacy are promoted for the purpose of spreading evil Marxian doctrines; economic development is pursued for the principal purpose of gaining military strength for geographic expansion—which is the theme of W. W. Rostow's book *The Prospects for Communist China*); to dire forecasts of imminent disaster based on little more than wishful thinking; and finally to data manipulation of the most questionable sort.

This strong propensity to treat China as the Enemy has led to some grossly distorted accounts of China's economic progress. The picture that is presented by these studies as a whole is one in which China, while making some progress for a time in certain areas, is just barely holding on to economic life. It is a picture of a China always close to famine, making little headway while the rest of the world moves ahead, being involved in irrational economic policies, and offering little reason for hope that the lives of its people will be improved. Our China experts, further-more, know what is wrong, and that, in a word, is communism. They seldom fail to pass judgment on some aspect or other of Chinese economic development, and this judgment is almost invariably capitalist-oriented. Thus national planning and government-controlled prices cannot be good because they do not meet the criteria of consumer sovereignty and competitive markets; communes violate individualism and private property; ideological campaigns upset order and harmony; the de-emphasis on material incentives violates human nature and so reduces individual initiative and economic growth; the breakdown of specialization lowers workers' productivity. This sort of thing pervades much of the economic literature on China.

Given all this—the narrow specialized studies that are sometimes useful but not often enlightening, the distortions by omission or commission, the capitalist-oriented approaches and assessments, not to mention those evaluations of Communist China that were inspired by a strong allegiance to Chiang Kaishek—given all this, it is little wonder that a fair picture of China's economic progress seldom gets presented. Seldom, not never: Barry Richman's book *Industrial Society in Communist China*, Carl Riskin's work—for example, in *The Cultural Revolution: 1967 in Review*—and several other researchers do approach Maoist theory in a serious way (though Richman and others reject it) by dealing with it as the ideology of the proletariat.

The truth is that China over the past two decades has made very remarkable economic advances (though not steadily) on almost all fronts. The basic, overriding economic fact about China is that for twenty years it has fed, clothed, and housed everyone, has kept them healthy, and has educated most. Millions have not starved; sidewalks and streets have not been covered with multitudes of sleeping, begging, hungry, and illiterate human beings; millions are not disease-ridden. To find such deplorable conditions, one does not look to China these days but, rather, to India, Pakistan, and almost anywhere else in the underdeveloped world. These facts are so basic, so fundamentally important, that they completely dominate China's economic picture, even if one grants all of the erratic and irrational policies alleged by its numerous critics.

The Chinese—all of them—now have what is in effect an insurance policy against pestilence, famine, and other disasters. In this respect, China has outperformed every underdeveloped country in the world; and, even with respect to the richest one, it would not be farfetched to claim that there has been less malnutrition due to maldistribution of food in China over the past twenty years than there has been in the United States. If this comes close to the truth, the reason lies not in China's grain output far surpassing its population growth—for it has not—but, rather, in the development of institutions to distribute food evenly among the population. It is also true, however, that China has just had six consecutive bumper grain crops (wheat and rice) that have enabled it to reduce wheat imports and greatly increase rice exports. On top of this, there have been large gains in the supplies of eggs, vegetables, fruits, poultry, fish, and meat. In fact, China today exports more food than it imports. The Chinese are in a much better position now than ever before to ward off natural disasters, as there has been significant progress in irrigation, flood control, and water conservation. The use of chemical fertilizers is increasing rapidly, the volume now being over ten times that of the early 1950s; there have been substantial gains in the output of tractors, pumps, and other farm implements; and much progress has been made in the control of plant disease and in crop breeding.

In education, there has been a major breakthrough. All urban children and a great majority of rural children have attended primary schools, and enrollments in secondary schools and in higher education are large, in proportion to the population, compared with those of pre-Communist days. If "school" is extended to include as well all part-time, part-study education, spare-time education, and the study groups organized by the communes, factories, street organizations, and the army, then there are schools everywhere in China.

China's gains in the medical and public-health fields are perhaps the most impressive of all. The gains are attested by many fairly recent visitors to China. For example, G. Leslie Wilcox, a Canadian doctor, a few years ago visited medical colleges, hospitals, and research institutes, and reported in "Observations on Medical Practices" (*Bulletin of the Atomic Scientists*, June 1966) that everywhere he found good equipment, high medical standards, excellent medical care—almost all comparable to Canadian standards. As William Y. Chen, a member of the U.S. Public Health Service, wrote in "Medicine in Public Health" (*Sciences in Communist China*), "The prevention and control of many infectious and parasitic diseases which have ravaged [China] for generations" was a "most startling accomplishment." He noted, too, that "the improvement of general environmental sanitation and the practice of personal hygiene, both in the cities and in the rural areas, were also phenomenal."

While all these gains were being made, the Chinese were devoting an unusually large amount of resources to industrial output. China's industrial production has risen on the average by at least 11 percent per year since 1950, which is an exceptionally high growth rate for an underdeveloped country. Furthermore, industrial progress is not likely to be retarded in the future by any lack of natural resources, for China is richly endowed and is right now one of the world's four top producers of coal, iron ore, mercury, tin, tungsten, magnesite, salt, and antimony. In recent years, China has made large gains in the production of coal, iron, steel, chemical fertilizers, and oil. In fact, since the huge discoveries at the Tach'ing oil field, China has become self-sufficient in oil and has offered to export some to Japan.

From the industrial, agricultural, and other gains, I would estimate that China's real GNP has risen on the average by at least 6 percent per year since 1949, or by at least 4 percent on a per capita basis. This may not seem high, but it is a little better than the Soviet Union did over a comparable period (1928–1940), much better than England's record during its century of industrialization (1750–1850), when its income per capita grew at one-half percent per year, perhaps a bit better than Japan's performance from 1878 to 1936, certainly much superior to France's 1 percent record from 1800 to 1870, far better than India's 1.3 percent growth from 1950 to 1967; more important, it is much superior to the postwar record of almost all underdeveloped countries in the world.

This is a picture of an economy richly endowed in natural resources, but whose people are still very poor, making substantial gains in industrialization, moving ahead more slowly in agriculture, raising education and health levels dramatically, turning out increasing numbers of scientists and engineers, expanding the volume of foreign trade and the variety of products traded, and making startling progress in the development of nuclear weapons. This is a truer picture, I believe, than the bleak one drawn by some of our China experts.

The failure of many economic experts on China to tell the

story of its economic development accurately and fully is bad enough. Even worse has been the general failure to deal with China on its own terms, within the framework of its own goals and its own methods for attaining those goals, or even to recognize the possible validity of those goals. Communist China is certainly not a paradise, but it is now engaged in perhaps the most interesting economic and social experiment ever attempted, in which tremendous efforts are being made to achieve an egalitarian development, an industrial development without dehumanization, one that involves everyone and affects everyone. All these efforts seem not to have affected Western economists, who have proceeded, with their income accounts and slide rules and free-enterprise values, to measure and judge. One of the most revealing developments in the China field is the growing belief among the economic experts that further research is hardly worthwhile in view of the small amount of economic statistics that has come out of China since 1958. Apparently, it does not matter that 775 million people are involved in a gigantic endeavor to change their environment, their economic and social institutions, their standard of living, and themselves; that never before have such potentially important economic and social experiments been carried out; that voluminous discussions of these endeavors by the Maoists are easily available. No, if GNP data are not forthcoming, if numbers can't be added up and adjusted, then the economy must be hardly worth bothering about.

What can be done? Probably not very much until a substantial number of younger economists become interested in China. It is a hopeful sign that many young economists are now breaking away from the stultifying atmosphere of present-day "neoclassical" economics and are trying to refashion the discipline into political economy, as it once was, so as to take account of the actual world and not the world of highly abstract models, scholastic debates, and artificial assumptions—all designed to justify the existing state of things and to accept without question the rather narrow, materialistic goals of capitalist society. This reformulation by the young will have to take place first, but once this task is well along, China is bound to be attractive to many of these "new" economists. Only then will we begin to get a substantial amount of research on China that makes sense.

The research that would make sense is any that takes Maoism seriously as a model of economic development, in terms both of its objectives and of the means employed to attain those objectives. A thoughtful consideration of Maoism means paying proper attention to Marxism-Leninism as well as to the Chinese past of Maoists. The Marxist-Leninist goal of the communist individual within a classless society in which each person works according to his ability and consumes according to his needs—this goal of the Maoists should be taken seriously in any economic analysis of what is now going on.

There is a core of development theory that would probably be accepted by both the capitalist and Maoist sides—that economic growth can be attained by increasing the amounts of labor, capital goods, and land used in production, by improving the quality of these factors of production, by combining them in more efficient ways and inspiring labor to greater efforts, and by taking advantage of economies of scale. Now, Maoism undoubtedly affects every one of these ingredients of economic growth, and often in ways quite different from the capitalist impact. For example, it is likely that Maoist ideology discourages consumption and encourages saving and investment, and so promotes the growth of the capital stock; it does this by preventing the rise of a high-consuming "middle class," by fostering the Maoist virtues of plain and simple living and devoting one's life to helping others rather than accumulating "pots and pans."

As another example, it is possible that Maoist economic development, by de-emphasizing labor specialization and reliance on experts and technicians, reduces the quality of the labor force and so slows the rate of economic growth. On the other hand, as Adam Smith once suggested, labor specialization, while increasing productivity in some narrow sense, is often at the expense of the worker's general intelligence and understanding. It was Smith's view that the person "whose whole life is spent in performing a few simple operations . . . generally becomes as stupid and ignorant as it is possible for a human creature to become." The difference between the most dissimilar of human beings, according to Smith, is not so much the cause of the division of labor as the effect of it. Consequently, while an economy might gain from the division of labor in some small sense, it could lose in the larger sense by creating people who are little more than passive and unreasoning robots. A major aim of the Maoists is to transform people from this alienated state into fully aware and participating members of society. The emphasis on "Reds" rather than experts is just one part of this transformation which, it is felt, will release "an atom bomb" of talents and energy and enable labor productivity to take great leaps.

In addition to this argument, which is based on the Maoists' interpretation of their own history and experience, it is also possible that the "universal being" in an underdeveloped economy would provide more flexibility to the economy. If most people could perform many jobs—manual and intellectual, urban and rural—moderately well, the economy might be better able to cope with sudden and large changes; it could with little loss in efficiency mobilize its labor force for a variety of tasks. Furthermore, since experience in one job carries over to others, workers might be almost as productive, in the sense of job proficiency, in any one of them as they would be if they specialized—a peasant who has spent some months in a factory can more easily repair farm equipment, and so on. Finally, a Maoist economy might generate more useful information than a specialist one, and so lead to greater creativity and productivity. When each person is a narrow specialist, communication among different kinds of specialists is not highly meaningful. When, on the other hand, each person has basic knowledge about many lines of activity, the experiences of one person enrich the potentialities of many others.

The point is that this issue—which, I should stress, includes not only labor productivity (that is, the development of material things by human beings) but also the development of human beings themselves—this issue of generalists versus specialists, communists versus experts, the masses versus bureaucrats, or whatever, is not to be laughed away, as it has been, in effect, by some China experts. How human beings in an industrial society should relate to machines and to one another in seeking happiness and real meaning in their lives has surely been one of the most important problems of the modern age. There is also another basic issue here: whether modern industrial society, capitalist or socialist, does in fact diminish the essential powers of human beings, their capacity for growth in many dimensions, even though it does allocate them "efficiently" and increase their skills as specialized inputs. Is human nature given, say, in Lockean fashion, so that people must forever react passively to outside forces, simply adjusting to disequilibrium forces from without? Or is human nature essentially subject to change, as Marxists allege, so that people, through revolutionary practice, can shake off their oppressors and their passivity and transform themselves into active, powerful, highly productive agents? If the latter, how are these powers released?

Maoists claim that the powers exist and can be released. If they are right, the poor of the world will soon learn of it and be greatly affected; the imperialists of the world will also feel the shock waves.

2

The Formation
of Mao's Economic Strategy,
1927–1949

Since 1949, China's economic progress has been vigorous, not only in the central sectors of industry and agriculture but also in such diverse areas as military production, medical care, and education. China's economic achievements have elevated China to a world power, raised the living standards of the vast majority of the Chinese far above their pre-1949 levels, and given the Chinese people greater security in their daily lives by virtually eliminating famines and epidemics. Much of the economic advancement has been contributed by the women of China, whose own lives have accordingly been greatly improved.

A large share of the credit for these accomplishments belongs to Mao Tse-tung, who, from 1949 on, has shaped much of China's economic-development efforts. Mao's ideas about how his country should develop after liberation were fashioned from his voracious reading and practical experiences during the previous three decades. Those were the years in which his early economic theories and policies were formulated, both in the quiet contemplation of Marxian literature and in the fiery crucible of the Chinese revolution.

When Mao gained power in 1949, decades of economic experience lay behind him: in land reforms; cooperative and mutual-aid efforts; the regulation of prices, rents, and interest payments; and production campaigns. Unlike Lenin and the Bolsheviks, whose practical experiences with economic problems prior to 1917 were almost nil, Mao and his party were in a position at the very beginning to apply nationally what they had already achieved regionally. As it turned out, they had much more to learn, but what they had absorbed in their revolutionary days was generally put to good use.

This essay covers the formative years—1927 to 1949—of Mao's ideas on economic strategy. It attempts to explain the development of his economic theories and programs and thus to serve as a vehicle for a better understanding of the economic policies of China after 1949.

Revolution and Economics

The main objective of the Chinese Communists was to capture power from the ruling propertied classes in order to destroy the semicolonial and semifeudal basis of the country and on these ashes to build a socialist society in which the lives of workers and peasants would be noticeably improved. Until 1927, the Communists attempted to do this primarily by organizing urban workers around their immediate demands and by shaping these groups into a revolutionary force. The repeated failures of this policy led Mao Tse-tung and others to shift the focus of the movement to the countryside, where they established rural base areas. These bases were protected militarily and developed socially, politically, and economically, and from them the revolution was expected to spread across the land, back to the cities and the urban workers.[1]

The soviet areas, as the rural bases were called, were under almost constant military attack. They were first assaulted by Kuomintang forces in 1930, and in 1934, after four years of encirclement campaigns, the Kuomintang finally drove the Communists from their bases in Kiangsi, Fukien, and neighboring provinces and forced them into the Long March to the northwest. In this region, which centered on Shensi province, as well as in other areas, the Communists again had to defend themselves against Kuomintang military onslaughts and blockades and later against Japanese invaders. Thus, while military engagements were not the raison d'être of the Communists, such engagements came to occupy most of their time and energy and to become their number one problem. As a result, Mao has written more on military matters than on economic issues. In fact, the military guerrilla tactics he worked out strongly molded his view of how economic development should be contrived, the Great Leap Forward of 1958–1960 being a spectacular case in point.[2]

Despite this preoccupation with military affairs, Mao often asserted that such victories necessitated the support of the masses, which was best earned by improving their welfare through campaigns on the political, economic, and ideological fronts. As early as March 1929, in his prescient report on the peasant movement in Hunan province, Mao outlined the sequence that should be followed in conducting the coming struggles in the rural areas: first, win the political struggle, so that the landlords are completely overthrown; second, engage in the economic struggle in order to redistribute land to poor peasants and to solve their other economic problems; finally, eliminate other systems of authority (clan, supernatural, and so on) and their supporting ideologies of "natural" inequalities, superstition, and religion.[3] Economic successes themselves would produce not only peasant and worker supporters of the military front but also increasing material resources for these revolutionary battles. Economic victories, Mao insisted, were necessary for military victories.[4]

Mao castigated those comrades who felt that economic work was improvident, that it was possible in peaceful and tranquil times but should not divert their energies from the military front in perilous periods. Mao warned:

> If the workers and peasants become dissatisfied with their living conditions, will it not affect the expansion of our Red Army and the mobilization of the masses for the revolutionary war? Therefore it is utterly wrong to think that no economic construction should be undertaken in the midst of the revolutionary war.[5]

During the Anti-Japanese War (1937–1945), Mao urged productive efforts even in the guerrilla zones, which were Communist-controlled but unstable and fluid areas: "The army and the people in the guerrilla zones can and must conduct large-scale production campaigns. . . . War is not only a military and political contest but also an economic contest."[6]

The economic objective was to raise the enthusiasm and efficiency of the peasants so as to increase their labor productivity, and to do this largely by fashioning a more egalitarian and democratic society. To attain such a society, the Maoists proposed to alter the class structures of the areas they controlled by revolutionizing the ownership and use of land, by raising the political consciousness of the peasants through encouraging them to investigate land and wealth ownership, by introducing economic institutions that would stimulate cooperative rather than individualistic behavior, and by mobilizing into the labor force people who had hitherto been outside it, such as women, youth, vagabonds, bandits, and the unemployed. Thus the Maoists set their sights on large gains in economic output through decisive changes in the social relations of production, though these efforts became less radical after 1937, during the period of the second united front with the Kuomintang. In addition, the Maoists attempted by direct means to increase the productive forces in these areas: the quantity and quality of the labor supply, the stock of capital equipment, and the supply of natural resources. Although there was little progress along these lines in the 1927–1934 period, more was accomplished during the later Yenan years.[7] Finally, throughout the entire period, this economic program was buttressed by campaigns to change the ideology, habits, political institutions, and aspirations of the peasants—to alter essential elements of the superstructure. These campaigns culminated in the so-called Rectification Movement of 1942–1944 in Yenan, when Marxist theory as applied to China was formally taught to thousands of cadres and others at precisely the time when the base areas were being hit hardest by enemy military forces. In Mao's view, military victories required politically conscious cadres who could successfully carry out production campaigns.

The Productive Forces

It has long been Mao's belief that, although the ordinary saving-investment techniques are important in building up a society's productive forces, those forces can be greatly expanded mainly through the release of powerful latent energies and abilities of the masses of peasants and workers, and that this reservoir of energy can be liberated if oppressive social institutions are swept away, along with various systems of authority and their debilitating ideologies.

The "ordinary" economic processes of saving and investment are invoked essentially to gain increasing margins between total output and the consumption of that output, and to invest the differences in beneficial ways. These surpluses can be realized through increases in total output or through reductions in consumption. Although Mao at times advocated reductions in consumption, he generally urged expansion of output as the preferred policy—that is, all-out efforts to work harder and more effectively, spurred on by production campaigns. In that way, he indicated, both consumption and investment could be increased at the same time.

This preference was also revealed in his attitude toward the financial difficulties of an economy—such as monetary excesses, budget deficits, and inflation—that are often reflections of conflicts among groups over their respective shares of the national output. One solution for such financial maladies is to reduce the demands of the various groups for national output and, by so doing, enable the groups to get their budgets into better balance. Mao called this the "conservative way." He claimed that in the end financial difficulties could not be solved in this way; they could be solved only by production campaigns that achieved large increases in national output. Mao's concentration was on the expansion of output, on building up the productive forces, on "real" factors overcoming the financial ones. Answering his critics on this point, Mao stated:

> They do not know that while a good or a bad financial policy affects the economy, it is the economy that determines finance. Without a

well-based economy it is impossible to solve financial difficulties, and without a growing economy it is impossible to attain financial sufficiency. . . . Financial difficulties can be overcome only by down-to-earth and effective economic development. To neglect economic development and the opening up of sources of finance, and instead to hope for the solution of financial difficulties by curtailing indispensable expenditures, is a conservative notion which cannot solve any problems.[8]

Mao has continued through the years to fight against the "conservative notion" of cutting back, of hobbling along like a woman in bound feet; instead, he has called for upsurges, aiming high, and bigger and better efforts. When economic problems mount, Mao's response has almost always been to leap ahead on the production front.

Moreover, Mao's belief has been that to achieve large gains in the productive forces, mass participation in production campaigns is indispensable, not only by workers and peasants but also by the army and everyone else. Each group should not only perform its assigned tasks but should also become self-reliant in food, clothing, and other necessities. All should try to become proficient in several tasks at once. Mao realized that this violates the sacred principle of specialization—the theory that greater results come from finer divisions of labor—but he noted that when army units, for example, are engaged in "all three contests" (military, political, and economic), they accomplish their military duties much better for having taken part in political and economic work. Despite Mao's conviction, there were times when he seemed to be on the defensive in justifying his call for such universal abilities:

> In our circumstances, production by the army for its own support, though backward or retrogressive in form, is progressive in substance and of great historic significance. Formally speaking, we are violating the principle of division of labour. However, in our circumstances—the poverty and disunity of the country—what we are doing is progressive.[9]

What Mao visualized was the possibility that labor productivity could be raised dramatically when workers perform a variety of tasks to achieve self-sufficiency, even though each worker becomes somewhat less adept at each particular undertaking. The productivity gains would result from greater enthusiasm, the contribution of each task to the knowledge needed by the worker for other tasks, greater discipline, and improved relations among various groups of the population as they intermingle in the several projects.[10]

Despite these expectations, there was in fact no sustained progress during the early years (1927–1934). The rural areas were typically very backward, with a grossly inadequate infrastructure of roads, communications, and other facilities as well as stultifying feudal social relations. Military demands on the Communists were often too intense to permit them to give adequate attention to economic matters, and Communist control over the various areas seldom lasted long enough for economic programs to coalesce and mature.

Nevertheless, some programs to increase productive forces did succeed in part, especially after the Communists moved in 1929 from the primitive Chingkang Mountains area to a central base on the border of Kiangsi and Fukien, where they found higher land fertility and more resources.[11] The programs included efforts to generate additional saving through sales of economic-construction bonds and other securities, the imposition of progressive commercial and agricultural taxes, the accumulation of profits by army and state enterprises, and the confiscation or requisition of wealth from "feudal exploiters." Some of these funds were used for economic development. At the same time, the Maoists increased the size of the labor force through the mobilization of women and the requirement that army and government personnel engage in productive work whenever feasible. They also promoted trade with the White (Kuomintang) areas to increase supplies of necessities, brought additional land under cultivation, established small experimental farms and agricultural research schools, improved irrigation and grain storage facilities, and encouraged handicraft and small industrial establishments.[12]

But even so, economic conditions were not good in any of these areas, for the most part, and improvement, while evident, was slow. Mao stressed the poverty and difficulties on several occasions:

> Trade between the two areas [Red and White] has almost entirely ceased; necessities such as salt, cloth and medicines are scarce and costly, and agricultural products such as timber, tea and oil cannot be sent out, so that the peasants' cash income is cut off and the people as a whole are affected. [13]
>
> There has been a decline in production in many handicraft industries in the Red areas, notably tobacco-curing and paper-making. [14]
>
> The Red Army has to fight the enemy and to provision itself at one and the same time. It even lacks funds to pay the daily food allowance of five cents per person, which is provided in addition to grain; the soldiers are undernourished, many are ill, and the wounded in the hospitals are worse off. [15]

At other times Mao was more encouraged and called attention to the improved living conditions of the poor peasants. He observed that agricultural output usually dropped in the first year or two after a Red area was established, because of unsettled conditions, but that it picked up again later on. He cited instances of such output gains, and he also pointed to increases in living standards that resulted from declines in the prices of essential commodities. In January 1934, still heartened, he stated: "The living conditions of the peasants have been much improved. . . . In the past, many peasants lived on tree bark or grain husks for several months a year. This situation no longer prevails and there is no more starvation in the Soviet areas. The life of the peasants is improving from year to year. They are no longer in rags." [16] Such improvements were also noticed by visitors to these areas in 1933 and 1934, [17] but Mao's vivid account shows how very low those standards really were.

The productive forces were also meager in the later Communist base areas in the northwest. In 1937, the border region of Shensi-Kansu-Ninghsia comprised no more than twenty-six counties covering about forty thousand square miles; there were perhaps one and a half million inhabitants, 80 percent of whom lived in small villages and hamlets. The area had low population density but also low land fertility and a very backward state of technical development, the combination of which resulted in low levels of labor productivity with little more than subsistence income for the population. Almost all of the people were illiterate; most were in poor health. There were very few handicraft industries in the area; the only "modern" enterprise was an oil field and refinery.

Edgar Snow, in his renowned visit to the area in 1936, painted a rather dismal picture of its economic resources:

> North Shensi was one of the poorest parts of China I had seen. . . . There was no real land scarcity, but there was in many places a serious scarcity of real land—at least real farming land. . . . The farms of Shensi may be described as slanting, and many of them also as slipping, for landslides are frequent. The fields are mostly patches laid on the serried landscape, between crevices and small streams.[18]

> There is no machine industry of any importance in the North-west. The region is far less influenced by industrialism than the eastern parts of China; it is farming and grazing country primarily, the culture of which has been for centuries stagnant.[19]

> For hundreds of miles around there is only semi-pastoral country, the people live in cave-houses exactly as did their ancestors milleniums ago, many of the farmers still wear queues braided round their heads, and the horse, the ass and the camel are the last thing in communications. Rope-oil is used for lighting here, candles are a luxury, electricity is unknown, and foreigners are as rare as Eskimos in Africa.[20]

Even as late as 1944, Gunther Stein's survey of the capital, Yenan, suggested a continuing shortage of the basic necessities:

> Here was Yenan—with only 40,000 people, of whom 12,000 were soldiers, government and party officials and students; without electricity and modern machinery; with no other motor traffic than four or five ancient trucks; with practically no roads, and without a navigable river; without any planes bringing in supplies from the outside world.[21]

Still, in the years 1935 and 1936, the Communists could see that the area had potentialities: its substantial quantities of unutilized natural resources, including salt, iron, coal, and oil; its crops, especially cotton, which could be improved with irrigation; its handicraft industries—spinning and weaving—which could be greatly expanded; and its population, whose energies and talents could be developed and better employed. [22]

Just as in the years of the Kiangsi soviets, the Maoists in Yenan used the "ordinary" saving-investment techniques to take advantage of these potentialities. Accordingly, they turned to taxation, confiscation, and bond issues to gain revenue and command over economic resources, monetary expansion to finance additional investment activities, and external trade and smuggling to obtain goods that could not be produced locally. They increased the area of cultivated land, the number of draft animals, and the participation of women in the labor force, and established small industries throughout the area. The productive forces were also increased by immigration into the area, by internal migration from labor-surplus to labor-deficit regions, and by the rehabilitation of vagrants and other idlers. For a short time, subsidies from the Nationalist government paid for larger imports of desperately needed commodities to the area. Moreover, Snow reported that the Communists captured most of the machinery they had in 1936 and 1937 from forays into neighboring areas: "During their expeditions to Shansi province last year, for example, they seized machines, tools and raw materials, which were carried by mule all the way across the interminable mountains of Shensi, to their fantastic cliff-dwelling factories." Besides this type of "primitive accumulation," the Communists had brought with them on their Long March many lathes, turning machines, stampers, dies, and the like. They had also brought dozens of Singer sewing machines to equip their clothing factories, silver and gold from the Red mines in Szechuan, and lithographing blocks and light printing machines. [23]

The chief fruits of the Yenan years were moderate gains in agriculture and large increases in clothing and other output from handicrafts, manufacturing, and mining. In addition, there was much road building, and "travelers reported a great deal of housing construction, especially in the form of cave digging, and a mushrooming of trade and service establishments." [24]

Social Relations of Production

When the Communists moved in and began to control a base area, their very presence immediately disrupted the class structure and hierarchical authority, which were dominated by landlords, militarists, village bosses, and the gentry. The Communists sided with the middle and poor peasants, farmhands, and other impoverished people who constituted the majority of the population. Thus the Communist presence tended to shift the balance of power directly from the wealthy to the poor. To consolidate and deepen this shift, the Communists swiftly introduced programs to change the social relations of production in the area—that is, the class structure and supporting institutions closely associated with the work process. These programs almost always included land reforms; they were often extended to the formation of state enterprises and cooperatives and to the replacement of feudal social relations—which discouraged useful work by women and other potential workers—with more democratic institutions and practices.

Land Reforms

During the years from 1927 to 1934, the Communists sporadically controlled several base areas. Their land reforms in these areas were all different, since conditions were dissimilar from one area to the next. Even the reforms enacted under the direction of Mao himself were not uniform. Furthermore, there were serious doctrinal differences among factions of the party regarding the proper way to carry out the land policies, and these disputes were mirrored in the provisions of the laws, including those enacted under Mao's general guidance. Mao's power was greatly curtailed during the later years of this period, which meant that he was often following orders rather than giving them. Consequently, it is difficult to discern exactly what Mao then favored.

His policies appear to have included: (1) only a limited amount of land confiscation, (2) redistribution of land on the basis of the township and equal amounts per person, (3) private ownership of land and its cultivation by individual families (not collective), and

(4) enlistment of the support of rich peasants, small merchants, and others in the "intermediate classes." Mao told Edgar Snow in 1937:

> In this Soviet [Ch'a-ling], and subsequently, we promoted a demo-cratic programme, with a moderate policy, based on slow but regular development. This earned Chingkangshan the recriminations of putschists in the Party, who were demanding a terrorist policy of raiding, and burning and killing landlords, in order to destroy their morale. [We] refused to adopt such tactics, and were therefore branded by the hotheads as "reformists." I was bitterly attacked by them for not carrying out a more "radical" policy.[25]

Mao's policies at this time were based on his view that China was a semifeudal, semicolonial country whose peasantry consti-tuted most of the population and whose immediate task was to fight against imperialism and feudalism, not against capitalism. Mao saw his forces as engaged in a protracted bourgeois-democratic revolution that needed to enlist the support of as much of the population as possible—to "win over the many"—and that would lead to the transitional stage of new democracy. Mao later denounced ultraleftist doctrines that were in opposi-tion to the basic ideas of his new democracy because these doc-trines promoted policies consistent with a socialist revolution, including all-out struggle against the bourgeoisie as a whole and the elimination of the rich-peasant economy.[26] For Mao, socialism lay in the distant future, after the bourgeois-democratic revolution, with its helpful capitalist elements, had been won and consolidated.

This prospect clearly explains some of Mao's agrarian policies: for example, his proclivity for striking mainly at the landlords while trying to enlist as many rich peasants and "intermediate classes" as possible on the side of the revolution and his insistence on at least de facto private ownership and family cultivation of the land. His other priorities merit further discussion.

One of Mao's policies was to redistribute the land—either its ownership or its use rights—to the poor and others on a per capita basis. Amounts of land equal in productive power were given to each person, young and old, male and female, worker and con-sumer. This method of land distribution was vigorously disputed by Mao's opponents, but one of his land laws defended it in the following ways: (1) If the old and the young receive smaller shares of land before the government has completed its preparations for caring for them, they will be unable to survive unless the government puts aside an appropriate amount of land for public-welfare purposes. In that event, the land might just as well be given to them to begin with. (2) Dividing the land according to the number of persons in each family is the simplest and most convenient method. (3) The number of families with neither old nor young is very small. Therefore, the simple redistribution scheme will cause no great inequity.[27]

A few years later, an apparently Maoist document stated that "equal distribution" would in fact stimulate production because

> the poor peasants and the jobless masses have devoted all their manpower to the land they have received. All former nonproductive parasites in the villages, like landlords and idlers, are obliged to farm now or else they will have nothing to eat. The labor power of some of the poor peasants which was formerly left unused for lack of land is being put to use, now that land has been assigned them.

Moreover, it was claimed, the poor peasants, knowing that the land now belonged to them, were willing to do deep plowing and frequent weeding, to improve irrigation, and to repair ponds and ditches.[28]

These were meant as telling arguments, mainly against base areas that redistributed land only to those able to work it. Mao may have succumbed to a variant of this labor-power method for a time, at least on paper, "so that a person with labour-power is allotted twice as much land as one without."[29] In this system, land gravitated to those who could work it, thereby tending to raise efficiency and agricultural output but to reduce the distributional equity of land use and land income. Another method advocated but probably not much used,[30] which was even more heavily biased toward efficiency and away from equity, was redistribution according to labor power *and* ownership of capital assets (primarily tools and draft animals)—on the ground that persons possessing these would have the greatest ability to make the land produce. Land allocation based on these criteria would, of

course, greatly favor the richer peasants, as the Land Law of the
Soviet Republic, November 1931, warned:

> The well-to-do peasantry seek to have the land distributed according
> to the means of production. The First [All-China Soviet] Congress
> considers this to be a counter-revolutionary effort on the part of rich
> peasants to hinder the development of the agrarian revolution and
> to further their own ends, and it must be strictly prohibited.[31]

In some cases the village was the basic unit of land redistribution, in others a group of villages within each *hsiang* (township).
For example, the Land Law of February 7, 1930 (a Maoist document), made the *hsiang* the basic unit and based land redistribution on an initial estimate of rice output per capita in the *hsiang*
as a whole. Each person was then given sufficient land, of varying
fertility, to yield rice of this average amount. If, in a rich village
with highly fertile land, land was left over after such redistribution, whenever possible it would be transferred to a poorer, ad-
joining village with a shortage of land. If this was not feasible,
villages within the *hsiang* might be merged for purposes of land
redistribution. As a last resort, people might be moved from the
poorer to the richer villages.[32] Consequently, a greater measure
of equity could be achieved within the *hsiang* than within the
individual village. In early 1930, Mao also introduced his twin
principles of land reform: "Take from those who have much to
help those who have little, and take from those who have fertile
land to help those who have poor land." John Rue explained how
these principles, incorporated in the Land Law of February 7,
1930, worked in practice:

> The amount of land apportioned to the poor from property
> confiscated from landlords rarely sufficed to create even approxi-
> mate equality at harvest time. Land was therefore to be taken from
> the rich peasants and some of the middle peasants and distributed
> among the poor and landless. Usually the rich peasants agreed to
> surrender only some of their poorer land, so that even after this step
> the poor peasants would possess land yielding a smaller harvest than
> that of the rich peasants. Dissatisfied, the poor peasants would
> support the next step in the struggle for greater equality, which was
> to take from those who had rich land to help those who had poor

land. Land was to be classified into three grades, and every family was to be allotted some of each. This step was at the expense of the rich and middle peasants, who usually owned the more fertile lands.[33]

The Communists were forced out of their base areas in the south in October 1934 and, after the Long March of six thousand miles, arrived in Shensi, in the northwest, about a year later. The Land Law of the Northwest Soviet Government was passed in December 1935. It provided for the confiscation of all of the rich peasants' land that was not cultivated by the owners themselves. Snow reported on this:

> Both the landlord and rich peasant were allowed as much land as they could till with their own labor. In districts where there was no land scarcity—and there were many such districts in the North-west—the lands of resident landlords and rich peasants were in practice not confiscated at all, but the wasteland and land of absentee owners was distributed, and sometimes there was a re-division of best quality land, poor peasants being given better soil, and landlords being allotted the same amount of poorer land.[34]

Snow further reported that the goal was not to equalize land-ownership but to give each family enough land to guarantee it a decent livelihood. Every enlisted man in the Red Army was given a portion of the redistributed land, which was tilled by his family or his local soviet in his absence. If he was not a native of the soviet districts, his income came from the "public lands," which were tilled by villagers in the local soviets, such labor being obligatory. Snow added:

> The land problem—confiscation and redistribution—was greatly simplified in the Northwest by the fact that big estates were formerly owned by officials, tax-collectors, and absentee landlords. With the confiscation of these, in many cases the immediate demands of the poor peasantry were satisfied, without much interference with either the resident small landlords or the rich peasants.[35]

Mark Selden has demonstrated, however, that in one township "the major consequence of the land revolution . . . was to destroy large concentrations of wealth and substantially enlarge the middle peasantry by distributing the land and property of rich peasants and landlords to the poor." [36] He goes on to say that no landlords survived the land reform (most fled) and that only four rich peasant families of the original sixteen were in the area five years later, though several former middle and poor peasants had in the meantime become rich peasants. The economic lot of the very poor was substantially improved. But Selden's data corroborate Snow's contention that land and other assets were by no means distributed equally. Rich- and middle-peasant families not only acquired more land but also retained most of the draft animals, and, moreover, they hired additional labor, thereby accentuating inequalities in productive power. [37] Still, the previous political and social dominance of the landlords and rich peasants was broken. They "no longer constituted a dominant socioeconomic elite controlling the destinies of the poor and monopolizing military and political power." [38]

This Maoist land revolution in the Shensi area, which began in late 1935, was effectively suspended in early 1937 (officially, in September 1937), when a second united front with the Kuomintang was being formed against the Japanese. Despite some weaknesses, the land revolution accomplished much in this short period:

> It had been carried to completion in ten to twelve districts and in significant parts of a dozen or more others comprising most of the area of northern Shensi and the Shensi-Kansu-Ninghsia border. In a few districts which were contested even after the formation of the Second United Front, the economic and political problems of landlordism remained unsolved. However, throughout most of the twenty-three districts which eventually comprised the border region, land revolution was the crucial first step in the creation of a new egalitarian order which featured large-scale peasant participation in a growing network of political and military organizations. [39]

Although the Communists had toned down their land policies as early as December 1935, they brought the land revolution to a halt only after they had concluded that the "principal contradiction" was the one between the Chinese masses and the Japanese imperialist invaders. Their new land program, consonant with the second united front, called for the cessation of the program of confiscating land without compensation. It then became the policy of the Communists to help the peasants reduce feudal exploitation but not to eliminate it. Accordingly, rent and interest rates were reduced, but the collection of these payments by landlords and lenders was guaranteed. Furthermore, landlords who joined the anti-Japanese struggle were assured that their civil liberties and other rights would be respected. The new policy recognized that

> the capitalist mode of production is the more progressive method in present-day China and that the bourgeoisie, particularly the petty bourgeoisie and the national bourgeoisie, represent the comparatively more progressive social elements and the political forces in China today. The mode of production of the rich peasants bears capitalist characteristics; they are the capitalists in the rural areas and are an indispensable force in the anti-Japanese war and in the battle of production. . . . Therefore the policy of the Party is not to weaken capitalism and the bourgeoisie, nor to weaken the rich peasant class and their productive force, but to encourage capitalist production.[40]

The party aspired to reduce most rent payments to landlords by 25 percent, generally from 50 percent of the crop to a maximum of 37.5 percent, and all rents were to be collected after the harvest. Interest rates were generally set near a ceiling of 15 percent per year. If a debtor had already paid his creditor large amounts of interest on the original loan, further interest payments, and at times even the principal, were canceled.

This moderate land policy replaced the more radical one as conditions changed. As Mao put it, the main question had become not whether the land should belong to the landlords or to the peasants but whether it would belong to the Japanese or to the Chinese. For this reason, the Maoists felt it necessary and possible to ally themselves with most of the bourgeoisie and with many landlords and rich peasants. Despite grave provocations from the Kuomintang, they never wavered throughout the war in seeing Japan as the principal contradiction and the Kuomintang as the secondary one. Their economic policies were fashioned from this broader analysis of world forces.

In late 1945, after Japan had been defeated and before full-scale civil war had begun, Mao directed the party to launch large-scale rent reduction campaigns "so as to arouse the revolutionary fervour of the great majority of the peasant masses."[41] He cautioned that rent reduction must not be a favor bestowed by the government but the result of mass struggle. He also reminded the cadres once again that the present policy was to reduce rents, not to confiscate land.

In the winter of 1945–1946 these moderate measures were tentatively changed to the more radical policy of land confiscation and distribution, but the change was gradual and was applied only in a few areas. The movement culminated, however, in the new land directive of May 4, 1946. Mao's editors explained it as follows:

> After Japan's surrender, in view of the peasants' eager demand for land, the Central Committee decided to change the land policy of the period of the War of Resistance, that is, to change from the reduction of rent and interest to confiscation of the land of the landlords and its distribution among peasants. The "May 4th Directive" marked this change.[42]

Another observer wrote that this directive ordered that the landlords' land be distributed among the landless, "with the landlords allowed to keep a larger-than-average share of land. It also warned against trespassing upon the properties of the rich peasants."[43]

A short time after the issuance of the directive, and a month after Chiang Kai-shek's all-out offensive against the Communists began, Mao counseled the party cadres to unite with as broad a spectrum of the people as possible and to distinguish carefully between traitors, bad gentry, and local tyrants on the one hand, and ordinary rich peasants and middle and small landlords on the other. He added that, where the land problem had been largely solved, the party should adopt a moderate attitude toward the landlord class as a whole. "In order to reduce the number of hostile elements and to consolidate the Liberated Areas, we should help all those landlords who have difficulty in making a living and induce runaway landlords to return to give them an opportunity to earn a living." Mao extended this policy of unity to the cities, in which he urged the party to isolate the reactionaries and unite with just about everyone else. He also broadened it to include the Kuomintang armed forces, where "we should win over all the possible opponents of civil war and isolate the belli-cose elements." [44] Thus, although the May 4th Directive reestab-lished the land policy of confiscation-redistribution, it did not attempt to eliminate the rich-peasant economy and it was toler-ant toward many landlords; it was consistent with Mao's policy of a broad united front.

Nevertheless, the directive did lead to some "left" excesses toward the middle peasants and others, for in early 1947 Mao found it necessary to reiterate the policy of uniting firmly with the middle peasants, including the well-to-do middle peasants, and of treating rich peasants and middle and small landlords leniently. We must unite, Mao stated, with more than 90 percent of the masses and isolate only the small number of feudal reactionaries who oppose land reform.

By February 1947, Mao could report that the new land policies had been widely applied with some success despite continued shortcomings:

In about two-thirds of the territory in each Liberated Area, the Central Committee's directive of May 4, 1946, has been put into effect, the land problem has been solved and the policy of land to the tillers has been carried out; this is a great victory. There remains around one-third of the territory, however, where further efforts must be made to arouse the masses fully and put the policy of land to the tillers into effect. In places where the policy of land to the tillers has been carried out, there are still shortcomings insofar as the solution was not thorough—mainly because the masses were not fully aroused, so that the confiscation and the distribution of land were not thorough and the masses became dissatisfied. In such places, we must check carefully and must "even up" to ensure that the peasants with little or no land obtain some and the bad gentry and local tyrants are punished. [45]

The party convened a National Land Conference in Sep-tember 1947. On October 10, 1947, the Outline Land Law was issued by the conference. This law, which Mao may not have executed himself, showed less consideration for landlords, hit harder at the rich peasants, and was in general a more "leftist" document than the May 4th Directive.[46] However, in February 1948 some changes were made by the Central Committee. In the old and semi-old Liberated Areas (the former liberated before the Japanese surrender, the latter liberated between September 1945 and August 1947), where the feudal system had already been overthrown, there would be no further land confiscation or equalization of land distribution. These methods would be limited to areas in which the feudal system still existed, and even there they would be confined to the land of landlords and the surplus land of old-type rich peasants (peasants who were rich prior to the area's liberation):

> In all areas, it was permissible to take the surplus land of middle peasants and new-type rich peasants [those who had become so in the revolutionary base areas] for the purposes of readjustment only if this was absolutely necessary and if the owners really consented. In the land reform in the new Liberated Areas [those liberated since the general counteroffensive by the Communists in August 1947], no land was to be taken from any middle peasant.[47]

In April 1948, because of several "left" deviations from the policy, Mao repeated that the general line of land reform was to rely on the poor peasants, unite with the middle peasants, avoid encroaching on the interests of *new* rich peasants, and eliminate the feudal landlords as a class. He declared that the immediate goal of land reform was the development of agricultural production. With the consummation of land reform, the party must transfer all available forces to the countryside, organize mutual aid and cooperatives, build irrigation works, and promote seed selection. These measures, on the basis of private ownership, would raise agricultural output and lay the foundation for the transformation of China from an agricultural into an industrial society.[48]

In a directive of May 25, 1948, the Central Committee removed from land reforms for the remainder of the year areas still designated as unstable guerrilla zones, areas in which the masses were not yet politically ready for such measures, and areas in which there were not enough party cadres to carry out such reforms. Generally speaking, this directive tended to divert attention from further land reforms and to emphasize instead the need to raise agricultural production. The directive probably marked the end of the period of increasing radicalization in land policy which had begun after the defeat of the Japanese, and a swing toward more moderate policies leading to agricultural improvement. This was particularly true in the new Liberated Areas, where the masses of peasants were unprepared to take the initiative in land reform. For these areas, which were rapidly expanding as the Communist counteroffensive swept south, Mao laid down a conservative set of policies:

> We should apply the social policy of reducing rent and interest and properly adjusting the supplies of seed and food grains and the financial policy of reasonable distribution of burdens . . . we should not immediately apply the social reform policy of distributing movable property and land. . . . Moreover, hasty dispersal of social wealth is to the disadvantage of the army. Premature distribution of land would prematurely place the entire burden of military requirements on the peasants instead of on the landlords and rich peasants. In the sphere of social reform, it is better not to distribute movable property and land but instead to reduce rent and interest universally so that the peasants will receive tangible benefits, and in financial policy we should effect a reasonable distribution of burdens so that the landlords and rich peasants will pay more. . . . After one, two or even three years, when the Kuomintang reactionaries have been wiped out in extensive base areas, when conditions have become stable, when the masses have awakened and organized themselves and when the war has moved far away, we can enter the stage of land reform—the distribution of movable property and land as in northern China. The stage of rent and interest reduction cannot be skipped in any new Liberated Area, and we shall make mistakes if we skip it.[49]

To summarize, Mao's agrarian reforms, which were on the whole moderate, did not set out to annihilate large segments of the population but rather to win over the great majority. Such policies were consonant with his theory that the Chinese revolution was in the bourgeois-democratic stage and not the proletarian-socialist stage. Consequently, agrarian policies had to be consistent with capitalism as a progressive force and not "jump over" a stage to socialism. Accordingly, Mao promoted private ownership of land, individual family cultivation, and the buying and selling of land.

As Mao saw them, the principal contradictions during the early period, 1927 to 1934, were feudalism (contradictions between landlords and peasants) and imperialism (contradictions between capitalist-imperialist nations and the Chinese masses). Although some classes—for example, the national bourgeoisie and the rich peasants—were frightened by the Communists' revolutionary drive against wealthy Chinese, at the same time they favored the Communists' anti-imperialist policies. As a result, under certain conditions those classes, or some of their members, could be won over to the Communists' side if the Communists' economic policies did not alienate them excessively. Following this reasoning, Mao selected economic programs that would satisfy the basic demands of the poor while not unduly antagonizing those with whom the Communists might unite.

When the principal contradiction of the bourgeois-democratic revolution became Japanese imperialism, Mao altered his economic policies so as to achieve unity with all possible anti-Japanese forces. Thus his land policies then prescribed reductions of rent and interest and guarantees of these reduced payments to the landlords and moneylenders. Land confiscation was suspended. Other economic programs were similarly readjusted to the new phase of the revolution. After the defeat of Japan, the more radical land policies were resumed. But on the eve of victory against Chiang Kai-shek, when large new territories fell to the Communists, Mao's policy became mainly to protect agricultural output from an excessively radical land program.

Basically, Mao followed Lenin in being particularly wary of "ultraleftist" policies. He insisted that the "historic stages" be followed and constantly attempted to unite with as many people as possible. At the same time, he demanded that such unity be combined with struggle against "enemies" within the revolutionary bloc, so that the party could maintain its own initiative and independence. "Struggle within unity" was his key motto.

The Land Verification Movement

During the summer and early fall of 1933, the land verification movement was launched in the Kiangsi areas under Mao's direction. The main purpose of the movement was to "investigate classes"—that is, to determine the class status of individuals. This effort was directed especially toward former landlords and rich peasants, who were escaping punishment or asset-confiscation by posing as toiling peasants, and toward outright counter-revolutionaries. In the process, Mao expected the masses to be mobilized and aroused in ways that would raise their class consciousness.

The land verification movement, however, was to apply only to certain areas. According to Mao's analysis, as a result of uneven economic and political development there were now three types of areas within the soviet territories: (1) the newly developed areas (the least developed), (2) the comparatively retarded struggle areas (of average development), and (3) the advanced struggle areas (the most developed). In the first type, the tasks of the Communists were to overthrow the landlords and to confiscate and redistribute their land; to establish revolutionary committees, form mass organizations, and build up the armed forces; and to annul debts and burn land deeds and promissory notes. In the second type, their main task was to carry out the land investigation movement, the above tasks having already been accomplished. In the third type, their principal task was to promote agricultural production. Thus Mao's priorities, in time sequence, were land revolution, land investigation, and agricultural development.[50] A shift in political power and the awakening of the masses had to precede serious economic efforts. There is nothing more important than that conception in Mao's economic strategy.

With regard to the land investigation movement, Mao advised his followers "to rely on the poor peasants, ally with the middle peasants, and make the hired farm hands play a leading role so as to annihilate the landlord class completely and frustrate the attempt of the rich peasants to steal the benefits of the land revolution and weaken their economic power."[51] Mao threw out a few warnings about the necessity of treating rich peasants differently from landlords. Rich peasants should be opposed, not annihilated; their property should not be entirely confiscated; their labor power should be recognized and appreciated.[52] At this time, Mao was reluctantly carrying out Stalin's tough line on rich peasants, which was transmitted to the Chinese through the Communist International, and he appeared to be concerned about ultraleftist actions against them.

Although it was stated repeatedly that the land investigation movement was not a land redistribution drive, some of the land and other property of landlords and rich peasants was nevertheless redistributed. The explanation is probably that land investigation was not intended to carry through another full-scale land reform in the areas affected, but rather to discover and then redistribute land and other assets that had escaped detection the first time around. When initiated and carried out by the poor peasants, such efforts would increase their understanding of class struggles and of their own role within the revolutionary movement.

John Rue sees this movement differently—as primarily one to gain revenue for the revolutionary war effort, which had been greatly intensified at the time.[53] Han Suyin, on the other hand, states that the movement was meant by Mao to mitigate the "left" line in land reform and in economic policy,[54] and there seems to be some evidence for this. Schram, however, is probably closer to the heart of the movement's aims when he views its goal as primarily political and only secondarily economic:

> The purpose of the "land verification movement," launched by Mao on a large scale in June 1933, was, as the name suggests, to verify whether the redistribution had been properly carried out. But this economic objective was less important in Mao's mind than the political aim of promoting class struggle. . . . The land verification movement, in Mao's view, would play a key role in opening the peasant's eyes to the true class nature of these hidden enemies. . . . The total confiscation of the landlords' property destroyed the economic basis for their existence as a class; the mobilization of the peasant masses to "struggle" against them was intended to destroy the roots of their position in tradition and habit . . . it reflects

Mao's conviction that land reform is a political quite as much as an economic measure, and at the same time a process of education of the peasantry.[55]

Cooperatives and Mutual Aid

In his 1927 "Report on an Investigation of the Peasant Movement in Hunan," Mao declared: "The peasants really need co-operatives, and especially consumers', marketing and credit co-operatives."[56] He explained to his comrades that the peasants were being cheated by merchants, moneylenders, and others, that cooperatives would free them from these exploiters, but that the peasants did not yet know how to establish and manage cooperatives. "Given proper guidance," Mao concluded, "the co-operative movement can spread everywhere along with the growth of peasant associations."[57]

Such efforts did not get under way, however, until 1933–1934, near the close of the Kiangsi soviet period. In the essay "Our Economic Policy," written about that time, Mao noted that "in many places mutual-aid groups and ploughing teams have been organized to adjust the use of labour-power in the villages, and co-operatives have been organized to overcome the shortage of draught oxen."[58] Though the mutual-aid groups and ploughing teams were based on individual farming, not cooperative or collective farming, they nevertheless encouraged the peasants to get together voluntarily to help one another and in this way to use their labor power, implements, and draft animals to better advantage. The teams also "gave preferential treatment to the families of Red Army soldiers and worked for bereaved old folk without any pay except for meals during the work."[59]

In the same essay, Mao stated that cooperative enterprises in the Kiangsi and Fukien soviets were growing rapidly. "Consumers' co-operatives and grain co-operatives head the list, with producers' co-operatives coming next. Credit co-operatives have just started functioning. When the co-operative and the state enterprises become co-ordinated and grow over a long period of time, they will become a tremendous force in our economy and will gradually prevail and assume leadership over the private sector."[60]

During the Yenan period too, Snow had reported that the cooperative movement was being pushed vigorously as early as 1936:

> These activities extended beyond production and distribution co-operatives, branching out to include co-operation in such (for China) novel forms as the collective use of farm animals and implements—especially in tilling public lands and Red Army lands—and in the organization of labour mutual-aid societies. . . . In busy periods the system of "Saturday Brigades" was used, when not only all the children's organizations, but every Soviet official, Red partisan, Red guard, women's organization, and any Red Army detachment that happened to be nearby, were mobilized to work at least one day a week at farming tasks.[61]

Snow went on to explain that the cooperative movement was regarded by the Communists "as an instrument to resist private capitalism and develop a new economic system—that is, to prepare the conditions for socialism."[62]

Gunther Stein, a visitor to Yenan and Shensi in 1944, disclosed that half of all the peasants in the border region were in labor exchanges:

> The movement started some four years ago when the increasing requirements of the army, of industries, cooperatives, and new administrative organizations began to make the lack of labor in the fields more and more acute. . . . There are different forms of Labor Exchange Brigades. . . . In some cases whole villages work together in various tasks. In others small individual groups are formed for a long period to deal with special jobs like land reclamation and dike building. Sometimes they get together for short periods during rush seasons. They use each other's tools and draft animals, which greatly increases their working capacity. . . . The Labor Exchange Brigades lend every three of their members the productive capacity of four or five farmers working in family groups or individually. They make work more pleasant and efficient. And in creating a new community spirit they do much to overcome the proverbial individualism and clannishness of the farmers.[63]

Stein heard a speech given by Mao at the Conference of Cooperatives in 1944. In it Mao claimed that the Chinese were developing new types of cooperatives, ones that were universal and many-sided: "They must help in the development of our economic life, our social life, our education . . . using the initiative of the masses of the people to supplement the activities of the government." Mao also spoke approvingly of insurance sections for cooperatives that would prevent families from going bankrupt by paying for large funeral expenses in the event of a member's death:

> As you know, everybody eats so much at those big feasts. . . . But this is not only a matter of insurance. We must also change our attitude toward such matters: nobody should take advantage of old customs any longer. In our new society the people must help each other. If they do that, they'll feel better. Even better than if they eat as much as they can put away at funeral feasts of poor farmers.

Mao then urged everyone to invest in cooperatives whatever could be spared—"money, the draft animals and implements they do not use all the time, or what land they cannot cultivate themselves." He told his audience not to be afraid of landlords and capitalists, that they too could invest in cooperatives, not only to their own advantage but also to the benefit of all the members. He ended with a plea to

> keep this in mind: the most important economic organizations in our areas are not the few factories we have, but our many small cooperative enterprises. The Border Region is not like Shanghai. In all our regions we must rank the importance of the cooperatives very high in every respect. . . . I know that some of our cadres still consider cooperative work beneath their dignity and prefer government or party work. They are wrong and must correct this mistaken idea.[64]

A conviction that Mao has expressed a number of times is that cooperatives can break down the traditional system of individual economy that prevailed for thousands of years in rural China, with each family more or less on its own as a productive unit. In one article, for example, he stated:

This scattered, individual form of production is the economic foundation of feudal rule and keeps the peasants in perpetual poverty. The only way to change it is gradual collectivization, and the only way to bring about collectivization, according to Lenin, is through co-operatives. . . . Ours is a new-democratic economy, and our co-operatives are still organizations for collective labor based on an individual economy (on private property).

Mao then went on to discuss four types of cooperatives: the collective, mutual-aid cooperative for agricultural production, the multipurpose cooperative, the transport cooperative, and the handicraft cooperative.

With these four kinds of co-operatives among the masses and the collective labour co-operatives in the army, the schools and government and other organizations, we can organize all the forces of the people into a great army of labour. This is the only road to liberation for the people.

Mao hoped that the benefits of cooperation would not be confined to production but would be distributed over many aspects of the peasants' lives:

Once production groups become the usual practice, not only will output increase and all kinds of innovations emerge, but there will also be political progress, a higher educational level, programs in hygiene, a remoulding of loafers and a change in social customs, and it will not take long before the implements of production will be improved, too.[65]

It is clear, then, that Mao saw sweeping advantages to cooperatives. At one time or another, he has claimed that they would: (1) free peasants from the exploitative nature of the individual, private-property economy; (2) enable peasants to use labor power, tools, and draft animals more effectively; (3) permit economies of scale; (4) stimulate work enthusiasm; (5) increase peasant solidarity, make life active and morale high; (6) break down traditional systems of the individual economy; and (7) favorably affect other aspects of life—social, political, and educational.

Mao's major point, however, has been that cooperatives tend

to shatter the individual form of production which kept peasants in perpetual poverty, both because that form of production was inefficient and because it could be dominated by landlords and their feudal ideas and values, thus serving to disorganize and immobilize the peasants. Small-scale farming was a "technology," Mao thought, that the landlords encouraged in order to maintain their rule.

Social Relations and the Labor Force

The economic assignment of the Maoists during the 1927–1934 period was to change radically the social relations of production in their rural base areas so as to release the energy of the masses for productive work. Land reform, land investigation, and the cooperative movement were spearheads in the attack on peasant apathy. Beyond that, the Maoists worked pertinaciously to destroy old customs that restricted the productive labor of women.

In his famous 1927 report on the peasants, Mao noted with indignation that although men were subjected to three systems of authority—political, clan, and religious—women were subjected not only to these but also to a fourth—male authority. However, he continued, the authority of the husband was generally weaker among poor peasants than it was within the richer classes because, out of economic necessity, poor peasant women did more manual labor and so had greater power within their families. Moreover,

> with the increasing bankruptcy of the rural economy in recent years, the basis for men's domination over women has already been weakened. With the rise of the peasant movement, the women in many places have now begun to organize rural women's associations; the opportunity has come for them to lift up their heads, and the authority of the husband is getting shakier every day.[66]

Notwithstanding Mao's sentiments, little was done to expand the economic role of women during the early days of the rural base areas. The emphasis, instead, was on drawing women into the revolutionary struggles against the landlords. As an example of this emphasis, the 1928 Resolution of the Sixth National Congress on the Peasant Movement stated:

> In the struggle of the peasant movement towards victory, it is very important to absorb peasant women into the struggle. They participate directly in the economy of the village, constitute an important element among the hired farm hands, and play a very important role in the life of the peasants. Therefore it is imperative that they join the movement.[67]

Three years later, however, in the Constitution of the Soviet Republic, the work and rights of women were discussed more fully:

> It is the purpose of the Soviet government of China to guarantee the thorough emancipation of women; it recognizes freedom of marriage and will put into operation various measures for the protection of women, to enable women gradually to attain to the material basis required for their emancipation from the bondage of domestic work, and to give them the possibility of participating in the social, economic, political, and cultural life of the entire society.[68]

A few years afterward, Mao stated that "women are taking part in production in great numbers."[69] We do not know whether this was true, but it is beyond doubt that the Maoists were most concerned to achieve such a result.

This interest in women intensified during the Yenan years. One author has described the progress of women under the Communists at that time as follows:

> The social reforms in the rural areas under Communist control during the war centered on the improvement of the status of peasant women, the abolition of undesirable customs and habits such as superstitious practices, opium-smoking and gambling, and the reform of loafers in the villages. . . . Women's right to inherit property, chiefly in regard to land, was guaranteed. They were given equal rights with men to participate in political activities, and many of them were elected to village administrative offices. Monogamous marriage was made the rule. . . . Divorce was made easier for the peasant women, but it was not encouraged. Also discouraged were the practices in the rural districts of keeping slave-maids and child

daughters-in-law. The elevation of the status of peasant women came mainly from their better economic position as a result of property inheritance, from subsidiary occupations such as weaving, and from increased opportunity to receive education. . . . Literacy enhanced both their social mobility and prestige.[70]

The author tells the story of women too calmly, for the change in status that the Communists achieved, or at least commenced, during the Yenan period was no small thing; it was in fact a revolution. For centuries, Chinese women had been the mere possessions of men, especially in the propertied classes. They were sources of material wealth, often bought and sold like cattle or slaves, trained and beaten into submissive, subservient attitudes, uneducated, degraded by enforced prostitution, concubinage, and compulsory marriage. Jack Belden's classic account of a young peasant girl, Gold Flower, tells of the terror imposed on her by her husband and other males: she endured repeated beatings, was forced to her knees before males in acts of submission, and suffered material and spiritual deprivation as a maidservant to her husband. Gold Flower's "liberation" from most of this is the heart of the story, and the Communists played a decisive role in it. Belden, writing in 1948, commented:

> The fact that the pain, anguish and despair of Chinese womanhood has been transmitted by revolutionary fires into new feelings of joy, pride and hope is a phenomenon of tremendous significance for all the world. The revolt of woman has shaken China to its very depths and may shake the foundations of even this strong country. Yet political commentators ignore these peasant women as if they had no part in the drama now being enacted on the stage of world history.[71]

The Communists lifted many of the burdens from the backs of women, organized them into women's associations, and encouraged them to participate in production, especially home industry, and in guerrilla struggles against the Japanese. Mark Selden did not miss the significance of this:

> Through the cooperative and textile movements [home industry] and, in the rear-area bases, above all as a result of their valuable contributions to the guerrilla struggle, the role of Chinese women

was being transformed. . . . The resistance period was . . . crucial in bringing Chinese women out of the home and into the mainstream of Chinese society. It marked a period of major advance in the achievement of women's political, educational, and economic rights, commensurate with their positive new social contributions.[72]

With regard to political rights, women gained many elected and appointed positions, and many actively participated in political discussions and community decisions. Nevertheless, as Selden observed, despite all the progress made in the Yenan years, many of the age-old problems remained intractable.

The Superstructure

In Marxian theory, the superstructure consists of the ideology, systems of authority, and other institutions designed to support the existing class structure of society. When class structures are thoroughly changed, as they were in the Communists' base areas, pressure is also exerted to transform the main elements of the superstructure. Mao recognized this in his 1927 report on the peasants, as I have indicated in discussing the role of women. These passages are so illuminating in showing how Mao blended Marxism with his Chinese background that they are well worth quoting at length.

A man in China is usually subjected to the domination of three systems of authority: (1) the state system (political authority), ranging from the national, provincial and county government down to that of the township; (2) the clan system (clan authority), ranging from the central ancestral temple and its branch temples down to the head of the household; and (3) the supernatural system (religious authority), ranging from the King of Hell down to the town and village gods belonging to the nether world, and from the Emperor of Heaven down to all the various gods and spirits belonging to the celestial world. As for women, in addition to being dominated by these three systems of authority, they are also dominated by the men (the authority of the husband). These four authorities— political, clan, religious and masculine—are the embodiment of the whole feudal-patriarchal system and ideology, and are the four thick ropes binding the Chinese people, particularly the peasants. . . .

At the present time . . . the peasants are concentrating on destroying the landlords' political authority. Wherever it has been wholly destroyed, they are beginning to press their attack in the three other spheres of the clan, the gods and male domination. But such attacks have only just begun, and there can be no thorough overthrow of all three until the peasants have won complete victory in the economic struggle. Therefore, our present task is to lead the peasants to put their greatest efforts into the political struggle, so that the landlords' authority is entirely overthrown. The economic struggle should follow immediately, so that the land problem and other economic problems of the poor peasants may be fundamentally solved. As for the clan system, superstition, and inequality between men and women, their abolition will follow as a natural consequence of victory in the political and economic struggles.[73]

The development strategy expressed so clearly in this early work was closely followed by Mao from that time on: politics first, then economics, and finally the superstructure. This was roughly the line of attack organized by the Maoists during the Kiangsi soviet period. After the political or class struggle was more or less won, the Maoists tried to generate larger economic output, not primarily through direct increases in the productive forces of the base areas but through radical alterations of social institutions intimately related to the work process—the structure of land use and ownership, agricultural work organizations, consumer organizations, and so on. But the Maoists also used land reforms to further the political struggle; in this and other ways the economic and political struggles were intertwined.

Beyond this, and mostly with regard to the superstructure, serious efforts were made to raise labor productivity by increasing the peasants' dedication to and enthusiasm for their work, as well as the efficiency and rationality with which they did it. For the Maoists, this required not only that old systems of authority be dissolved but that "correct ideas" be taught to both the cadres and the masses and also that the cadres, in their contacts with the masses, employ correct methods of formulating policies and of translating them into actions and results. Ideas and systems of authority responsive to the needs of the peasants were to be established.

Perhaps the most striking aspect of economic policy in this period was the Maoists' belief that to raise labor productivity correct ideas and correct methods of work are just as important as the specification of the tasks to be accomplished. Although they made a great effort, for example, to state clearly what was to be achieved in a land reform, it is distinctive of the Maoists that they exerted an even greater effort to specify why the land reform should be carried out and exactly how to do so. This effort moved the reform program from the desk to the earth.

Correct Ideas

It is a Marxian concept that the ruling ideas of a society are, by and large, the ideas of the ruling classes—ideas that support the privileged positions of these classes and hold the lower classes in subservient positions. Since such ruling-class ideology is meant to immobilize the masses and induce them to accept their lot, however miserable, it is imperative, as Marxists see it, that this ideology be destroyed when the masses—or their vanguard—have overthrown the old ruling classes and are for the first time in a position to substantially improve their lives. It is then necessary for the masses, if their promise is to be fulfilled, to sweep away and replace old ideas, habits, and customs. Marxists claim that this can be done only if the masses actively participate in changing their world at the same time they study the debilitating effects of the old systems of authority and ideas; only through a combination of theory and practice can new ideas become potent forces in the everyday lives of the people.

In 1927, Mao was already scrutinizing the world with Marxian eyes: he praised the peasants who were struggling against the old ruling classes and what he called "patriarchal ideas."[74] One such idea was that any threatening, excessive behavior by the peasants must be denounced as a terrible thing. Mao explained that this reaction

is obviously a theory for combating the rise of the peasants in the interests of the landlords; it is obviously a theory of the landlord class for preserving the old order of feudalism and obstructing the establishment of the new order of democracy, it is obviously a counter-revolutionary theory.[75]

And then Mao pronounced the corrective: "Proper limits have to be exceeded in order to right a wrong, or else the wrong cannot be righted." The "proper limits" were always established by the classes benefiting from the perpetuation of the wrong. Mao's editors noted that

the old Chinese phrase, "exceeding the proper limits in righting a wrong," was often quoted for the purpose of restricting people's activities; reforms that remained within the framework of the established order were to be permitted, but activities aiming at the complete destruction of the old order were to be forbidden. . . . It is a convenient doctrine for reformists and opportunists in the revolutionary ranks.[76]

These old ideas, of course, excluded revolution, as Mao explained in a famous passage: "A revolution is not a dinner party, or writing an essay, or painting a picture, or doing embroidery; it cannot be so refined, so leisurely and gentle, so temperate, kind, courteous, restrained and magnanimous." These were the refined virtues of Confucius and, Mao implied, they supported the landlord class by ideologically disarming the peasants.[77]

For the same reason, Mao attacked the superstitious ideas of the peasants, which came from their subjection to the supernatural system and inculcated passivity and resignation. In judging the new peasant associations, Mao said, the middle peasants

knit their brows and think to themselves, "Can the peasant associations really last?" "Can the Three People's Principles prevail?" Their conclusion is, "Afraid not!" They imagine it all depends on the will of Heaven and think, "A peasant association? Who knows if Heaven wills it or not?"[78]

Mao related that, while in the countryside for his investigation, he did some propaganda work against superstition. In this marvelous blend of Marxian class struggle and old Chinese traditions, he talked with the peasants:

If you believe in the Eight Characters [a method of fortune-telling in China], you hope for good luck; if you believe in geomancy [the superstition that one's fortunes are influenced by the location of his ancestors' graves], you hope to benefit from the location of your ancestral graves. This year within the space of a few months the local tyrants, evil gentry and corrupt officials have all toppled from their pedestals. Is it possible that until a few months ago they all had good luck and enjoyed the benefit of well-sited ancestral graves, while suddenly in the last few months their luck has turned and their ancestral graves have ceased to exert a beneficial influence? The local tyrants and evil gentry jeer at your peasant association and say, "How odd! Today, the world is a world of committeemen. Look, you can't even go to pass water without bumping into a committeeman!" Quite true, the towns and the villages, the trade unions and the peasant associations, the Kuomintang and the Communist Party, all without exception have their executive committee members—it is indeed a world of committeemen. But is this due to the Eight Characters and the location of the ancestral graves? How strange! The Eight Characters of all the poor wretches in the countryside have suddenly turned auspicious! And their ancestral graves have suddenly started exerting beneficial influences! The gods? Worship them by all means. But if you had only Lord Kuan [a warrior widely worshiped as the god of loyalty and war who lived about A.D. 200] and the Goddess of Mercy and no peasant association, could you have overthrown the local tyrants and the evil gentry? The gods and goddesses are indeed miserable objects. You have worshiped them for centuries, and they have not overthrown a single one of the local tyrants or evil gentry for you! Now you want to have your rent reduced. Let me ask, how will you go about it? Will you believe in the gods or in the peasant association?

Mao reported that these words "made the peasants roar with laughter."[79]

Mao was worried about the tendency of the new political executive committees and councils in the Chingkang Mountains area to become dictatorial and manipulative. He attributed this to the fact that

the evil feudal practice of arbitrary dictation is so deeply rooted in the minds of the people and even of the ordinary Party members that it cannot be swept away at once; when anything crops up, they choose the easy way and have no liking for the bothersome democratic system.

Mao then implied that propaganda alone would not correct this:

Democratic centralism can be widely and effectively practised in mass organizations only when its efficiency is demonstrated in revolutionary struggle and the masses understand that it is the best means of mobilizing their forces and is of the utmost help in their struggle.[80]

Ruling-class ideas among the peasants arose not only from the desire of the higher classes to maintain their privileged positions but also from the structure of society's economic base. Mao indicated that the poverty of China's means of production served to hold the economy in a peasant (poor agricultural) status in which small-scale, individual-family farming and handicrafts predominated within a survival atmosphere. This petty-bourgeois world led to the acceptance of ideas of ultrademocracy—to people going their own way, excessively criticizing others, and "doing battle" in a hostile world against their neighbors' own necessities.[81]

For Mao, the correct ideas were proletarian ideas, Marxist-Leninist ideas which reflected the interests of the working classes. Mao stressed that the cadres and the masses should adopt democratic centralism; make careful class analyses of problems, investigating them thoroughly by gathering all the facts, and putting them into a wide context so that they took on more meaning; and acquire unity of purpose, discipline, selflessness, and modesty.[82] The critical task was to shake off the old systems of authority, which mystified and distorted the world, and to look at the world rationally.

Correct Methods of Work

I have already intimated that Mao considered methods of work as important as the tasks to be accomplished. In early 1934, he expressed the issue this way:

We are the leaders and organizers of the revolutionary war as well as the leaders and organizers of the life of the masses. To organize the revolutionary war and to improve the life of the masses are our two major tasks. In this respect, we are faced with the serious problem of methods of work. It is not enough to set tasks, we must also solve the problem of the methods for carrying them out. If our task is to cross a river, we cannot cross it without a bridge or a boat. Unless the bridge or boat problem is solved, it is idle to speak of crossing the river. Unless the problem of method is solved, talk about the task is useless.[83]

The first requirement was to discover the correct method of organization for any unit, and this method was democratic centralism, a method of democracy under central guidance. Mao elucidated the method carefully. First, there had to be centers of leadership that would give a correct line of guidance, based on familiarity with the life of the masses; the decisions of those centers must be promptly transmitted to the lower bodies and carried out by them after discussion meetings with the lower cadres and the rank and file regarding the meaning of the directives and the methods of carrying them out.[84]

Second, it was necessary to train large numbers of cadres for the work of implementing the centers' decisions and maintaining close contact with the masses.

Third, the masses had to be mobilized when any important policy was to be carried out:

Our objectives cannot be attained unless we use various organizational means to mobilize the masses and conduct propaganda among them . . . that is to say, unless the presidiums and the economic and finance departments of the government bodies at all levels actively attend to discussing and checking up on the work of economic construction, unless they spur the mass organizations into action and hold mass propaganda meetings.[85]

Fourth, the cadres must not be bureaucratic: they must use practical and concrete methods. In a striking passage, Mao warned: "Bureaucratic leadership cannot be tolerated in economic construction any more than in any other branch of our revolutionary work. The ugly evil of bureaucracy, which no comrade likes, must be thrown into the cesspit."[86] Furthermore, the cadres must not be "bossy" in carrying out their tasks: "We must reject commandism; what we need is energetic propaganda to convince the masses, and we should develop the co-operatives, promote the sale of bonds and do all the work of economic mobilization in accordance with the actual conditions and the real feelings of the masses."[87] Some years earlier, Mao had alluded to this problem of commandism when he expressed concern about how to sweep away the peasants' superstitions and religious idols:

> It is the peasants who made the idols, and when the time comes they will cast the idols aside with their own hands; there is no need for anyone else to do it for them prematurely. The Communist Party's propaganda policy in such matters should be, "Draw the bow without shooting, just indicate the motions." It is for the peasants themselves to cast aside the idols, pull down the temples to the martyred virgins and the arches to the chaste and faithful widows; it is wrong for anybody to do it for them.[88]

Finally, the cadres must make correct, rational analyses of the situations they faced. They should always gather the facts, investigate all sides of a problem, and try to place the problem in a broad context so that it could be better understood. The cadres must pay attention to the fact that everything depends on everything else.[89] In brief, as we shall now see, they should learn to judge the world in a Marxist-Leninist way.

The Rectification Movement

The Rectification Movement of 1942–1944 taught large numbers of party members the fundamentals of Marxism and their application to the Chinese revolution. The party issued study papers, organized discussion groups, and conducted general examinations. This was followed by a period for the investigation of party work and, finally, by a period "in which members in the individual organs and schools were to draw conclusions on the quality of their comrades' work, then submit reports to higher levels for approval."[90]

The need for this movement grew out of the huge increases in party membership from 1937 to the early 1940s—from 40,000 to

800,000—and of the new members' ignorance of the Marxian basis of the party. The theme of the Rectification Movement was the union of "the universal truths of Marxism-Leninism with the concrete reality of the Chinese revolution."[91] Mao demanded that Marxism be made Chinese. The specific target of the movement was the group of party leaders who had studied in Moscow and who, Mao felt, on returning to China had used Marxism-Leninism in a dogmatic way which had little relevance for the concrete conditions of China's revolution. Mao believed that greater ideological unity in party work was essential, given the intensified military demands imposed on the party at that time by the Kuomintang and the Japanese. "The rectification movement was born of the crisis precipitated by the Japanese offensive and the intensified Kuomintang blockade," Selden stated.[92] It was during these difficult times that the entire party went to school.

The prevailing opinion about the Rectification Movement is that it sought to increase the efficiency of party work through unity of thought and tight discipline. There is evidence to sustain this view, for the Reform Documents, which contained the study papers, were expressed in exactly that way. For instance, in Mao's speech of February 1, 1942, he stated:

> Why must there be a revolutionary party? There must be a revolutionary party because the world contains enemies who oppress the people and the people want to throw off enemy oppression. In the era of capitalism and imperialism, just such a revolutionary party as the Communist Party is needed. Without such a party it is simply impossible for the people to throw off enemy oppression. We are Communists, we want to lead the people in overthrowing the enemy, and so we must keep our ranks in good order, we must march in step, our troops must be picked troops and our weapons good weapons.[93]

In this address Mao also criticized party members who did not understand democratic centralism:

> They do not realize that the Communist Party not only needs democracy but needs centralization even more. They forget the system of democratic centralism in which the minority is subordinate to the majority, the lower level to the higher level, the part to the whole and the entire membership to the Central Committee.[94]

Accordingly, the Rectification Movement can be visualized as a purge of wrong views and a closing of ranks ideologically, for the purpose of "defeating the enemy."

There is also evidence, however, that by instructing cadres in Marxism-Leninism and encouraging them to apply this world outlook to Chinese problems, the movement was also meant to increase the cadres' powers of analysis, their ability to see the world correctly and hence their ability to pursue realistic and sensible goals, and their general intelligence. Thus the movement's intention was to present a valid picture of the modern world so as to enable the cadres to make correct decisions and to act in a rational, scientific way. Mao expressed this in a remarkable passage:

> Our comrades must understand that we do not study Marxism-Leninism because it is pleasing to the eye, or because it has some mystical value, like the doctrines of the Taoist priests who ascend Mao Shan to learn how to subdue devils and evil spirits. Marxism-Leninism has no beauty, nor has it any mystical value. It is only extremely useful.[95]

The usefulness of Marxism-Leninism, according to Mao, lay in uniting its universal truth to the concrete practice of the Chinese revolution,[96] in showing it not as a dogma but as a guide to action.[97] The materialism of Marxism-Leninism tells us, Mao wrote in 1942, that "being determines consciousness, that the objective realities of class struggle and national struggle determine our thoughts and feelings."[98] It instructs us that one's social practice—that is, all activity in the struggle for production, in class struggle, and in scientific and artistic pursuits—"exerts a profound influence on the development of man's knowledge."[99] Mao later expressed these thoughts in a passage that became famous:

> Where do correct ideas come from: Do they drop from the skies? No. Are they innate in the mind? No. They come from social practice, and from it alone. . . . It is man's social being that determines his thinking. Once the correct ideas characteristic of the advanced class are grasped by the masses, these ideas turn into a material force which changes society and changes the world . . . the one and only purpose of the proletariat in knowing the world is

to change it. Often, a correct idea can be arrived at only after many repetitions of the process leading from matter to consciousness and then back to matter, that is, leading from practice to knowledge and then back to practice. Such is the Marxist theory of knowledge, the dialectical materialist theory of knowledge.[100]

Mao is a Marxist dialectician, and dialectics is the study of contradictions. As Mao observes the world, contradiction is universal and absolute; it permeates the processes of development of all things at all stages of their development. "The law of contradiction in things, that is, the law of the unity of opposites, is the basic law of materialist dialectics."[101] All things change and develop; the cause is primarily internal—the development of their internal contradictions; external causes of change become operative through internal causes.

Every form of society and every form of ideology, Mao has written, has its particular contradictions. In order to reveal the special attributes of the contradictions in any ongoing process, it is necessary to look closely at the two aspects of each contradiction. A process, for example, the Chinese revolution, has a continuing fundamental contradiction; when it changes, the process becomes a new one—in our example, the essence of the Chinese revolution changes. Within each process, there are stages in which secondary contradictions change. If people do not pay attention to the stages in a thing's development they cannot deal properly with the contradictions in that development. There are many contradictions in the development of a complex thing, one of which is necessarily the principal contradiction, whose existence and evolution influence the existence and evolution of the other contradictions. Finally, in any contradiction, principal or secondary, the development of the contradictory aspects is uneven; one aspect is principal, the other secondary.[102]

Because Mao was continually immersed in dialectical reasoning, and because teaching it played a central role in the Rectification Movement, it would seem best to illustrate Mao's analysis with concrete examples from the "process" which occupied most of his time, the revolution itself. In the scheme below, I picture the Chinese revolution as having only two contradictions and each contradiction as having only two aspects. Thus, in the

Chinese revolution, feudalism and imperialism were the two contradictions, one of which was the principal contradiction at any given time. But the situation was not static; feudalism might be the principal contradiction today, imperialism tomorrow. The two aspects of feudalism, landlords versus peasants, differed from the two aspects of imperialism, Japanese versus Chinese. In each contradiction, there was a principal aspect—for example, the landlords might completely dominate the peasants. But, once again, the situation was not static, for tomorrow the peasants might be the principal aspect in that contradiction. Finally, there was both unity and struggle between the two aspects; each existed only because of the presence of the other, but there was struggle within this unity.

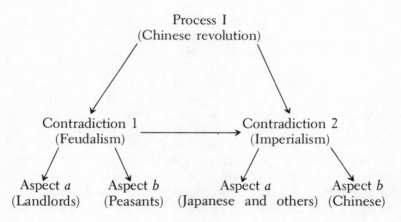

Since Mao saw the world dialectically, it is evident that his policies for resolving contradictions would differ from one period to the next as the nature of the contradictions changed. No one set of economic or social policies could be considered technically superior or optimal at all times. The concrete situation had to be analyzed in each case: Exactly what is the principal contradiction and its principal aspect? How is the contradiction developing? How is it influencing the other contradictions? The following passage reveals Mao's dialectical viewpoint and specifies the policies required to deal with each contradiction:

Qualitatively different contradictions can only be resolved by qualitatively different methods. For instance, the contradiction between the proletariat and the bourgeoisie is resolved by the method of socialist revolution; the contradiction between the great masses of the people and the feudal system is resolved by the method of democratic revolution; the contradiction between the colonies and imperialism is resolved by the method of national revolutionary war; the contradiction between the working class and the peasant class in socialist society is resolved by the method of collectivization and mechanization in agriculture; [the] contradiction within the Communist Party is resolved by the method of criticism and self-criticism; the contradiction between society and nature is resolved by the method of developing the productive forces. Processes change, old processes and old contradictions disappear, new processes and new contradictions emerge, and the methods of resolving contradictions differ accordingly. . . . The principle of using different methods to resolve different contradictions is one which Marxist-Leninists must strictly observe. The dogmatists do not observe this principle; they do not understand that conditions differ in different kinds of revolution and so do not understand that different methods should be used to resolve different contradictions; on the contrary, they invariably adopt what they might imagine to be an unalterable formula and arbitrarily apply it everywhere.[103]

Mao believed that the dialectical viewpoint enables one to understand reality and to handle its contradictions. This viewpoint also encompasses a broad historical approach to current problems. In outlining the program to educate a 1942 Central Committee resolution the cadres noted:

Apart from a mastery of specialized work, department conditions, and policy, the purpose of political education is the understanding of general conditions and policy, the broadening of vision, and the avoidance of prejudice and the error of narrow specialization without an understanding of the general situation.[104]

Poor, ineffective thinking, Mao instructed, came from the "three ill winds" of subjectivism, sectarianism, and stereotyped party writing—all of which were a reflection of petty-bourgeois ideology in the party.[105]

Subjectivism indicates errors in the style of study, and it takes the two forms of dogmatism and empiricism, the former being theory and book learning without concrete practice or experience and the latter being ample experience without a theoretical foundation.

The dogmatists "fancy themselves very learned and assume airs of erudition"; they know and can recite a great many Marxist-Leninist books, but they do not know how, or make little attempt, to apply the theory to "the realities of China's history and revolution."

> Our achievements on the theoretical front will be poor indeed if, as members of the Communist Party of China, we close our eyes to China's problems and can only memorize isolated conclusions or principles from Marxist writings. If all a person can do is to commit Marxist economics or philosophy to memory, reciting glibly from Chapter I to Chapter X, but is utterly unable to apply them, can he be considered a Marxist theorist? No! He cannot.[106]

At the opposite end, the empiricists have much practical experience but they come to grief by misusing their experiences because of lack of theory. They have perceptual knowledge, which is partial, and lack rational knowledge, which is comprehensive.

> Thus, there are two kinds of incomplete knowledge, one is ready-made knowledge found in books and the other is knowledge that is mostly perceptual and partial; both are one-sided. Only an integration of the two can yield knowledge that is sound and relatively complete.[107]

Mao pressed on to explain that book learning must develop in the direction of practice and that those who are rich in experiences must take up the study of theory. Theory and practice must be combined—in reality and not just in talk. Subjectivism, in both of its polar forms of dogmatism and empiricism, can be combated by the teaching of materialism and dialectics.[108]

Just as subjectivism indicates errors in the style of work, sectarianism indicates errors in the style of party relations; it is "an expression of subjectivism in organizational relations"[109] and assumes the general form of favoring small groups and individual activities. It means, in its internal manifestations, putting oneself or one's small group ahead of the party, not understanding the party's system of democratic centralism, and stressing the part and neglecting the whole. In its external manifestations, sectarianism means exclusiveness toward people outside the party, a closed-door attitude, disrespect for "outsiders." Sectarianism can be overcome if party members realized that the enemy cannot be defeated unless the party is put first and they unite with as many revolutionary forces as possible.

Finally, stereotyped party writing is the "instrument of propaganda or form of expression" for subjectivism and sectarianism.[110] It is a type of writing and speechmaking that lacks the critical spirit of dialectical materialism: it is purely formal in that it regards what is bad as wholly bad and what is good as wholly good. This bourgeois formalism mouths empty phrases, makes a false show of authority to instill terror, uses insipid language, categorizes thoughts in an empty one-two-three fashion, and fails to keep the target or objective in mind.[111]

Mao traced this party formalism to the May 4th Movement of 1919, which "opposed the traditional [Confucian] dogmas and advocated science and democracy."[112] The old dogmas constituted old formalism which compelled people to write in the literary style and to believe in a set of Confucian doctrines.[113] The May 4th Movement overcame the old formalism but itself succumbed to newer types of formalism—right formalism associated with the bourgeois branch of the May 4th Movement and left formalism associated with the Marxist branch. The Marxist movement had within it the correct method of dialectical materialism, but it also had the incorrect method of formalism. This left formalism, as already noted, produced the species of subjectivism, sectarianism, and stereotyped party writing. "So it can be seen," Mao said, in a show of dialectics, "that stereotyped Party writing is no accident, but is, on the one hand, a reaction to the positive elements of the May 4th Movement and, on the other, a legacy, a continuation or development of its negative elements."[114] This style of writing, Mao thought, reflected incorrect ways of learning and incorrect human relations, and it was "unsuitable for expressing the revolutionary spirit," not "vigorous, lively, fresh and forceful," as was the Marxist-Leninist style of writing.[115]

Mao's analysis can be shown schematically in the following way:

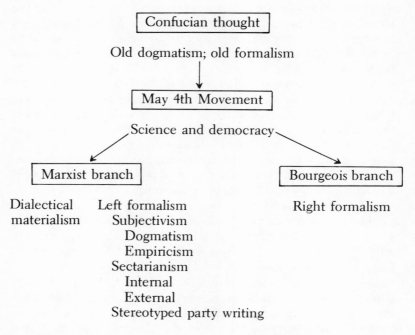

Confucian thought

Old dogmatism; old formalism

May 4th Movement

Science and democracy

Marxist branch   Bourgeois branch

Dialectical   Left formalism   Right formalism
materialism   Subjectivism
                   Dogmatism
                   Empiricism
                   Sectarianism
                   Internal
                   External
                   Stereotyped party writing

Thus Mao desired not only unity and discipline but also cadres who could view the world correctly and act rationally and intelligently. Since the three evils of subjectivism, sectarianism, and stereotyped party writing blocked these possibilities for many cadres, they had to be eradicated by means of an intensive study of Marxism-Leninism and its application to China. But, Mao insisted, "if there is not a comparatively high cultural level, the mastery of Marxist-Leninist theory is impossible."[116] And by culture Mao meant literacy and a general knowledge of history, geography, social and political science, and natural science. Thus the study of current affairs, historical research, and the application of Marxism-Leninism to China were necessary. There had to be more solid research and investigation in many fields by the cadres, for, as Mao stated, "After political policy has been determined, the cadres are the all-decisive factor."[117] Consequently, the Rectification Movement, in its economic dimensions, raised the ability of the party cadres and the party rank and file to deal effectively with problems of economic construction and reform. And it was expected that Marxist-Leninist thinking, a superior kind of thought, would lead to more correct answers, fewer mistakes, and in general to higher labor productivity.

In mid-1949, on the eve of complete victory, Mao wrote: "Communists the world over are wiser than the bourgeoisie, they understand the laws governing the existence and development of things, they understand dialectics and they can see farther."[118] That was the conviction behind the Rectification Movement.

Conclusions

In this final section, I wish first to explain what Mao meant by economic policymaking and then, on that basis, to summarize the overall economic strategy he preferred during the formative years 1927 through 1949. This is followed by a discussion of the role of the "mass line" in policymaking and by a short reminder of Mao's emphasis on "man" as the most powerful productive force. Then I review the reasons why Mao occasionally changed his economic tactics, within his general strategy, an explanation founded on Mao's examination of the development of the Chinese revolution. Finally, there is a brief account of Mao's look into the future, as he appraised the situation in the years 1947 to 1949, just before he and his party gained complete control of China.

Economic Policies and Contradictions

The distinctive features of Mao's policymaking issue from his dialectical-materialist world outlook. The theory of materialist dialectics states that development arises primarily from the contradictions within a thing, from its internal and necessary self-movement, and only secondarily from its interactions with other things, and that such development frequently results in the transformation of one quality into another, in qualitative leaps rather than continuous quantitative changes. Mao has proposed that this world outlook "teaches us primarily how to observe and analyse the movement of opposites in different things and, on the basis of such analysis, to indicate the methods for resolving contradictions."[119]

Each contradiction has a particular essence that makes it qualitatively different from other contradictions. "Qualitatively different contradictions," Mao tells us, "can only be resolved by qualitatively different methods."[120] But the important methods of resolving contradictions are all forms of struggle, including revolutionary wars, cultural revolutions, radical changes in social relations, increases in the productive forces, criticism, and self-criticism. A contradiction is resolved by first developing it, through some appropriate form of struggle, into a state of qualitative change in which disharmony and disequilibrium exist and each aspect of the contradiction is transformed into its opposite, thereby dissolving the contradiction as an entity. A contradiction cannot be resolved when it is in a state of only quantitative change, when harmony and equilibrium prevail, for then each aspect of the contradiction, though in struggle with its opposite, maintains its identity without changing the basic nature of the contradiction. To be eliminated, a contradiction must first be intensified.

Policymaking is the act of choosing the form of struggle most suitable for resolving a contradiction. An economic policy is a form of struggle that is intended to expand society's productive forces by resolving a contradiction. Economic policies may affect the productive forces directly, or they may do so indirectly, by first influencing other elements of the economic base. Other policies—social, cultural, political, and military—directly impinge on the superstructure. Nevertheless, if those policies are intended to enlarge the productive forces ultimately, they can be termed quasi-economic policies.

As Mao sees it, economic policies initiated by the state—whether direct, indirect, or quasi—are intended to increase the productive forces in ways that strengthen the position of the ruling class, and they are effective in doing so to the extent that they resolve the contradictions facing that class. But since the contradictions change with the historical development of society—in fact, society is pushed forward by the development of its contradictions—economic policies must change with changes in the concrete conditions. Hence, no single set of economic policies is technically optimal at all times. The best policy for a ruling class is the one that best resolves the particular contradiction blocking further expansion of the productive forces. Resolving that contradiction will solidify the position of the ruling class. Thus, by helping to resolve contradictions, effective economic policies aid the advancement of society, which in turn generates new contradictions that require new economic measures for their resolution.

The particular economic policy appropriate for resolving the contradiction that hinders development of the productive forces depends on the nature of the contradiction and its principal aspect. Thus, if the major contradiction is between the productive forces and the relations of production, the principal aspect must first be identified. Then an economic policy can be designed to work through that aspect to resolve the contradiction successfully. As Mao stated in examining this problem: "When it is impossible for the productive forces to develop without a change in the relations of production, then the change in the relations of production plays the principal and decisive role." In this case, the appropriate policy is an indirect one; in the contrary case, direct economic programs would be most suitable. Similarly, to turn to Mao again, "When the superstructure (politics, culture, etc.) obstructs the development of the economic base, political and cultural changes become principal and decisive." [121] To achieve such changes, quasi-economic programs, to use our terminology, are called for.

Consequently, a society's productive forces can be expanded by means of direct, indirect (through the relations of production), or quasi (through the superstructure) economic policies. Mao's broad view of economics, which is not limited to direct measures, does not signify, he has explained, an antimaterialism.

> The reason is that while we recognize that in the general development of history the material determines the mental and social being determines social consciousness, we also—and indeed must— recognize the reaction of mental on material things, of social consciousness on social being and of the superstructure on the economic base. This does not go against materialism; on the contrary, it avoids mechanical materialism and firmly upholds dialectical materialism. [122]

In fact, from 1927 to 1949 Mao's strategy was not confined to direct policies to expand the productive forces. Instead, whether out of necessity or conviction, his strategy was considerably more elaborate, as he explained in stating what he believed to be the general law of social development: "Historical experience has proved that only by first creating revolutionary public opinion and seizing political power, and then changing the relations of production, is it possible to greatly develop the productive forces." [123] If the working classes do not first seize political power, they have no base on which to construct new relations of production; and if new relations of production are not established, the development of the productive forces will be obstructed. Therefore, indirect policies must be followed before policies aimed directly at the productive forces can be carried out. And, we may add, a cultural revolution to change the superstructure may also be necessary to lower further the barriers to continued progress in the economic base.

These actions, in temporal sequence, can be schematized as follows:

Policies	*Area of impact*
First	
Win the political (revolutionary) struggle	The state in the superstructure

Second

Win the economic (production) struggle	Economic base
(*a*) carry out land reform	
(*b*) carry out land investigation	Relations of production
(*c*) promote mutual aid and cooperatives	
(*d*) achieve agricultural (and industrial) development of the productive forces	Productive forces

Third

Win the cultural and ideological struggle	Superstructure

It should be stressed that, in practice, Mao's general strategy was not so rigid that one struggle had to be completed before the next began, for there was in fact a great amount of overlapping among policies. But the above portrays accurately what Mao considered to be the optimal strategy for raising the living standards of the working classes in ways that would simultaneously strengthen their advantage over former oppressors.

Economic Policies and the Mass Line

Economic policies, we have just seen, are meant to increase the productive forces in ways that strengthen the desired relations of production. A distinctive feature of Maoism is its "mass line," which is a method of involving the masses in policy formulation and implementation for the purpose of achieving that desideratum. The mass line enables the party leaders to unearth what the masses are thinking and so to fashion correct policies with their support. Mao expressed this feature of the mass line in 1943:

> In all practical work of our party, correct leadership can only be developed on the principle of "from the masses, to the masses." . . . The basic method of leadership is to sum up the views of the masses, take the results back to the masses so that the masses can give them their firm support and so work out sound ideas for leading the work on hand.[124]

In addition, new economic policies change the social environment in which the masses live and work. Such changes can endure and bear fruit only if the masses have been actively involved in formulating and implementing the very policies which initiated those social changes. For example, peasants can benefit lastingly from a land reform that radically transforms the social conditions only if they have changed themselves from passive, resigned, and superstitious vassals of their "natural" masters into a politically aware, vigilant, and class-conscious rural proletariat. And this is possible only if the peasants themselves, under the leadership of dedicated cadres, actively participate in all phases of the land reform and thus come to understand the class structure of their society and the institutions and ideas bolstering that structure. This understanding will enable them to comprehend their own oppression and the solution to it.

Thus the Maoist view is that economic policies succeed when they change both the objective conditions and "man" himself, and that "man" is changed by his own attempts to change the world. These two phases are brought into focus in the mass line.

Economic Policies and Human Beings

Economic policies are directed at the expansion of a society's productive forces, with the ultimate aim of raising its output and, given the proper social relations, the living standards of the working classes. Output per capita can be increased if the growth of the productive forces raises the productivity of the working classes. The traditional bourgeois ways of doing that are to provide workers with more and better capital goods and to achieve more efficient management and organization of the work. In addition, higher productivity is realized by having the workers themselves become better educated, healthier, and more skillful.

Mao has not scorned these productivity-enhancing modes, but, following Marx, he believes that people are by far the most important productive force of all. By that he means that workers' productivity can be greatly enhanced only if the masses are aroused by revolutionary forces and inspired by stimulating purposes, if they are imbued with the desire and need for hard work to complete tasks which they deem eminently worthy of them as human beings. Mao recently referred to this in speaking of China's socialist and technological revolutions of the 1950s: "Our revolutions are like battles. After a victory, we must at once put forward a new task. In this way, cadres and the masses will forever be filled with revolutionary fervour." [125] Revolutionary fervor, Mao would argue, is a factor many times more powerful than new machinery, chemical fertilizers, or modern buildings—or even an atom bomb.

In discussing Britain's lagging labor productivity, Joan Robinson, the distinguished British economist, once told me, "Just think what we could do if people really wanted to work." This is the simple lesson that Mao learned long ago, a lesson that still seems to be hidden from most bourgeois economists, within the dark chambers of the "residual" element in their production functions.

Economics and the Chinese Revolution

Mao's strategy called for an attack on the economic base after political power had been assured. But this attack could take many different forms. The problem was to choose the best economic measures that would, directly or indirectly, enlarge the productive forces while furthering the leadership of the revolutionary classes in China's revolutionary movement. Mao solved this problem by means of an analysis of the historical development of the Chinese revolution, an analysis that indicated to him the specific types of policies that would be consistent with the revolution's particular stages of development.

As Mao studied his country's historical progress, he concluded that China gradually changed from a feudal society to a semicolonial, semifeudal society after the Opium War of 1840, when foreign capital began its invasion of the country. Mao supposed that China would have slowly developed into a capitalist country in any case, owing to the growth of its productive forces and thus the development of internal contradictions which in time would have dissolved feudalism, but that the penetration of foreign capital accelerated the process. For various reasons, the penetration was incomplete, which meant that China became a semicolony rather than a full-fledged one. At the same time, the penetration established and fostered only some capitalist elements in Chinese society, thereby failing to transform it into a full capitalist economy. Hence, China remained semifeudal.[126]

From 1931 to 1945, the new element of "colonialism" was added by the Japanese invaders who began full colonization of northeast China at that time. Mao analyzed the new development in late 1939: "China today is colonial in the Japanese-occupied areas and basically semi-colonial in the Kuomintang areas, and it is predominantly feudal or semi-feudal in both."[127] Consequently, during those years Mao called China a colonial, semicolonial, and semifeudal country. Presumably, after the Japanese had been defeated, in 1945, China reverted to its semicolonial, semifeudal status and it finally shed that status when the Communists liberated the country in 1949. China then became a society of "new democracy," which was succeeded by a socialist society in 1956.[128]

As Mao surveyed and interpreted the historical revolutionary scene, the rising capitalist classes in Western Europe had carried out bourgeois revolutions against the old feudal classes. Eventually the proletariat of the Western European countries would carry out socialist revolutions against their capitalist classes. Prior to the Bolshevik Revolution of 1917, the revolutionary movements in the countries of the underdeveloped world, including China, were bourgeois-democratic, in that they were led by rising national capitalist classes against the old order with the objective of establishing a bourgeois society in each country. After the Bolshevik Revolution, however, the situation in the underdeveloped world changed drastically. From that moment the proletariat and the peasantry began to assume command of the revolutionary movements, aided by the emergence of the Soviet

Union, with the objective of establishing a proletarian-socialist society, though only after a coalition of revolutionary classes (including parts of the bourgeoisie) had swept away feudalism and imperialism and paved the way with a transitional stage of "new democracy."

Consequently, after 1917, the Chinese revolution was transformed into a new-democratic revolution, which, as Mao explained, had the following characteristics:

However, in present-day China the bourgeois-democratic revolution is no longer of the old general type, which is now obsolete, but of a new special type. We call this type the new-democratic revolution and it is developing in all other colonial and semi-colonial countries as well as in China. The new-democratic revolution is part of the world proletarian-socialist revolution, for it resolutely opposes imperialism, *i.e.*, international capitalism. Politically, it strives for the joint dictatorship of the revolutionary classes over the imperialists, traitors and reactionaries, and opposes the transformation of Chinese society into a society under bourgeois dictatorship. Economically, it aims at the nationalization of all the big enterprises and capital of the imperialists, traitors and reactionaries, and the distribution among the peasants of the land held by the landlords, while preserving private capitalist enterprise in general and not eliminating the rich-peasant economy. Thus, the new type of democratic revolution clears the way for capitalism on the one hand and creates the prerequisites for socialism on the other. The present stage of the Chinese revolution is a stage of transition between the abolition of the colonial, semi-colonial and semi-feudal society and the establishment of a socialist society, *i.e.*, it is a process of new-democratic revolution. . . . A new-democratic revolution is an anti-imperialist and anti-feudal revolution of the broad masses of the people under the leadership of the proletariat. Chinese society can advance to socialism only through such a revolution; there is no other way.[129]

Mao went on to point out that the new-democratic revolution was different from the old type because it would not result in a dictatorship of the bourgeoisie, as the bourgeois-democratic revolution did in Europe and America, but in a dictatorship of the united front of all revolutionary classes under the leadership of the proletariat. These revolutionary classes were the proletariat, the peasantry, the urban petty bourgeoisie, and at times, the national bourgeoisie (capitalists who had not sold out to imperialism but had retained strong nationalist leanings).[130] The new revolution would result in new democracy, not in capitalism; it would prepare the way for socialism.

The new-democratic revolution was also vastly different from a socialist revolution in that it would not destroy "any section of capitalism which is capable of contributing to the anti-imperialist, anti-feudal struggle."[131] Also it would not culminate in the dictatorship of the proletariat; it would not sweep away capitalism but would use it during a transition period.

Since the revolution was of the new-democratic type, Mao's economic policies were rather consistently within the bounds of capitalist private ownership. In agriculture, Mao's basic policy was to achieve a more equal *private* ownership of land and to encourage cooperative efforts among peasants who retained privately owned assets. This policy was often extended to the rich peasants and some landlords. In industry, Mao's purpose was to allow private operation of industrial firms rather than to nationalize them, but to improve the working conditions and raise the wages of their employees. He usually made a sharp distinction between landlords' assets in the rural areas and the industrial and commercial concerns they owned in the urban areas (based, respectively, on feudal relations and on capitalist relations); the former were confiscated, the latter untouched. In trade and commerce, Mao preferred to encourage or at least tolerate, much private trading, though he certainly favored strict controls over commercial abuses.

In keeping with the new-democratic nature of the revolution, Mao's policies generally did not include acute struggles between the working classes and the owners of capital: "In the stage of democratic revolution, there are limits to the struggle between labour and capital."[132] Accordingly, his policies embraced some reduction in working hours for the proletariat but not nationalization of the firms; moderate increases in the wages and living standards of workers but not the abolition of private profitmaking or the collection of rents and interest; limitations on property returns, not their elimination; progressive income taxes, not the abolition of high incomes. Speaking in 1940, when his mild, reformist policies were at their peak, Mao outlined in a most striking way the bourgeois type of policies that were being carried out:

> There must not be excessive increases in wages or excessive reductions in working hours. . . . Once a contract between labour and capital is concluded, the workers must observe labour discipline and the capitalists must be allowed to make some profit. . . . Particularly in the rural areas, the living standards and wages of the workers should not be raised too high, or it will give rise to complaints from the peasants, create unemployment among the workers and result in a decline in production . . . this is not the time for a thorough agrarian revolution . . . our present policy should stipulate that the landlords shall reduce rent and interest . . . but the reductions should not be too great. . . . The reduction in interest on loans should not be so great as to render credit transactions impossible. . . . Taxes must be levied according to income . . . the burden shall be carried by more than 80 percent of the population, including the workers and peasants, and not be placed entirely on the landlords and capitalists. . . . Capitalists should be encouraged to come into our anti-Japanese base area and start enterprises here if they so desire.[133]

Not surprisingly, Mao depicted his policies as consistent with capitalism, not socialism: "Our policy, including the confiscation of the land of the landlords and the enforcement of the eighthour working day, never went beyond the bounds of capitalist private ownership; our policy was not to put socialism in practice then."[134] Of course, land confiscation without compensation does go beyond capitalist bounds by violating private property rights, but Mao was correct in saying that he stayed within those bounds in the redistribution phases of the land confiscation program by making private ownership of land more widespread. The land confiscation itself broke up whatever feudal relationships still prevailed and so prepared the way for a more capitalistic development of agriculture.

Although Mao's policies were within the limits of capitalism, they were intended to prepare the way for socialism, the main objective. Mao described it thus:

We mean that the target of this revolution is not the bourgeoisie in general but national and feudal oppression, that the measures taken in this revolution are in general directed not at abolishing but at protecting private property, and that as a result of this revolution the working class will be able to build up the strength to lead China in the direction of socialism, though capitalism will still be enabled to grow to an appropriate extent for a fairly long period. "Land to the tiller" means transferring the land from the feudal exploiters to the peasants, turning the private property of the feudal landlords into the private property of the peasants and emancipating them from feudal agrarian relations, thereby making possible the transformation of an agricultural country into an industrial country. Thus, "land to the tiller" is in the nature of a bourgeois-democratic and not a proletarian-socialist demand.[135]

These moderate policies were constantly being attacked by other revolutionaries, by some of Mao's comrades, both from the right and from the left. Rightist tendencies, as Mao saw them, were those promoting leadership of the revolution by the bourgeoisie, those that stressed unity with the bourgeoisie but not struggle against it—"all alliance and no struggle." Rightist tendencies resulted in retreatism, capitulationism, and opportunism; they permitted the bourgeoisie and the landlords to gain the initiative and thus to put an end to any movement toward socialism.

On the other hand, from Mao's point of view, leftist tendencies were policies that "jumped over" the bourgeois-democratic stage of the revolution to the socialist stage. They were policies of "all struggle and no alliance"—of refusing to have anything to do with the nonproletarian elements, of making no concessions—policies looking to the "immediate" establishment of socialism and the "immediate" demise of nonproletarian classes.

Although both rightist and leftist tendencies in the party were dangerous, Mao was normally more concerned about the latter. As early as 1928, for instance, he mentioned, without pressing the issue, that up until February 1928 "we applied our policy towards the petty bourgeoisie fairly well." Then, he noted, in March the party was criticized for rightist policies—for not burning and killing enough and "for having failed to carry out the so-called policy of 'turning the petty bourgeois into proletarians and then forcing them into the revolution.' " Mao added that, against his advice, some of these ultraleftist actions were then carried out. "This ultra-Left policy of attacking the petty bourgeoisie drove most of them to the side of the landlords, with the result that they put on white ribbons and opposed us. With the gradual change of this policy, the situation has been steadily improving." [136]

Mao's battle against ultraleftist actions continued throughout the 1930s and 1940s. [137] In late 1947, looking back at some of the ultraleft policies, he observed:

> It is absolutely impermissible to repeat such wrong ultra-left policies towards the upper petty bourgeois and middle bourgeois sectors in the economy as our Party adopted during 1931–1934 (unduly advanced labour conditions, excessive income tax rates, encroachments on the interests of industrialists and merchants during the land reform, and the adoption as a goal of the so-called "workers' welfare," which was a short-sighted and one-sided concept, instead of the goal of developing production, promoting economic prosperity, giving consideration to both public and private interests and benefiting both labour and capital). To repeat such mistakes would certainly damage the interests both of the working masses and of the new-democratic state. [138]

In 1948, Mao amplified his list of left deviations, most of which he had fought previously:

> At present the "Left" deviations consist chiefly in encroaching on the interests of the middle peasants and the national bourgeoisie; laying one-sided stress in the labour movement on the immediate interests of the workers; making no distinctions in the treatment of landlords and rich peasants; making no distinctions in the treatment of big, middle and small landlords, or of landlords who are local tyrants and those who are not; not leaving the landlords the necessary means of livelihood as required by the principle of equal distribution; overstepping certain demarcation lines of policy in the struggle to suppress counter-revolution; not wanting political parties which represent the national bourgeoisie; not wanting the enlightened gentry; neglecting the tactical importance of narrowing the scope of attack in the new Liberated Areas (that is, neglecting to neutralize the rich peasants and small landlords); and lacking the patience to work step by step. [139]

Such warnings amounted to an admonition to unite with as many as possible. At one time, Mao carried "unity" so far as to suggest that the party should unite with some traitors and pro-Japanese elements![140]

On the whole, Mao's policies reflected both alliance and struggle. He insisted on simultaneous unity with and struggle against the national bourgeoisie and other social strata. Thus he urged that an economic policy of simultaneously lowering and guaranteeing landlords' rents be accompanied by educational efforts among the peasants to explain the exploitative nature of *all* rents, high or low. Mao described such policies as dual policies.

> In labour policy, it is the dual policy of suitably improving the workers' livelihood and of not hampering the proper development of the capitalist economy. In agrarian policy, it is the dual policy of requiring the landlords to reduce rent and interest and of stipulating that the peasants should pay the reduced rent and interest.[141]

Mao Looks into the Future

From late 1947 until the Communists came to power throughout China, Mao gave increasing attention to how China would develop economically after the liberation. He regarded the capitalist sector as an indispensable part of the economy and believed that there would also be a rich-peasant sector in the rural areas. But these sectors would be dominated by the "huge state enterprises" taken over by the Communists from the bureaucrat-capitalist class and by the vast agricultural economy liberated from feudalism. In December 1947, Mao visualized three sectors in the economic structure of the new China: "(1) the state-owned economy, which is the leading sector; (2) the agricultural economy, developing step by step from individual to collective; and (3) the economy of small independent craftsmen and traders and the economy of small and middle private capital."[142]

A year later Mao explained that although capitalism would be allowed to develop, it "will not be unrestricted and uncurbed as in the capitalist countries."[143] Moreover, individual agriculture would have to be gradually transformed into cooperative agriculture.

If there were only a state-owned economy and no co-operative economy, it would be impossible for us to lead the individual economy of the labouring people step by step towards collectivization, impossible to develop from the new-democratic society to the future socialist society and impossible to consolidate the leadership of the proletariat in the state power.[144]

In June 1949, however, Mao expressed the belief that it would not be possible to consolidate the victory without the help of the Soviet Union.[145]

After liberation, "the people" would comprise workers, peasants, the urban petty bourgeoisie, and the national bourgeoisie. The monopoly capitalist class and the landlords would be "eliminated for good." The national bourgeoisie could eventually be educated to accept socialism. "When the time comes to realize socialism, that is, to nationalize private enterprise, we shall carry the work of educating and remoulding them a step further."[146] The peasantry's education was the serious problem. There would have to be socialization of agriculture, for without it "there can be no complete, consolidated socialism. The steps to socialize agriculture must be co-ordinated with the development of a powerful industry having state enterprise as its backbone."[147]

Mao was apprehensive about entering the cities.

The centre of gravity of the Party's work has shifted from the village to the city. . . . We must do our utmost to learn how to administer and build the cities. . . . If we do not pay attention to these problems . . . we shall be unable to maintain our political power, we shall be unable to stand on our feet, we shall fail.[148]

Mao had come full circle. In the 1920s he had turned his back on the cities and discovered revolutionary fires in the countryside. The fires had eventually spread across the lands of China until Mao stood once again facing the cities and once again fearful of them. The cities were destined to haunt Mao in the coming years as they had puzzled and frustrated him in the past.

Notes

1. Mao's rural strategy has aroused much controversy. The position associated with Trotsky is that Mao was not only divorced from the urban proletariat after 1927 but really had no firm class basis at all. Mao's armies, it is claimed, were initially composed in the main of lumpenproletarians, including local bandits, jobless agricultural laborers, and mutinous soldiers, and only later of large numbers of peasants. Even the few urban workers in these armies were imported into the base areas. In view of these weaknesses, the argument concludes, the Chinese Communist Party was bound to smother the emergence of urban democracy—a workers' state— and to develop into a totalitarian party, since it had, at best, only a petty-bourgeois base. Mao's movement was in the countryside, not in the cities. See Harold R. Isaacs, *The Tragedy of the Chinese Revolution* (Stanford, Calif.: Stanford University Press, 1961), pp. 30–31, 52, 309–28. See also Leon Trotsky, *Problems of the Chinese Revolution* (Ann Arbor: University of Michigan Press, 1967), and Isaac Deutscher, "Maoism—Its Origins and Outlook," in *Ironies of History* (London: Oxford University Press, 1966).

   The same view of Mao's class basis has also been expressed in Nikita Khrushchev's memoirs, *Khrushchev Remembers* (Boston: Little, Brown & Co., 1970):

   > When Mao's victorious revolutionary army was approaching Shanghai, he halted their march and refused to capture the city. Stalin asked Mao, "Why didn't you take Shanghai?"
   > "There's a population of six million there," answered Mao. "If we take the city, then we'll have to feed all those people. And where do we find food to do it?"
   > "Now, I ask you, is that a Marxist talking?" [Stalin asked].
   > Mao Tse-tung has always relied on the peasants and not on the working class. That's why he didn't take Shanghai. He didn't want to take responsibility for the welfare of the workers. Stalin properly criticised Mao for this deviation from true Marxism. But the fact remains that Mao, relying on the peasants and ignoring the working class, achieved victory. Not that his victory was some sort of miracle, but it was certainly a new twist to Marxist philosophy since it was achieved without the proletariat. In short, Mao Tse-tung is a petty-bourgeois whose interests are alien, and have been alien all along, to those of the working class. (pp. 462–63)

2. The Great Leap Forward, in particular, embodied guerrilla tactics: an emphasis on the human will rather than on weapons and

machines; on local mobility (large units marching to economic tasks, such as water control projects) and on self-reliance in local areas; on a centralized strategic command but a decentralized command in campaigns and battles; on the concentration of forces against an enemy's weakness, in this case agriculture's weak industrial base. The Great Leap was so thoroughly a guerrilla operation that "central headquarters" lost track of many of the local "battles."

3. Mao Tse-tung, "Report on an Investigation of the Peasant Movement in Hunan," in *Selected Works of Mao Tse-tung* (Peking: Foreign Languages Press, 1965), 1: 46. Hereafter, these selected works will be denoted by S.W. and the volume number.

4. See, for example, Mao, "Pay Attention to Economic Work," S.W., 1: 135–36, and Mao, "The United Front in Cultural Work," S.W., 3: 235, where it is stated: "In our work the war comes first, then production, then cultural work."

5. Mao, "Pay Attention ———," S.W., 1: 130.

6. Mao, "Production Is Also Possible in the Guerrilla Zones," S.W., 3: 250.

7. That some attention, nevertheless, could be given in this early period to increasing the productive forces is made clear in Mao, "Pay Attention ———," S.W., 1: 131.

8. Mao, "Economic and Financial Problems," S.W., 3: 111–12.

9. Mao, "On Production by the Army for Its Own Support and on the Importance of the Great Movements for Rectification and for Production," S.W., 3: 326.

10. Ibid., pp. 327–28.

11. Han Suyin, *The Morning Deluge* (Boston: Little, Brown & Co., 1972), p. 216.

12. See Mao, "The Struggle in the Chingkang Mountains," S.W., 1: 90; "Pay Attention ———," S.W., 1: 129–33; "Our Economic Policy," S.W., 1: 141–45. See also V. A. Yakhontoff, *The Chinese Soviets* (New York: Coward-McCann, 1934), pp. 269–71, 279–80.

13. Mao, "The Struggle ———," S.W., 1: 89.

14. Mao, "Our Economic Policy," S.W., 1: 143.

15. Mao, "Why Is It that Red Political Power Can Exist in China?" S.W., 1: 69. See also Edgar Snow, *Red Star Over China* (New York: Random House, 1938), p. 154.

16. Mao, "Our Economic Policy," S.W., 1: 141–42; and Kuo-chun Chao, *Agrarian Policy of the Chinese Communist Party* (Bombay and New York: Asia Publishing House, 1960), pp. 33–34.

17. Yakhontoff, *Chinese Soviets*, p. 162. See also Isaacs, *Tragedy*, pp. 339–42.

18. Snow, *Red Star*, p. 57.
19. Ibid., p. 211.
20. Ibid., p. 243.
21. Gunther Stein, *The Challenge of Red China* (New York: McGraw-Hill, 1945), p. 87.
22. Peter Schran, "Guerrilla Economy," (unpub. ms.) pp. 3.42–3.43.
23. Snow, *Red Star*, p. 245.
24. Schran, "Guerrilla Economy," pp. 7.57–7.59.
25. Snow, *Red Star*, pp. 151–52.
26. See "Resolution on Certain Questions in the History of Our Party," *S.W.*, 3 (1965 ed.): 177–220. The moderate nature of Mao's policies is best seen in this statement from the resolution (which does not appear in later editions):

> He [Mao] pointed out that after the big bourgeoisie's betrayal of the revolution [April 1927] there was still a difference between the liberal bourgeoisie and the comprador bourgeoisie; that there were still broad strata of people who demanded democracy and especially demanded a fight against imperialism; that it was therefore necessary to treat the various intermediate classes correctly and do everything possible to make an alliance with them or neutralize them; and that in the countryside it was necessary to treat the middle and rich peasants correctly ("taking from those who have a surplus and giving to those who have a shortage and taking from those who have better and giving to those who have worse") while firmly uniting with the middle peasants, protecting the well-to-do middle peasants, providing certain economic opportunities for the rich peasants and also enabling the ordinary landlord to make a living). (p. 195)

However, Chao, *Agrarian Policy*, p. 18, states that Mao's policy was to show no mercy to the rich peasants. Although Mao may in fact have acted this way at one time or another, this cannot be said to have been his policy. Mao later said that all of his policies were within the framework of the bourgeois-democratic revolution, which included the maintenance of a rich-peasant economy. But from time to time, he did carry out Moscow's tough line on the rich peasants, for example, in the land investigation movement. On this, see Tso-liang Hsiao, *The Land Revolution in China: 1930–1934* (Seattle: University of Washington Press, 1969), pp. 291-92.

Mao's ideas about the class structure of China were worked out at an early date but were refined later on, at the end of the 1930s. This class structure was as follows:

1. Landlords
   a. Big landlords (along with the big bourgeoisie, called the bureaucrat-capitalist class, monopoly capital, or diehards)
   b. Middle and small landlords
   c. Enlightened gentry (individual landlords and rich peasants with democratic leanings)
2. Bourgeoisie
   a. Comprador or big bourgeoisie, including pro-Japanese; and pro-European, pro-American
   b. National bourgeoisie (also called the middle bourgeoisie)
3. Petty bourgeoisie
   a. Intellectuals and students
   b. Small tradesmen
   c. Handicraftsmen
   d. Professionals
4. Peasantry
   a. Rich peasants (rural bourgeoisie)
   b. Middle peasants, including well-to-do peasants and others
   c. Poor peasants
   d. Farm laborers
5. Proletariat
   a. Modern industrial workers
   b. Others
6. Vagrants, prostitutes, criminals

See Mao, "The Chinese Revolution and the Chinese Communist Party," *S.W.*, 2: 319–26.

27. John E. Rue, *Mao Tse-tung in Opposition: 1927–1935* (Stanford, Calif.: Stanford University Press, 1966), pp. 83–84.
28. Hsiao, *Land Revolution*, pp. 160–61, in the document "The Rich-Peasant Problem."
29. Mao, "The Struggle," *S.W.*, 1: 90. See also Rue, *Mao in Opposition*, pp. 112, 198.
30. See, however, Benjamin I. Schwartz, *Chinese Communism and the Rise of Mao* (New York: Harper and Row, 1951), pp. 175, 177, and 181, which indicates that in 1930 an anti-Mao faction in Kiangsi called for opposition to "the practice of dividing land on the basis of the possession of tools and labor power"—as though Mao were doing this. This faction also called for a policy of dividing the land equally.
31. C. Brandt, B. Schwartz, and J. K. Fairbank, *A Documentary His-*

tory of Chinese Communism (London: Allen & Unwin, 1952), p. 226.

32. Rue, *Mao in Opposition*, p. 201.
33. Ibid.
34. Snow, *Red Star*, p. 216.
35. Ibid., p. 217.
36. Mark Selden, *The Yenan Way* (Cambridge, Mass.: Harvard University Press, 1971), p. 80.
37. Ibid., p. 86. See Selden's data on pp. 84, 86.
38. Ibid:, p. 87.
39. Ibid., p. 100.
40. Brandt et al., *Documentary History*, p. 278. The document is the "Decision of the Central Committee on Land Policy in the Anti-Japanese Base Areas," January 28, 1942.
41. Mao, "Rent Reduction and Production Are Two Important Matters for the Defense of the Liberated Areas," *S.W.*, 4: 71–72.
42. Mao, "A Three Months' Survey," *S.W.*, 4: 118.
43. Chao, *Agrarian Policy*, p. 77.
44. Mao, "Smash Chiang Kai-shek's Offensive by a War of Self-Defense," *S.W.*, 4: 89–90.
45. Mao, "Greet the New High Tide of the Chinese Revolution," *S.W.*, 4: 123–24.
46. Mao, busy with other things elsewhere, may not have been consulted about this land law, and so its leftist orientation may have been directed and fashioned by others. See Jerome Ch'en, ed., *Mao* (Englewood Cliffs, N.J.: Prentice-Hall, 1969), p. 93, n. 14.
47. Mao, "The Present Situation and Our Tasks," *S.W.*, 4: 174–75.
48. Mao, "Speech at a Conference of Cadres in the Shansi-Suiyuan Liberated Area," *S.W.*, 4: 237–38. In this speech, Mao clarified his past policies by emphasizing the reactionary nature of measures leading to absolute egalitarianism:

> We support the peasants' demand for equal distribution of land in order to help arouse the broad masses of peasants speedily to abolish the system of landownership by the feudal landlord class, but we do not advocate absolute equalitarianism. Whoever advocates absolute equalitarianism is wrong. (pp. 235–36)

49. Mao, "Tactical Problems of Rural Work in the New Liberated Areas," *S.W.*, 4: 251–52.
50. Hsiao, *Land Revolution*, pp. 79–80, 82–83, and 202–5. The important document is "The Land Investigation Drive Is the Central

Task of Great Magnitude in Vast Areas," pp. 202–5, presumably written by Mao in June 1933.

51. [Mao?], "Conclusions Reached by the Conference of Responsible Soviet Authorities by Eight Counties on and above the District Level on the Land Investigation Drive," June 29, 1933, in Hsiao, *Land Revolution*, p. 218.

52. Mao, "Preliminary Conclusions Drawn from the Land Investigation Drive," August 29, 1933, in Hsiao, *Land Revolution*, pp. 247–49.

53. Rue, *Mao in Opposition*, p. 259.

54. Suyin, *Morning Deluge*, p. 255.

55. Stuart Schram, *Mao Tse-tung* (Baltimore: Penguin Books, 1967), pp. 166–68.

56. Mao, *S.W.*, 1: 54–55.

57. Ibid., pp. 52–55.

58. Ibid., p. 142.

59. Ibid., p. 145, n. 2.

60. Ibid., p. 144.

61. Snow, *Red Star*, p. 218.

62. Ibid., pp. 221–22.

63. Stein, *Challenge of Red China*, pp. 165–66.

64. Ibid., pp. 211–15.

65. Mao, "Get Organized!" *S.W.*, 3: 156–57.

66. Mao, "Report," *S.W.*, 1: 44–46.

67. Brandt et al., *Documentary History*, p. 159.

68. Ibid., p. 223.

69. Mao, "Our Economic Policy," *S.W.*, 1: 142.

70. Chao, *Agrarian Policy*, p. 67.

71. Jack Belden, *China Shakes the World* (New York: Monthly Review Press, 1970), p. 316. Gold Flower's story is on pp. 275–309. Also see Jan Myrdal, *Report from a Chinese Village* (New York: Pantheon, 1965), for many stories of peasant women before and after liberation; Stein, *Challenge of Red China*, pp. 251–59; Harrison Forman, *Report from Red China* (New York: H. Holt & Co., 1945), pp. 67–70, 154–59.

72. Selden, *Yenan Way*, p. 260.

73. Mao, "Report," *S.W.*, 1: 44, 46.

74. Ibid., p. 25.

75. Ibid., p. 27.

76. Ibid., pp. 29, 56–57.

77. Ibid., pp. 28, 56. This reminds me of what Lenin once said about a

wealthy engineer, a former Bolshevik who had become fearful of a workers' revolution. "He was willing to accept the social revolution if history were to lead to it in the peaceful, calm, smooth and precise manner of a German express train pulling into a station. A sedate conductor would open the carriage door and announce: 'Social Revolution Station! All change.' " Lenin, "Can the Bolsheviks Retain State Power?" *Selected Works* (New York: International Publishers, 1967), 2: 409.

78. Mao, "Report," S.W., 1, pp. 31–32.
79. Ibid., pp. 46–47, 58.
80. Mao, "The Struggle," S.W., 1: 91. Mao's insistence that revolutionary practice is a necessary ingredient in the education of peasants shows up in his writings in many forms. He wrote, for example, that in eliminating the narrow geographic interests of peasants ("localism")

> reasoning can at best produce only limited results, and it takes White [Kuomintang] oppression, which is by no means localized, to do much more. For instance, it is only when counter-revolutionary "joint suppression" campaigns by the two provinces make the people share a common lot in struggle that their localism is gradually broken down. Localism is declining as a result of many such lessons. (Ibid., p. 93)

81. Mao, "On Correcting Mistaken Ideas in the Party," S.W., 1: 105–15.
82. See, for example, ibid., p. 112.
83. Mao, "Be Concerned with the Well-Being of the Masses, Pay Attention to Methods of Work," S.W., 1: 150.
84. Mao, "On Correcting Mistaken Ideas," S.W., 1: 107–9.
85. Mao, "Pay Attention," S.W., 1: 134.
86. Ibid., p. 134. See also Mao, "Be Concerned," S.W., 1: 150–51.
87. Ibid., pp. 135, 151.
88. Mao, "Report," S.W., 1: 46.
89. Mao, "Pay Attention," S.W., 1: 135–36.
90. Boyd Compton, ed., *Mao's China: Party Reform Documents, 1942–1944* (Seattle: University of Washington Press, 1952), p. xxxvii.
91. Ibid., p. xxxix.
92. Selden, *Yenan Way*, p. 188. It should be noted, however, that the background of the Rectification Movement extends at least to May 1937, when Mao called for raising "the Marxist-Leninist theoretical level of the whole Party." (See Mao, "The Tasks of the Chinese Communist Party in the Period of Resistance to Japan," S.W., 1:

275.) Mao again expressed the need for Marxist-Leninist study in October 1938:

> Generally speaking, all Communist Party members who can do so should study the theory of Marx, Engels, Lenin and Stalin. . . . [This theory] is universally applicable. We should regard it not as a dogma, but as a guide to action. . . . For us, therefore, the spreading and deepening of the study of Marxism-Leninism presents a big problem demanding an early solution which is possible only through concerted effort. . . . Another of our tasks is to study our historical heritage and use the Marxist method to sum it up critically. . . . For the Chinese Communist Party, it is a matter of learning to apply the theory of Marxism-Leninism to the specific circumstances of China. (Mao, "The Role of the Chinese Communist Party in the National War," S.W., 2: 208–9)

Furthermore, in early 1939 four thousand cadres and students were involved in a Marxist-Leninist study group in Yenan, and in 1941 Mao spoke a few times on the need for a Marxist-Leninist study campaign as a way to improve the party's work and spirit.

But the Rectification Movement itself was officially begun in a Yenan lecture hall on February 1, 1942, when Mao spoke to more than a thousand party members on the subject "Rectify the Party's Style of Work," S.W., 3: 35–51.

93. Mao, "Rectify," S.W., 3: 35. See also Compton, Mao's China, p. 9.
94. Mao, "Rectify," S.W., 3: 44.
95. Mao, "Reform in Learning, the Party, and Literature," in Compton Mao's China, p. 21. This speech was later officially titled "Rectify the Party's Style of Work." In this later version, Mao altered the passage cited, though it retained the same meaning.
96. Mao, "Resolution on Certain Questions," S.W., 3: 212.
97. Mao, "Rectify," S.W., 3: 43.
98. Mao, "Talks at the Yenan Forum on Literature and Art," S.W., 3: 73–74.
99. Mao, "On Practice," S.W., 1: 295–96.
100. Mao, "Where Do Correct Ideas Come From?" in K. Fan, ed., Mao Tse-tung and Lin Piao: Post-Revolutionary Writings (New York: Anchor Books, 1972), pp. 267–68. For an earlier statement of the same idea, see Mao, "On Practice," S.W., 1: 297.
101. Mao, "On Contradiction," S.W., 1: 311. In recent years, Mao has continued to use the law of contradiction to analyze economic matters. See his "On the Ten Great Relationships," in Ch'en, Mao, pp. 65–85.

102. Mao, "On Contradiction," *S.W.*, 1: 311–47. Many of the statements in the paragraph are in fact quotations from this article or close paraphrases.

103. Ibid., pp. 321–22. See also p. 325 for an example of how the principal contradiction can change within a given process.

104. "Resolution of the Central Committee of the Chinese Communist Party on the Education of Cadres in Service," in Compton, *Mao's China*, pp. 83–84. See also Mao, "Reform Our Study," *S.W.*, 3: 22, where Mao states that a Marxist-Leninist does not "chop up history."

105. Mao later referred to subjectivism, bureaucracy, and sectarianism as the three errors in one's way of thinking and style of work. See Fan, *Mao Tse-tung and Lin Piao*, pp. 204–5.

106. Mao, "Rectify," *S.W.*, 3: 37–39. See also "Resolution on Certain Questions," *S.W.*, 3: 210–13, 215–16.

107. Mao, "Rectify," *S.W.*, 3: 41.

108. Ibid., pp. 41–42, 49.

109. Ibid., p. 47. See also "All Sectarian Ideas Are Subjectivist," *S.W.*, 3: 49.

110. Mao, "Oppose Stereotyped Party Writing," *S.W.*, 3: 53.

111. Mao, "In Opposition to Party Formalism," in Compton, *Mao's China*, pp. 34–45. A revised version of this essay appears in *S.W.*, 3: 53–62, under the title "Oppose Stereotyped Party Writing."

112. Ibid., p. 54.

113. This is in the original version of the essay. See Compton, *Mao's China*, p. 34.

114. Mao, "Oppose," *S.W.*, 3: 55.

115. Ibid., p. 63.

116. "Resolution of the Central Committee of the Chinese Communist Party on the Yenan Cadre School," in Compton, *Mao's China*, p. 77. I assume that this resolution was written by Mao or at least that it faithfully reflected his views.

117. "Resolution of the Central Committee of the Chinese Communist Party on the Education of Cadres in Service," in Compton, *Mao's China*, p. 80. Mao quotes Stalin's saying "Cadres decide everything." In recent years, Mao has repudiated this saying by emphasizing that it leaves out the masses and is therefore elitist and one-sided. See also Mao, "Some Questions Concerning Methods of Leadership," *S.W.*, 3: 117–22; "On Coalition Government," *S.W.*, 3: 315–17.

118. Mao, "On the People's Democratic Dictatorship," *S.W.*, 4: 411.

119. Mao, "On Contradiction," *S.W.*, 1: 315.

120. Ibid., p. 321.
121. Ibid., p. 336.
122. Ibid.
123. I cannot locate the source of this quotation, but Mao has expressed this thought many times. See, for example, *Miscellany of Mao Tse-tung Thought* (Arlington, Va.: Joint Publications Research Service, 1974), pp. 195–96, 259, 269, 289.
124. Selden, *Yenan Way*, p. 274.
125. Mao, "Sixty Points on Working Methods," in Jerome Ch'en, ed., *Mao Papers* (London: Oxford University Press, 1970), pp. 62–63.
126. Mao, "Chinese Revolution," *S.W.*, 2: 307–9. This part of the essay was drafted by others but revised and approved by Mao. See also Mao, "On New Democracy," *S.W.*, 2: 341.
127. Mao, "On New Democracy," *S.W.*, 2: 341.
128. Ibid., pp. 342–44, 348.
129. Mao, "Chinese Revolution," *S.W.*, 2: 326–27.
130. See fn. 26 for Mao's analysis of classes.
131. Mao, "Chinese Revolution," *S.W.*, 2: 327.
132. Mao, "On Tactics against Japanese Imperialism," *S.W.*, 1: 169.
133. Mao, "On Policy," *S.W.*, 2: 445–47.
134. Mao, "Tasks," *S.W.*, 1: 271. See also "The Orientation of the Youth Movement," *S.W.*, 2: 242.
135. Mao, "On Coalition Government," *S.W.*, 3: 297.
136. Mao, "The Struggle," *S.W.*, 1: 98.
137. Mao, "Report to the Second All-China Soviet Congress," in Brandt et al., *Documentary History*, p. 235. See also Mao, "Problems of Strategy in China's Revolutionary War," *S.W.*, 1: 249–50, where Mao discusses the left opportunism of 1931–1934; "Our Study and the Current Situation," *S.W.*, 3: 165; and "Resolution on Certain Questions," *S.W.*, 3: 195.
138. Mao, "The Present Situation," *S.W.*, 4: 168–69. See also ibid., pp. 164–65.
139. Mao, "A Circular on the Situation," *S.W.*, 4: 219. See also "Speech at a Conference of Cadres in the Shansi-Suiyuan Liberated Areas," *S.W.*, 4: 228–29; "On Some Important Problems of the Party's Present Policy," *S.W.*, 4: 182–86.
140. Mao, "On Policy," *S.W.*, 2: 443. See also "Unity to the Very End," *S.W.*, 2: 437–39.
141. Mao, "Postscript to Rural Surveys," *S.W.*, 3: 14–15. See also "Speech at the Assembly of Representatives of the Shensi-Kansu-Ningsia Border Region," *S.W.*, 3: 32–33.
142. Mao, "The Present Situation," *S.W.*, 4, 168–69.

143. Mao, "Report to the Second Plenary Session of the Seventh Central Committee of the Communist Party of China," S.W., 4: 368.
144. Ibid., p. 369.
145. Mao, "On the People's Democratic Dictatorship," S.W., 4: 416–17.
146. Ibid., p. 419.
147. Ibid.
148. Mao, "Report to the Second Plenary Session," S.W., 4: 363–64.

3

A Survey of China's Economy Through Books

The story of China's economic progress from the first Opium War of 1839–1842 to the present can be told in many ways. I have adopted a rather unusual method of doing this by selecting more than two dozen recent books on China's economy, arranging them more or less chronologically and according to their topics, and then reviewing them. This method not only enables a story to unfold but also offers many opportunities to discuss some of the leading books on China's economy that have been published in the past few decades. The approach makes for certain gaps in the coverage since one is confined to the topics investigated by the authors; and a small amount of duplication of material has been unavoidable. Nevertheless, it has enabled me to present a narrative about China's successes and failures in economic development over more than a century which may be rewarding for the reader.

Naturally, it was not possible to include all the important works in this field. After a long drought, such a flood of economic studies on China has appeared that for this survey I have had to choose those which interested me most, including works I had previously reviewed at the request of journal editors. Most of the books covered examine aspects of Chinese economic development since 1949.

The authors of these books read many other books in order to write their own. As we now set out to gain an understanding of

China's economic development through books based on books, we should heed Mao's warning about the dangers of one-sided bookishness. We can learn something about imperialism, stagnation, revolution, and economic development from books, but not everything—and probably not enough.

The Ch'ing (and Later) and Stagnation

Chi-ming Hou, *Foreign Investment and Economic Development in China, 1840–1937*. (Cambridge, Mass.: Harvard University Press, 1965).

Frank H. H. King, *Money and Monetary Policy in China, 1845–1895*. (Cambridge, Mass.: Harvard University Press, 1965).

John K. Chang, *Industrial Development in Pre-Communist China*. (Chicago: Aldine, 1969).

The roots of the failure of China's economy to develop thoroughly during the 1800s and early 1900s were both many and deep and can hardly be found chiefly in the greed of foreign investors or in the deficiencies of China's "crazy" monetary system. Yet, foreign investment and monetary policies were important aspects of China's economy in those years, and they are essential to a general understanding of the economic events of that period. We can now approach that comprehension through the first two studies listed above.. In the third, John Chang quantifies the extent to which industrial growth did occur from 1912 to 1949, and explains why it was ineffective in lifting the millions of peasants out of the mire of disease and poverty.

Foreign Trade and Investment

Hou Chi-ming's principal point is that, while China did not really develop from 1840 to the 1930s, significant economic changes did take place; and foreign investment not only stimulated some of those changes but at the same time established the preconditions for later growth. Thus foreign investment had some good effects and did not have any serious bad effects.

Before examining this thesis, we should accompany Hou through some of the relevant background material.

Although China had traded with England, India, and other countries before the Treaty of Nanking, which ended the first Opium War, was signed in 1842, that treaty and later coercion and armed force opened the country considerably to foreign investors and traders—mainly to the British, French, German, Russians, Japanese, and Americans. Dozens of treaty ports were established in which foreigners were outside the jurisdiction of the Chinese authorities and in which foreign firms were freed from any Chinese control. From these enclaves, foreigners pushed on into the interior, illegally at first, to set up manufacturing firms and to build railroads and establish mining operations; and they received leased areas where they were immune from local control. As Hou summarizes the situation:

> Foreign direct investment took place under very favorable conditions. A foreigner who wished to trade with the Chinese or establish business firms in the open ports in China had no reason to fear Chinese laws or other Chinese control. . . . In certain ways the open ports in China were not much different from the colonies of foreign powers, except that a colony usually served only one master whereas China had to serve them all. (pp. 108–9)

Total foreign investment in China rose from virtually nothing in 1840 to about $1 billion in 1902 and then to more than $3 billion in the 1930s. Toward the end of this period, more than three-quarters of the total was direct investment in land and capital goods, almost all of the rest being financial investment by foreigners in the obligations of the Chinese government. In the mid-1800s, however, direct investment had been relatively less important.

Most of the direct foreign investment during the period was in enterprises having close connections with foreign trade: in trading companies and shipping, in banks to finance the trade, in coal mining for British steamers, in railroads, in treaty port public utilities, and in textiles and insurance. In 1931, 46 percent of the total direct investment was in Shanghai, 36 percent in Manchuria, and only 18 percent in the rest of China.

In addition to direct investments, foreigners made loans to the

Chinese government. Most of these loans were for military spending, indemnities arising from Chinese military defeats, and general administration; some were for railroad and industrial construction. Interest rates and other charges on the loans were generally high, and the other lending terms were favorable to the foreign lenders—including, for some loans, the pledge of customs and salt revenues as security, and the right to manage the enterprises during the loan period.

Hou insists that, despite all this activity, foreign investment in China was really quite small—only $6–$8 per capita in the 1930s and only a fraction of that in the 1800s. He shows that in the 1930s the per capita figures were higher for most other underdeveloped countries. However, Hou fails to stress that in 1936 the total amount of foreign capital in China was probably greater than the amount in any other underdeveloped country in the world—about $3½ billion. At that time, China's gross domestic product was around $35 billion (in prices of the time), so that foreign capital was 10 percent of the national output, which would seem to be no small proportion. More important, as Hou does demonstrate, foreign capital was dominant in many areas of the economy. Railroads were "in the main either foreign-owned or built with foreign funds" (p. 127); the same was true for water transportation; and foreign capital was also strong in iron and coal mining. In manufacturing industries as a whole, foreign-owned firms accounted for 35 percent of output in 1933. Still, it must be pointed out, the manufacturing sector was only a small part of an economy dominated by agriculture, and there was no foreign investment in agriculture.

Hou believes that the foreign investment had beneficial effects. The direct investments encouraged retaliatory efforts by the Chinese to build up their country militarily and to modernize the economy. Many Chinese imitated the foreigners by starting their own manufacturing firms. Through linkage effects, the direct investments created profitable opportunities for other Chinese firms, and the traditional sector, partly for this reason and partly because it was based on "cheap labor and the poverty of the masses" (p. 219), was able to live nicely alongside the modern sector. Hou sees some good in the railroad, military, and general administrative loans to the Chinese government, and elsewhere he has even entertained the notion that China's indemnities were beneficial in forcing it "to adopt measures to strengthen the Chinese economy . . . to meet the . . . payments."[1] But he quickly abandons the thought!

It is apparent that Hou would like to believe the very best about foreign investment in China, but the facts that he himself presents repeatedly weaken his case. Although there is copious evidence of change, some of it, I admit, induced by foreign investment, the paramount and damaging fact is that there was not a trace of sustained economy-wide development, or anything like it, during this long period.[2] Poverty, disease, and illiteracy in the 1930s were almost precisely what they were a century earlier. Theoretically and, I suppose, potentially, there were all sorts of good "effects" from foreign investment, such as retaliation, imitation, and linkage effects, but actually the whole panoply led to virtually nothing for the masses of Chinese; and Hou is not loath to acknowledge that the government's efforts to industrialize and to modernize agriculture were "pitifully small" (p. 217).

Despite all of Hou's speculation about how foreign investment might have been a boon to China, and despite all the data he marshals to demonstrate change, he is aware that there was no prolonged economic development in China—and, indeed, he wonders why. His provisional answer is that growth was retarded by inefficient and corrupt leadership, by a miserable tax system, by inhibiting social institutions, and by interminable wars.

Even as a "provisional" answer, this is not too satisfactory, for it is overly generous in ascribing a positive role to foreign investment, and it is too complete in isolating its effects from the negative, inhibiting influences of Chinese society itself. Thus Hou seems to conclude that if it had not been for the retarding social institutions of China and all the other backward features of that traditional society, the positive impact of foreign investment would have asserted itself and led eventually to extensive economic development. If only China had been strong enough to absorb the foreign medicine!

The fact is, however, that the foreign medicine aggravated China's illnesses in numerous ways. For one thing, the foreigners, by one device or another, propped up a government that was not committed to industrial development, and not committed precisely because any such development threatened the privileged positions of China's bureaucrats and ruling classes. The foreigners more than once supported these privileged groups against rebellious peasants who sought to improve their lives by radical changes in social institutions. At many other times, however, and despite their backing when the dynasty was under attack, the foreigners carried out aggression against the Chinese in order to increase their profit opportunities. The resulting defeats and indemnities greatly weakened China. The foreigners' aggression in quest of profits also led them, for a time, to push the sale of opium in China, which ultimately did great damage to human life and social intercourse.

Furthermore, foreign investment and trade weakened and even ruined certain domestic industries, and caused severe dislocation in cotton textiles. In general, foreign investments were much more profitable to the imperialist countries than they were to the Chinese, for these investments served to link the resources of China to the demands of foreign economies rather than to the needs of the Chinese economy.

Thus the truth seems to be more complex than Hou believes. The foreigners both built and preyed on China, both strengthened and weakened it. What the foreigners built was designed for their own profits, not China's welfare, but in the process some Chinese were aided. What the foreigners preyed on was deprivation and destitution, which they themselves intensified with cannon and dope, as they sought greater profits.

Ultimately, however, imperialism, by contributing to the deterioration of traditional Chinese society, made it possible for progressive forces to overthrow the Ch'ing dynasty in 1911, which later opened the way for Communist victories and for full-scale economic development. In the end, then, the foreigners' contribution to China turned out to be, not cannon and dope, but food and clothing; not capitalism, but communism.

Money and Banking

Frank King believes that China's failure to develop in the nineteenth century was no fault of its monetary system. Although the system was complex, mystified foreigners, and had many defects, King feels that on the whole it worked pretty well; to understand it, in fact, is to love it. But understanding it is no small matter the way King goes about his job; and a reader might well wonder at times whether King would just as soon not share his love of the system with others.

Although the book is difficult, it does contain a detailed description of monetary institutions and episodes, of monetary regulations and practices, written by a competent monetary theorist. Since that is what the book is all about, I will first present its main outlines of the monetary system and then make a few comments about the scope of monetary policy during the period it covers.

The money supply consisted of copper coins, silver coins (mostly foreign-minted), silver bullion (in the shape of "shoes"), paper money, and current deposits. As this suggests, the currency system was bimetallic: copper and silver. The unit of account was the *tael* when payment was made in silver; the *ch'uan*, when payment was made in copper (called cash). Ideally, a debt of 1 *tael* would be paid by 1 *liang* (a weight measure) of silver or by 100 *liang* of copper coins. If each copper coin weighed 1/10 *liang*, it would take 1,000 copper coins to pay the debt. In turn, the 1,000 copper coins (in China proper) were equal to 1 *ch'uan*, and so 1 *ch'uan* was equal to 1 *tael*. However, these relations changed intermittently and were different in different places at any one time.

The copper coins were "a mixture of old and contemporary, worn and new, heavy and light, legal and counterfeit, Chinese and foreign . . . each coin [was] the potential subject of long and protracted debate" (p. 53). The coins were strung together through their center square holes in substrings worth 100 *ch'ien*, and when ten of these were connected the result was a string worth 1,000 *ch'ien*. This amount was equal (in some places) to 1 *ch'uan*. Coins so strung, however, were usually worth more than the sum of the individual coins.

The 990 cash string would, however, be current only in certain markets, while in other markets strings containing some other number of good coins or some other number of coins of mixed quality would be current. . . . stringing was something of a skilled task requiring the recognition of each of the many types of cash coins in the market, the detection of tempered coins and counterfeits, and a knowledge of their current value. (pp. 56–57)

In the silver sector, as noted above, the *tael* was the unit of account. Monetary silver consisted mostly of ingots, each weighing about 50 *liang*, formed into the shape of a horse's hoof, or "shoe." The banks sent their imported bar silver to the silver shops to be melted and molded into these shoes. "When a payment required tender of portions of these ingots, the correct amount would be cut off and weighed. Such a process would eventually leave broken silver" (p. 72). Silver dollars minted outside of China also circulated, the principal ones being the Carolus dollar of Spain and the Mexican dollar.

The other forms of money were notes and current accounts, both supplied by the banking system, which included foreign banks and the so-called native banks (including, at times, some semiofficial institutions). The foreign banks issued paper money and deposits and financed foreign trade. The primary function of the native banks was either handling remittances (Shansi banks) or making loans to local merchants, but both types of institution issued notes and deposits. The banknote liabilities of the foreign banks were restricted by the terms of their charters—usually the maximum amount could not exceed paid-in capital, and a reserve in specie was required against the liabilities. The native banks, on the other hand, were not subject to such restrictions; but their notes usually had to be endorsed by the person passing them on, who then became responsible for payment if the bank failed.

The foreigners did not like the Chinese monetary system. Their complaints centered on

(1) the changing relationship of the copper coins to the silver bullion [the 100-to-1 ratio changed]; (2) the failure of coins to pass at par with their unit of account [more or less than 1,000 copper coins might be needed to pay a 1 *tael* debt]; (3) the variety of weights [a

copper coin might not weigh 1/10 liang], coins [many were counter-feits], and consequent exchange rates which increased the risk of doing business; and (4) the apparent lack not only of official standards but of any official supervision of the monetary system. (p. 49)

These complaints greatly annoy King. He feels that much of the grousing was due to ignorance of how the currency system was supposed to work. King is willing to admit that the system had many weaknesses; but he thinks that the complaining foreigners should have realized that the defects were inherent in the system, that the Chinese built it that way in the first place, and that if one wanted to remove the defects he had better scrap the entire system. The foreigners' complaints, in King's view, were not very constructive.

It is no doubt true that some of the grievances were piddling, similar to those voiced by any tourist when he is trying to sort out the strange coins he has just received. But it is also true that the system served the interests of merchants, middlemen, and speculators rather than those of producers and consumers. The complications of the system required a proliferation of unproductive specialists between those producing the goods and those consuming them. Furthermore, there were really no monetary authorities, no monetary policies, and no general monetary controls. During the second half of the nineteenth century, money was in general use throughout much of China; the monetary institutions were fairly sophisticated; and an extensive system of mints produced coins. But who was in charge? And of what?

Under the emperor, there were six administrative boards, one of them the Board of Revenue, which, among other things, supervised coinage; and this is as close as we will get to a "monetary authority." Two imperial mints in Peking were directly controlled by the Board of Revenue (and by the Board of Works), and the provinces had mints under their own authority. Thus the central authorities in Peking had only partial control over a supply of debased copper coins that, despite the numerous counterfeits, were almost always in short supply; the central authorities had virtually no control over the supply of silver money until the establishment of the Canton mint in 1889; and they had no control over paper money and deposits, much of this money being issued by foreign banks in the treaty ports.

So when all is said and done, the monetary authorities' control—and presumably their interest—extended little farther than the copper mines and the mints. Domestic copper output for the mints was usually inadequate, and the monetary authorities had their most trying days when the supplies were further reduced by local rebellions. To facilitate the output of copper and its transportation to the various mints, the authorities concentrated not only on squelching rebellions but on introducing new machinery in the mines, constructing new railroads, surveying mining areas more thoroughly, and training additional mining technicians. How could monetary authorities concern themselves with the entire money supply when the square holes of the copper coins caused so many headaches: "Unfortunately, technical difficulties arose over the punching of the center hole; the machines could not be properly adjusted to prevent at the same time the breaking of the coin itself" (p. 227). This was the stuff of monetary policy under the Ch'ing!

It is also the stuff of Frank King's book. Despite its title, King's study is mostly about coins. There is very little here on paper money and deposits, and almost nothing on bank credit and banking operations. King narrows his view to that of the mintmasters, and perhaps for that reason his book gives few clues on whether the monetary system aided or hindered the economy. However, King guesses that the defects of the system were not a key factor in China's failure to develop. His thesis is that the particular institutions of a country cannot explain such failure, for, when a country develops, its institutions are changed by underlying forces. So he importunes us to look at the deeper forces and not at the coinage system for an understanding of economic stagnation. In effect, his advice is—though I hesitate to say it—to look at the big Ch'ing and not at the small change.

Industrial Development

Turning from both the big Ch'ing and the small change to John Chang, we see that the author has set out to establish that, despite general underdevelopment of the Chinese economy in the first half of this century, China's modern industry recorded substantial growth rates from 1912 to 1949. The mystery is how the two—continued underdevelopment (even stagnation) and high industrial growth—could be paired. But before unraveling this enigma, we must first attend to the more prosaic data.

Chang's industrial-production index includes fifteen commodities in three sectors. In the sector of mining and metallurgy, it covers ten commodities, among them steel, coal, iron ore, and tungsten. The manufacturing sector comprises cotton yarn, cotton cloth, and cement. Fuel and power embraces only crude oil and electric power. The output indexes of the fifteen series are added together for each year, but each index enters the total with a weight that reflects the relative importance of the commodity in 1933 (determined by unit net value added). The fifteen commodities, while fairly representative, do not by any means cover all industrial output. Excluded for lack of good data are the products of such industries as construction, food and beverages, paper, flour milling, and all the handicrafts. Chang's basic index does include, however, certain industrial operations in Manchuria, where the Japanese, especially after 1931, realized considerable industrial progress.

Table 3.1 registers some of Chang's major findings. The central figure is the annual industrial growth rate of 5.6 percent over the full period. However, as one can see, this is an average of several different subperiod rates, which started high in the early years and then steadily declined until in 1942–1949 the growth rate was actually negative, an understandable ending when account is taken of the Sino-Japanese and civil wars. Thus the highest rate for the basic index is for 1912–1920, an interval consisting mostly of World War I and its immediate aftermath. Now this should engage the attention of radical economists who have asserted that imperialist powers generally strangle the growth potential of their colonies or neocolonies, and that only when the imperialist countries fight each other, as in the two world wars, does the relaxation of their death grip allow the dependencies to develop on their own. While Chang is no Marxist, he offers the same explanation, shorn of radical dialect:

Table 3.1
Annual Growth Rates of Industrial Output:
1912–1949
(in percent)

Period	Annual growth rates of industrial output			
	Basic index	Including handicrafts	Excluding Manchuria	Manchuria alone
1912–1949	5.6	2.3		
1912–1933	9.3	6.2		
1912–1920	13.4			
1912–1936	9.4			
1936–1942	4.5			
1942–1949	−4.8			
1926–1936	8.3		6.4	14.2
1931–1936	9.3		6.7	16.7

Source: John R. Chang, pp. 71, 95, 99.

The growth rate over the 1912–20 period is the highest among those calculated. During this period, especially during World War I, foreign competitors diverted their attention, though only temporarily, from Chinese markets. . . . Even after the war, the European powers could not recover sufficiently to return to the Chinese market immediately. As a result, the domestic industries of China made substantial gains during this period. (p. 72)

Table 3.1 further discloses that industrial growth rates decline remarkably if the output of handicraft industries is included in the basic index; and that they also fall considerably when Manchurian output is excluded from the basic index. These figures demonstrate that industrial growth was centered in modern (not traditional) industry and that it was heavily swayed by Japanese industrialization in Manchuria. Consequently, overall industrial growth in China proper was actually of modest proportions.

But Chang, fixing his sights on modern industry only, including Manchuria's, thinks differently: "The evidence suggests that the industrial growth of pre-Communist China could hardly be characterized as long-term stagnation or retardation" (p. 74).

Still, the evidence also indicates, Chang informs us, "that the Chinese economy as a whole remained largely undeveloped during the pre-Communist period, despite the rapid expansion of the modern industrial sector" (pp. 112–13). Why? Chang's sole answer in this study is that for decades the state, unenlightened and disorganized as it was, ignored or discouraged industrial growth, and that only when Chiang Kai-shek achieved a degree of political unification was the economy ready for the "great spurt." Thus, during the years 1928–1936 "the necessary foundation was being laid for modern economic transformation" (p. 115). It is a terrible pity, then, we are led to believe, that the Japanese invaders and the Communist bandits botched things up so dreadfully just when everything was being prepared for exponential flight.

In an article published two years before his book, Chang treats this question more fully.[3] He advances three reasons why industrial growth contributed so little to general development. The first is that, despite high industrial growth rates, the weight of modern industry in aggregate national output was quite small. In the 1930s, for example, modern industrial output comprised a mere 3–4 percent of national output, handicrafts contributing 7 percent, agriculture around 65 percent, and other sectors the remainder. Consequently, high growth rates in an insignificant sector meant little. Chang's second reason is that modern industry had few linkages to other areas of the economy: Shanghai, Tsingtao, and Manchuria were bound much more closely to foreign countries than to China itself. Finally, Chang proposes, whatever happened in modern industry, no thorough development could occur in the face of stagnation in agriculture, the largest sector of the economy. Modern industry was in fact a tiny island in a foul sea of rural poverty, and the bridges from this island led over this sea of rural misery to the happier lands of foreign enterprises and foreign creditors.

It is strange that Chang did not incorporate these good arguments in his book.

The Kuomintang and Inflation

Kia-ngau Chang, *The Inflationary Spiral, the Experience in China, 1939–1950* (New York: The Technological Press of MIT and John Wiley & Sons, 1958).

Chou Shun-hsin, *The Chinese Inflation 1937–1949* (New York: Columbia University Press, 1963).

Arthur N. Young, *China's Wartime Finance and Inflation, 1937–1945* (Cambridge, Mass.: Harvard University Press, 1965).

The Ch'ing dynasty fell in 1911. From that time to 1927, when Chiang Kai-shek's Nationalist government came to power, China had no strong central government to mend its political disunity. And even Chiang's regime, beset as it was by the Japanese invasion, frequent battles with local warlords, and continuing struggles against the Chinese Communists, was far from a completely unifying force. Nevertheless, in spite of the turmoil, there was, as we have just seen, some industrial growth in China from 1912 on, but it occurred mostly in the treaty ports and Manchuria. Industrial growth was confined to small areas and hardly touched the masses of Chinese. For China proper, there was little or no economic development during the 1930s and 1940s, but there was an abundance of inflation.

Each of the three books listed above is by an "insider" of sorts. Chang Kia-ngau held a key position with the Bank of China (then a powerful private bank) from 1917 to 1935, was later minister of communications, and in 1947–1948 was governor of the Central Bank of China. Chou Shun-hsin was a staff member of the Central Bank of China under Chang. And Arthur Young, an American, was financial adviser to China from 1929 to 1947. The earliest book of the three, by Chang, contains the most comprehensive account and the most sensible analysis of the inflation. Chou, whose book was published several years later, barely mentions Chang's work, and then only to criticize a very small point, while Young, writing still later, relies, for better or worse, on both Chang and Chou for much of his economic analysis. Chang's book is fairly well balanced; Chou's contains specialized analyses; and Young's tells who did what when, and how much.

The Chinese inflation was caused by rapidly mounting government expenditures, a grossly inadequate tax system, massive increases in the money supply to finance the resulting deficits, and eventually a "flight from money" as the public came to anticipate an acceleration of inflation—a classic case. The inflation got under way "slowly" in 1938, when prices rose by about 3 percent a month. The average monthly rate climbed to 5 percent in 1939 and to 7 percent in 1940. Prices rose 10 percent a month from mid-1941 to late 1944; and 20 percent a month from then to the war's end in 1945. From August 1945 to late summer 1948, prices rose 2,500 times, equal to their ascent during the previous eight years. And in the final months of the Nationalist regime, they went out of sight.

As Chang clearly points out, the price increases in the early war years were not entirely due to the rise in government spending for military purposes but were due in part to an absolute decline in tax revenues and to a sharp fall in the real output of goods and services. By the close of 1938, Japan had occupied one-third of China, including regions producing 40 percent of China's agricultural output and containing 92 percent of its industrial capacity. The decline in real output within "Free China" was only partly offset by a decline in demand for that output. Of course, real aggregate consumption declined within the reduced area of Free China because population as well as production was lost. However, this was offset to some extent by a large inflow of refugees into Free China. Aggregate investment and government spending, on the other hand, remained large—perhaps as heavy as just before the war. Many industries had to be moved to the interior, new ones established, housing built; in addition, the government spent heavily for transportation and communication facilities and to build up the armed forces to fight the war. Altogether, aggregate demand remained very high relative to supplies, though a good deal of the demand was concentrated not on consumption but on investment goods. This, along with a few good harvests in the early war years, held food prices in check until the end of 1939.

The loss of port areas and other centers of production to the Japanese cut heavily into the government's tax revenues. Cus-

toms revenues, which were 40 percent of all nonborrowed receipts in 1937, fell to practically nothing; the loss of territory
reduced the salt taxes (20 percent of total taxes in 1937) and
adversely affected other commodity taxes. As Chang points out,
"Collection of agricultural taxes was undertaken by the provinces,
while the central government based its tax system upon the urban
sector of the economy, collecting its revenues from foreign trade
and the production of industrial goods" (p. 89). And these were
precisely the areas that were lost to the Japanese. The result was
that in 1938 and 1939 revenues had declined to only half of the
1937 levels.

The loss of tax revenues and the rise in government spending
produced large and increasing deficits. The government's attempts to finance these through bond issues met with almost total
failure. Consequently, the deficits were covered by the creation
of money, as the government was forced to borrow directly from
the Central Bank. In addition to the attempted bond sales in the
early war years, the government extended the income tax (which
had an impossibly narrow base), introduced an excess-profits tax,
and imposed a limited set of price controls and rationing. None of
these measures proved to be of more than slight importance.

In terms of 1937 prices, tax revenues fell from CNC (Chinese
National Currency) $1.4 billion in 1937 to about CNC $0.1 billion
in 1941. In the latter year, the government finally made a serious
attempt to broaden and improve the tax system. In June, the right
to tax land was shifted from the provinces to the central government, and the tax became payable in kind; also, compulsory
lending in kind was imposed on farmers. In September, indirect
taxes were changed from a specific to an *ad valorem* basis. In
further actions, duties on the consumption of salt were raised,
and direct taxes were widened and strengthened. In 1942, the
government reimposed a limited set of price controls, promoted
savings campaigns, and tried to restrict bank credit expansion.
The tax measures led to a somewhat better revenue situation: the
decline in real tax revenues was stopped and even reversed for a
while. However, prices continued to accelerate as the public lost
confidence in any near-term stabilization, and a flight from
money developed during the remainder of the war.

When the Japanese were finally defeated, it was generally felt that the Chinese inflation was over. From 1941 to 1945, China had accumulated large amounts of foreign exchange and gold, and so was in a position to import greatly needed supplies of commodities. Moreover, it was believed that domestic production would expand quickly after the war, that the fighting and large-scale military spending were over, and that foreign aid would be forthcoming. Prices did in fact fall sharply for a few months after the Japanese surrender, and, after some controversy, price and other controls were dismantled. As Chang relates the situation:

> Foreign businessmen in China, especially Americans and British, took the view that the government was not sufficiently accomplished in techniques of control to apply restrictions efficiently, and that controls on commodity prices and on the movement of goods within China might easily obstruct the flow of international trade. Foreign loans to assist China's reconstruction were being discussed at the time, and the government did not wish to jeopardize its chances of receiving aid by inviting charges of corruption and incompetence in the administration of controls. (p. 68)

But foreign aid was slow in coming, and it was not large enough when it arrived; domestic output did not shoot up; and government expenditures hardly slackened off before they rose again because "of the necessity of maintaining a military force strong enough to contain the Communist expansion in Manchuria and China proper and rehabilitating the economy of previously occupied areas" (p. 71). The inflation gathered momentum once again, hardly pausing to notice the reimposition of controls in early 1947 and barely feeling the brakes of the tax system. From mid-1946 to mid-1948, prices rose almost six hundred times, and toward the end of this period they had almost succeeded in tracing out an absolute vertical path.

In desperation, the Nationalist government put together a monetary reform program in August 1948, "under the illusion that by waving this magic wand prices and wages would be restored to their previous levels" (p. 357). The reform introduced a new bank note, the gold *yuan*, each of which was equal to CNC $3 million of the old notes. The exchange of new for old notes was made at this rate, and a gold, silver, and foreign-exchange reserve of 40 percent was established behind the new note issue. Prices of all commodities were frozen at their levels on that day (in terms of gold *yuan*), and the public was not permitted to own gold, silver, or foreign exchange.

> In the three important districts of Shanghai, Tientsin, and Canton specially appointed high ranking officials assumed personal charge of the control system. In Shanghai the government imposed the most rigorous restrictions, enforced by secret police. For six weeks Shanghai was more or less terrorized into a state of monetary equilibrium. (p. 80)

But within a month or so, the mounting inflationary pressures broke loose and routed the secret police. And open inflation raged again.

Various attempts were made to save the situation—United States aid in 1948, another monetary reform in early 1949, bond sales. But the feverish ascent of prices continued until, near the end, the real value of currency was not significantly different from zero at the 1 percent confidence level. Chang put it well: "The ultimate rejection of the currency in the concluding stage of inflation was no more than an economic reflection of the impending downfall of the Nationalist government" (p. 85). Just when the price level took off for the Great Beyond, Chiang Kai-shek took off in another direction, for Taiwan.

Chang believes that the downfall of the Kuomintang was due essentially to its erroneous beliefs about economic forces, its overestimate of its own political influence as well as its gross underestimate of the Communist threat, and the steady erosion of confidence and support that resulted from inflation (pp. 364–66). On this last point, Chang describes the redistribution of real incomes and wealth during the inflation: the gainers were commercial entrepreneurs, speculators, smugglers, military officers, and some high government officials; the losers were civil servants, soldiers, teachers, and, to a lesser extent, urban laborers. Farmers probably held their own. Chang concludes:

> Thus inflation in China produced a particularly irresponsible class of war profiteers and reduced most classes, particularly civil servants,

teachers, and other salaried employees, to a state of misery far worse than that experienced during the depression of the early 1930s. Public servants and servicemen were demoralized by a degree of poverty extreme even for China and were antagonized by the growth of a wealthy class which had achieved its position by engaging in activities inimical to the general welfare. By its failure to avoid the economic conditions leading to this outcome and its further failure to correct the situation that emerged, the government earned the disaffection of the army and of the administrative services. These conditions led toward the loss of support which eventually brought the downfall of the Nationalist Government and the triumph of Communism in China. (pp. 65–66)

Chang's study is a nice one, even though its analysis never rises above the elementary level, and even though it is marred occasionally by bad theory—for example, that note issues are inflationary while increases in bank deposits are not. But his very interesting story tends to hide such blemishes.

Actually, Chang has written his book twice: the first hundred pages or so contain the essential facts and analysis; the next two hundred fifty embellish the story with many additional details. While this may be excusable, one wonders why Chou and Young decided to write the book for the third and fourth times, especially since their stories are basically the same as Chang's. But each of our three authors is an "insider" in a somewhat different way, and Chou's intention apparently was to analyze some of the data more thoroughly, while Young had further facts to present and some judgments to render.

As I have suggested, Chou's study is analytically more ambitious than Chang's. After briefly presenting the pattern of the Chinese inflation and the budgetary situation that fed it, Chou attempts to assess the extent to which consumption, private investment, foreign-exchange and trade policy, and the monetary system added to the inflationary pressures. He also analyzes the redistributional effects of the inflation, and the severity of China's inflation compared to that of other countries.

Most of the analysis is blemished. Despite Chou's stated intention, consumption demand is not really discussed—just the supplies of certain consumer goods—so his book provides only a slim basis for assessing the inflationary impact of this GNP component. Furthermore, investment spending is divided into "investment for use benefit" (investment in "bona fide" industrial and commercial enterprises) and "investment for ownership benefit" (accumulation of foreign exchange, excessive inventories, and so on). According to Chou, the former may not be inflationary, because it increases production, while the latter almost always is. This distinction, however, proves to be of little use. A better analysis would recognize that both types of investment spending added to the inflationary pressures; that the inflation itself distorted some investment decisions by distorting relative rates of return and so led to an inefficient pattern of investment spending; and that this in turn led to a lower level of national output than would have prevailed under more rational decision-making.

Chou's analysis of the monetary situation is particularly defective. He shows that banknotes rose much faster than bank deposits up to 1943 and that the trend was the other way from 1943 to 1946. Chou interprets this to mean that deposits "could not have intensified the inflationary spiral" (p. 213), in the first period, while "the expansion in bank deposits did have an amplifying effect" (p. 213) in the second period. This is pretty poor stuff. The fact is that the government deficits were financed by sales of IOUs to the monetary system, thus increasing the liabilities of that system. At given price levels, these monetary claims were in excess supply. The public was free to choose the types of financial claims it wanted to possess—currency, current accounts, savings deposits, and so on. To single out any of these claims as the "culprit" is to emphasize a decision of the public that was in fact relatively inconsequential to the inflation process.

Equally questionable is Chou's analysis of the income velocity of money. Since there are no good data on real output, and since Chou presents none for current deposits (though a series was available in Chang's book), all that he has left are data on currency and prices. He finds that prices rose substantially faster than currency, and therefore concludes that the income velocity of money rose. The conclusion is no doubt right, but all that is actually shown is that real currency holdings fell. This is an interesting point, but it cannot support Chou's elaborate analysis of income velocity.

The author presents an estimable account of foreign-exchange and trade policy during this period. In November 1935, China left the silver standard and adopted a managed-currency system with pegged exchange rates. During the initial years of the inflation, the pegged rates were defended most inadequately; official devaluation eventually came, together with somewhat improved defenses of the new rate in the form of import controls, stabilization funds, and the like; then further devaluation, and so on. Chou concludes from all this that the pegged rates of the early years were absurd because there were no effective controls over trade and payments, and that throughout the entire period the government put far too much faith in foreign-exchange operations as a means of stopping the inflation. On this last point, it seems to have been fairly widely accepted at the time that the depreciation of the currency on foreign-exchange markets was a cause of the inflation, which partly explains the excessive attention paid by the government to this aspect of the inflationary process.

As I have noted, Chou attempts to probe certain aspects of the Chinese inflation more deeply than do the two other authors, so his book is useful as a starting point for further studies in these areas. On the other hand, it does not present a good narrative of the inflation—as does Chang's book—because the chapter arrangement is awkward and the analysis fragmented, and especially because Chou is so involved in manipulating and adjusting the data that he seldom presents the basic information necessary for an understanding of what happened. Still, the book can be recommended as a supplement to Chang's work, even though Chou pointedly ignores it.

Arthur N. Young, who was financial adviser to the Nationalist government from 1929 to 1947, is the latest of our three chroniclers of the inflation, but since his story and conclusions are essentially the same as the others', I will not dwell on them. Young does present some well-organized data on the inflation, and he offers some strong opinions about it.

Unfortunately, his book does not deal so much with the basic causes of the inflation as with his and others' woefully ineffective efforts to contain it. The first part of the book sets out the facts regarding budget expenditures and receipts. The second part discusses the extent to which budget deficits were covered by borrowing from the public, borrowing abroad, and foreign aid. The third and longest part takes up the government's attempts to check the inflation by various monetary policies, exchange stabilization schemes, and price controls, and ends with an analysis of the causes and effects of the inflation.

Young concludes that the inflation was primarily due to excessive creation of money, that overall scarcity of goods was not an important element in the price spiral (the contrary view was widely held at the time in Washington), that among the heaviest losers were army personnel and civil servants, and that inflation, as usual, led to corruption and inefficiencies. Although Young is sympathetic to the Chiang regime, many passages in his book are devoted to the abuses, bribery, thefts, and extravagances of some of its officials and leaders.

Young's accounts of his battles with Washington over policy measures for China are particularly interesting. In one of these accounts, he accuses the U.S. Treasury—Harry Dexter White in particular—of "foot-dragging" during the period when the United States was sending gold to the Nationalist government so that it could be sold to the public in exchange for excess money balances. "The deliberate foot-dragging and obstruction of needed [gold] shipments, despite China's urgent pleas, was primarily the work of White and other subordinates," and "White's efforts in 1944–1945, while blocking gold shipments to China, to promote a U.S. $10 billion postwar loan to Russia, show a strong anti-Chinese and pro-Russian bias" (pp. 296–97, 298). Young concludes that the inflation was a major cause of the Communist victory and that those in Washington who aggravated the inflation "must bear part of the responsibility for the later tragic events" (p. 298). Aside from other dubious implications of this account, the implied efficacy of gold sales in China as an anti-inflationary device seems grossly exaggerated.

The Past in China's Present

Dwight H. Perkins, ed., *China's Modern Economy in Historical Perspective* (Stanford, Calif.: Stanford University Press, 1975).

The essays in this book suggest that Maoist economic development, although made possible only by a violent revolution against the old society, nevertheless contains much of that old society within it, along with its Marxist elements. No Hegelian or Marxist would take issue with that dialectical interpretation of Chinese historical development. Although the book is fairly successful in depicting the stagnant and retardatory forces of the old society, and in suggesting what was required to overcome them, it is not rich in examples or insights regarding the elements of the old society still retained in the new. As we shall see, some factor endowments, a few factories, a little traditional cooperation, and some persistent Chinese traits do not move the dialectic any great distance. But the movement is in the right direction, as is the movement of scholarship in this country on China's economy. The times they are a-changing.

Dwight Perkins, who ably edited this volume, announces in his introductory essay ("Introduction: The Persistence of the Past") that "the primary focus [of the book] is on the degree to which China's post-1949 economy [is] a product of the nation's own past." It is obvious that the answer is, "To a great degree," especially if one includes in "the nation's own past" the Communist revolutionary movements themselves. While Peter Schran takes this tack in his paper, "On the Yenan Origins of Current Economic Policies," Perkins and most of the other contributors are almost entirely concerned with the "traditional" dimensions of "the nation's own past," which appear to include only the more genteel activities of the Chinese and to exclude the many peasant revolutionary movements for equality, land redistribution, freedom from landlordism, elimination of foreign domination, and so on. The Taipings, secret societies, peasant associations, the Boxers, social banditry and rural terror, labor movements—none of these figures prominently as a part of "the nation's own past" to explain later Communist economic policies, attitudes, and aims.

Perkins believes that much in "traditional" Chinese society contributed positively to economic development after 1949. What he finds are certain values and traits—for example, the high value placed on education, widespread familiarity with commercial networks, a drive to achieve—"that made the Chinese people on the average effective entrepreneurs, workers, and organization men when given the opportunity" (p. 5). That opportunity was provided, he thinks, by the Communist revolution, which swept away an intensely conservative government, "steeped in the Confucian tradition," which could not or would not maintain social stability or mobilize resources for economic development. Thus, as Perkins views it, although many of the characteristics and institutions of the Chinese people were ideally suited to economic development, this occurred only fitfully before 1949 owing to the ineptness or recalcitrance of their government.

The government, however, was not the only actor in this arena; there were at least four others: the ruling classes, the exploited classes, foreigners, and the technological base. While Perkins' introductory essay moves among them all, it appears to place an unduly large share of the blame on the government for the lack of progress in improving general welfare. So too does Robert Dernberger ("The Role of the Foreigner in China's Economic Development, 1840–1949"), who, after absolving foreigners and paying brief tribute to a technological explanation, declares that "the Chinese government itself was the greatest and most obvious obstacle to economic development" (p. 47). It could also be reasoned, as Carl Riskin does in his essay, "Surplus and Stagnation in Modern China," that the stagnation was largely due to the fact that some classes extracted large economic surpluses from others and dissipated most of them. Of course, the official bureaucracy participated in this exploitation, but Riskin's view is directed more to the class structure of Chinese society and less to the ruling classes' political reflection, more to the dissolute ways of the ruling classes and less to the conservative responses of the government. Another answer is supplied by Mark Elvin

("Skills and Resources in Late Traditional China"), who guesses that, given population growth and the added pressure on land and mineral resources, the absence of dramatic technological change condemned China to its "familiar equilibrium," which is as close to a technological explanation as one can get. Alas, there is no one to argue the final case—that the ever-widening debilitating impact of private and public exploitation on the peasants left them drained and destitute, without the means to extricate themselves. The masses, whom Marx saw as the greatest productive force of all, were only potentially that: in truth, they were impoverished, ill, illiterate, and mired in superstition.

The full explanation of why so little progress was made during the century before 1949 would undoubtedly incorporate all of these pieces—and more. One fuller explanation would be that substantial economic surpluses were extracted by landlords, officials, moneylenders, and others from the peasants and workers, that the surpluses were largely funneled into wasteful nongrowth channels, that the peasants were ground down to impotence by this continuing exploitation, that the government participated in the exploitation and protected the class structure that allowed it, that foreigners also dipped their spoons into the surplus and so helped to support this entire edifice, and that all elements of this social formation—its values, social relations, and institutions—discouraged rapid technological advance. The heart of the explanation, however, would lie in the exploitative class structure of Chinese society and in the means for its continual reproduction.

Riskin's essay, which strikes me as a major contribution (but one that builds on Victor Lippit's fine work in this area), measures the size of the economic surplus siphoned off by the ruling classes just prior to the Communist victory. To obtain his answer, he first develops a new concept of this surplus—the potential economic surplus above mass consumption. This surplus (S_m) is defined as consisting of two parts: $S_m = (Y_a - C_m) + (Y_p - Y_a)$, where Y_p is potential net domestic product—that is, actual NDP (Y_a) plus the potential output of unemployed factors, including rentiers—and C_m is mass consumption, defined as the average wage rate (w) of workers applied to the total labor force (N) and to rentiers (R):

$w(N + R)$. Riskin assumes that actual profits, interest, and rents provide a fair measure of the first part $(Y_a - C_m)$ and that the second part $(Y_p - Y_a)$ can be estimated from data on unemployed and underemployed factors, underutilization of land, and so on. Taking 1933 data, Riskin finds that the economy had an actual surplus in that year of about 27 percent of NDP and was capable of adding another ten percentage points to this by producing to its potential. Although some of the calculations are based on very rough estimates, there seems little doubt that the economy had actually and potentially substantial margins above subsistence to work with. However, as Riskin demonstrates, most of this surplus was not used in growth-inducing ways but instead served to feed privileged consumption habits, hypertrophic bureaucracies, and foreign appetites.

Thus Riskin's findings are consistent with the view of the "distributional school" that "a major cause of the continuing rural stagnation . . . was the siphoning off of income from the tiller of the soil and its unproductive expenditure by a variety of parasitic elements" (p. 57). This view, based on an analysis of China's class structure, is at odds with that of the "technological school," which is best presented in Mark Elvin's book *The Pattern of the Chinese Past* and is hazily offered in his present essay. In his book, Elvin argued that, by the beginning of the 1800s, "the Chinese countryside was becoming predominantly a world of smallholders" in which landowners, having moved into urban areas, exercised little control over the peasants. Landless peasants were increasingly able to obtain extra income from handicrafts; social mobility increased greatly; some serfs could become richer and more powerful than many free persons. These trends, Elvin continued, eventually fashioned "a social continuum" in the countryside, within which there was no distinct socially dominant class: it was truly an egalitarian society. "Chinese rural society in the nineteenth and the early twentieth century was thus one of the most fluid in the world." However, Elvin added, although significant economic surpluses did not exist in the countryside, there was substantial capital in merchants' hands. To some extent, officials inhibited the productive use of this capital, but its failure to flow into agriculture was due more to the cheapness of rural labor relative to the cost of equipment and resources. In any case, Elvin concluded that the absence of dynamic technological breakthroughs in late traditional China resulted in diminishing returns and eliminated any agricultural surpluses above subsistence that may have existed previously. China was thus in a high-level equilibrium trap in which agricultural productivity per acre had reached its limits within the framework of the traditional technology—that is, in the absence of modern industrial-scientific inputs. But such inputs required an industrial revolution that could not be supported by the meager surpluses available.

Riskin refers to this thesis, summing it up by saying that

> a purely technological position seems to require demonstrating not only that diminishing returns put long-term pressures on the surplus, but that the absolute size of the surplus was so small as to render the question of its distribution and use inconsequential. (p. 64)

But if the "technological paradigm" is accepted, Riskin asks, "how do we explain the rapid attainment of very high levels of investment by the Chinese Communists immediately after their victory in 1949" (p. 50)? That is to say, gross domestic capital formation rose from about 5 percent of GDP in 1933—and presumably no more than that just before 1949—to 15–20 percent in 1952. Riskin's answer, of course, is that a substantial economic surplus was clearly available, that it was tapped by means of land reform, and that it was utilized for capital formation.

In his present essay, Elvin modifies his previous argument somewhat by noting that methods to revolutionize hydraulic technology *were* available and that the high-level equilibrium trap argument does not explain why they were not used. He surmises that cultural factors were important hindrances—that is, the Chinese may have been *too* practical to do much experimenting, or *too* suspicious of new mechanical contrivances. He does not attempt, however, to trace these attitudes to the society's class structure or to move any distance from the spit of land that his intense concentration on technology has confined him to.

Dernberger's objective is to determine whether foreigners

made a positive contribution, either direct or indirect, to China's economic development after 1840. He mistakenly believes that the Marxist-Leninist position assigns first place (the fundamental cause) "to the foreigner as a factor in China's failure to industrialize" (p. 23). To begin with, this was certainly not the opinion of Marx, who believed that the mission of Europeans was to revolutionize a static Asiatic mode of production that had no internal mechanisms of change. Thus, for Marx, Europeans fulfilled a double mission—one destructive, the other regenerative; one accompanied by brutalities and actuated by the vilest of interests, the other as "an unconscious tool of history" in laying the foundations for future Asian progress. In *A Short History of China*, the Chinese Marxist Lin Yi departs from Marx but nevertheless does not take Dernberger's position. For Lin places equal weight on foreign aggression *and* domestic feudalism as forces retarding China's development. Nor was Lenin's position that described by Dernberger. Lenin assuredly regarded capitalist imperialism as exploitation of colonial areas, but at the same time he saw it as Marx did—as a progressive force that was awakening Asia and generating struggles of new classes. Indeed, Lenin viewed this positive side of imperialism "as a fresh confirmation of Marxism." It is fair to say that, in general, Marxists do not relegate to a secondary position an underdeveloped country's mode of production—including its class structure and its political forms—when analyzing that country's lack of development; and most Marxists do not consider foreigners to be the fundamental cause of the difficulties of poor countries. More to the point, Mao's analyses consistently referred to China as semicolonial *and* semifeudal, thereby putting equal emphasis on both foreign and domestic exploiters. Dernberger's caricature of the Marxist position would appear to fit more closely the thesis advanced by Chiang Kai-shek.

In any case, Dernberger contends, as does Elvin, that China was in a high-level equilibrium trap, presumably with little or no economic surplus to apply to development—though Dernberger seems to argue inconsistently on this last issue. He believes that its escape could have been effected only through a technological revolution. China, in other words, was in a domestic trap and not in the death grip of foreigners. Much of Dernberger's essay is a worthy reevaluation of the foreigners' role. He finds that, on the whole, the foreigners made a direct though limited positive contribution to China's domestic economy and that they provided "an exogenous shock to induce modernization." Admittedly, he writes,

> the forces of imperialism worked real and often unfair hardships on the Chinese peasantry. At the same time, to the extent that foreign exports and production weakened Chinese handicrafts, the foreigner served as the vital catalyst for the disruption of China's high-level equilibrium trap and the ensuing search for economic development. The long-run solution of a higher standard of living for the Chinese peasant lay not in the protection of the traditional economy from the forces of modernization, but in the industrial development of China. (p. 36)

In the end, ironically, Dernberger's conclusions are rather close to Marx's.

In six other essays, the authors find several other bases for support of the proposition that the contemporary economy is largely a product of its past. Perkins' second essay, "Growth and Changing Structure of China's Twentieth-Century Economy," asserts that China's traditional factor endowments (much labor and little land) explain the present low returns in agriculture, despite heavy investment, as well as the stability of real-wage rates. Perkins goes on to argue that the distinguishing feature of Chinese communism during the 1950s was its income redistribution policies, which substantially improved the living standards of the masses, even though overall per capita income in 1957 was only 20 percent higher than the 1933 level (pp. 125–128). While this is a good point, in my view the postrevolutionary Chinese economy has *not* been distinguished primarily by its redistribution policies but rather by the political power of the workers and peasants and their control of the production process. Everything helpful to the masses comes from that. The remainder of Perkins' essay is an excellent account of economic development after 1949.

Kang Chao shows (in "The Growth of a Modern Cotton Textile Industry and the Competition with Handicrafts") that the
People's Republic inherited a modern textile industry, which
grew up after 1890, and that textile handicraft weaving survived,
despite the growth of its modern counterpart, because each sector was using a noncompeting set of resources. That is, he shows
rather convincingly that supply, not demand, factors explain the
survival of this handicraft sector. It was, Chao claims, the Communists who actually destroyed these handicrafts by eliminating
surplus labor in the rural areas. Chao seems displeased by this
"premature elimination of handweaving," presumably for the
bizarre reason that *if* surplus labor had continued to exist it would
have been efficiently absorbed in an inefficient industry. Seem-
ingly, therefore, he is berating the Communists for eliminating
this beautiful solution to a problem by eliminating the problem
itself!

Thomas Rawski's solid story ("The Growth of Producer Industries, 1900–1971") is that Chinese industrialization after 1949 was
significantly shaped by the growth of producer goods industries
after 1900. The inherited foundation of the Communists, he
writes, "now appears considerably stronger than previous studies
. . . would suggest" (p. 232). He shows that the engineering sector
in Shanghai grew strongly over time, but that ferrous metallurgy
did not measure up because the iron and steel industry, unlike
engineering, initially required much capital, which was in short
supply. "Indivisibilities, business fluctuations, and scarce capital
combined to thwart the development of an iron and steel industry
in Republican China's market economy" (p. 216). He also shows
that some of these difficulties, stemming from free-market forces,
were overcome in Manchuria by state action that overrode them.

Rawski finds that the output spurt of producer goods during the
years 1952–1957 was due to the restoration of political and
monetary stability, government programs, and socialist economic
organization that swept away "restraints formerly imposed by the
market" (p. 226). But the startling performance of the machinery
sector in those years was based on an inherited foundation consisting of many firms, established before 1949, that were already

at the threshold for the takeoff. Finally, the small enterprises that were inherited by the Communists from the pre-1949 days played an important role in overcoming some problems of the 1960s. Rawski notes that the "learn from Shanghai" campaigns were essentially promoting the small industries established many years earlier in that urban area.

Ramon Myers' essay, "Cooperation in Traditional Agriculture and Its Implications for Team Farming in the People's Republic of China," makes only one point: that the cooperative aspects of family farming before 1949 contributed to the success of production cooperatives and communes after 1949. Myers cites instances of farming cooperation found by Japanese surveys conducted between 1939 and 1942; some cooperative efforts in Taiwan during the Ch'ing dynasty; and cooperation in controlling water in Hopei, Kwangtung, Kiangsu, and elsewhere. He alleges that "cooperation was part of rural life in much of China," only because peasant families, after close calculations of benefits and costs, found certain cooperative endeavors profitable (p. 270). He then qualifies this by stating that the benefits and costs were such that it took unusual circumstances to induce peasant families to cooperate with one another: they strongly preferred private transactions on markets. He then returns to his first position by noting that it was easy for the Communists to build on the "strong family-farm cooperative tradition" in China. At the end, the reader is too dizzy to calculate the benefits and costs of the essay.

Peter Schran, in the article previously noted, demonstrates that the "Yenan way" established strong lines of continuity from the 1930s to the present day. This "way" included the Yenan spirit of hard struggle, self-reliance, and selfless behavior. It also comprised economic policies of self-sufficiency, cooperation in production and collective organization of consumption, production drives, income redistribution, and measures relying on reservoirs of talent and energy in the peasant masses. Schran believes that the Yenan model was implicit in several policy initiatives of the 1950s and 1960s which modified the Soviet style of development: Mao's dictum that collectivization should precede agricultural mechanization; many aspects of the Great Leap; the negative reaction to bureaucracies and highly centralized decision-making; the *hsia-fang* movements; the various ideological campaigns (reminiscent of the Rectification Movement of 1942–1944); and the emulation campaigns. Schran concludes that in the final analysis the Yenan model envisions great benefits from major changes in relations of production which had reduced the vast potentialities of workers, coupled with only minor alterations in the productive forces. The vision, in short, is that of the new socialist "man." This is a readable and interesting study.

The essay by John Fei—"The 'Standard Market' of Traditional China"—takes as a basis William Skinner's well-known work to develop an economic theory of the standard market. Fei employs the principles of minimizing transportation costs and of the efficiencies of large-scale production. In his model, "the optimum market area is the one that maximizes consumer welfare by balancing the low-transportation cost of the small area against the efficiency of large-scale production in the large area" (p. 247). He then considers regional differences in land fertility and natural resources. In more fertile areas, population density is higher and a higher proportion of the labor force is engaged in industrial work. But the efficiencies of large-scale industrial production decline as the industrial labor force grows. Consequently, the market area shrinks to economize transportation costs in the more fertile areas.

This essay was probably included because it implied that the Communist policies of economic self-sufficiency and decentralization have a traditional Chinese basis—the "standard market" as a self-sufficient unit. The implication is that basic economic principles, as much as Maoism, determine the economic environment. And that is the message several authors of the book wish to convey. Perkins' volume, though limited by its exclusion of the unsavory behavior of the ill-bred, does succeed very well in making its point about the continuing influence of China's past on its present.

The Communists and Economic Development

The hyperinflation was finally halted by the Communists by mid-1950, clearing the road for economic reconstruction and development. As it turned out, the new People's Republic of China had one of the fastest-growing economies in the world during the 1950s. The annual growth in its rate of output was probably around 10 percent, though this figure was influenced by the depressed levels of economic activity at the beginning of the decade and by the frenzied output drives of the Great Leap Forward at the end of the decade. Output growth was slowed, and the economy was finally tilted downward, by a succession of disastrous harvests starting in 1959 (due mainly to unfavorable weather conditions), by disincentives growing out of life in the communes, by inefficiencies resulting from the Great Leap, and by the abrupt departure of almost all Soviet technicians in mid-1960. Output very likely fell slightly in 1960, and it assuredly declined, perhaps considerably, in 1961. After the extension of the depression into 1962, there was a resumption of growth, at a rate below that of the 1950s, until 1966–1967, when the Cultural Revolution began to interfere with urban industrial production. Economic growth again resumed in 1968, this time at a brisk pace powered by heightened activity in rural industrialization.

The spectacular gains of the 1950s resulted largely from a bounteous investment program, especially in the industrial sector. Gross domestic investment averaged around 25 percent of gross output, and the ratio was higher than that if investment in human capital is included. At least half of this figure was capital formation in heavy and light industry. For one of the world's poorest countries in terms of income per capita, this was an extraordinary achievement.

The relatively large investment expenditures in the industrial and transportation sectors, which grew especially fast in the early years of the decade, created strong inflationary pressures for consumer goods and services, particularly food products. Since comparatively little state investment went into agriculture, the party leadership endeavored to increase agricultural output mainly by social and political reorganizations that were intended to raise incentives and efficiency. Land reforms, mutual-aid teams, elementary and advanced agricultural producer cooperatives, and communes were the principal innovations. These methods were quite successful in attaining their aims, but at the end of the decade socialization was thrust forward too rashly. Since 1961, the party has placed less stress on reorganization, mainly because the collectivization of agriculture had been largely achieved, and has accentuated agricultural investment from an industrial base that has become increasingly capable of supplying the rural areas with modern machinery, electrical power, and chemical fertilizers.

These measures served to expand supplies of consumer goods. On the demand side, the heavy investment program of the 1950s required restraint of demand for consumption or, what is the same thing, sufficient saving to match the investment. The Communists, having just witnessed the devastation produced by the hyperinflation on which they rode to power, were determined not to obtain the required saving through an inflationary process. Instead, they greatly increased tax receipts and held down government consumption, thereby generating saving in the government sector; they used direct controls and established prices and wage rates at levels that would realize large profits in the state enterprises, most of which reverted to the budget and so swelled government saving; they encouraged individual saving by creating attractive financial assets with purchasing power clauses, lottery features, and so on, and by spreading thousands of new banking offices around the country; and for a time they were able to tap some foreign saving for their investment program. Although the supply of consumer goods expanded at only a moderate rate after 1953, demand was restrained sufficiently to prevent any significant increase in prices. This balance has been largely maintained over the last decade or more.

This brief excursion into Chinese development, especially during the 1950s, may serve as an introduction to the discussion below of recent work on the new Chinese economy. I shall begin with several specialized studies of China's national income and growth during the 1950s and then append a few works that cover China's development up to more recent years. After that, I shall review studies of particular facets of the economy, including price and wage policies, agriculture, foreign trade, taxation, and money and banking. Along the way, I shall present sufficient data for the reader to judge the performance of the Chinese economy from 1949 to the early 1970s.

National Income and Growth during the 1950s

Shigeru Ishikawa, *National Income and Capital Formation in Mainland China* (Tokyo: Institute of Asian Economic Affairs, 1965).

Ta-chung Liu and Kung-chia Yeh, *The Economy of the Chinese Mainland: National Income and Economic Development, 1933–1959* (Princeton, N.J.: Princeton University Press, 1965).

Kang Chao, *The Rate and Pattern of Industrial Growth in Communist China* (Ann Arbor: University of Michigan Press, 1965).

Choh-ming Li, *The Statistical System of Communist China* (Berkeley: University of California Press, 1962).

One intention of Ishikawa's book is to bring together the various published official statistics relating to national income. Ishikawa devotes a large part of his study to a discussion of the concepts and methodology of the national-income accounts of the Chinese, and to the presentation of the actual official figures. Liu and Yeh, on the other hand, in their massive work done for the RAND Corporation, are principally involved in adjusting these figures. Ishikawa has served up the meal, but Liu and Yeh, in their dissatisfaction, have returned much of it to the kitchen.

Table 3.2 presents some of the data on China's aggregate national output contained in these two books. The figures in column 1, from Ishikawa, are China's official estimates of its net domestic material product at market prices (expressed in constant 1952 prices, as are all of the figures in the table). This concept of national output is narrower than that of net national (or domestic) product, which is generally used in noncommunist countries. The main difference is that net material product includes only the value added by the "material-producing" sector, excluding

Table 3.2
Some Estimates of China's National Output,
1949–1959
(in billions of *yuan*; 1952 prices)

	(1) Ishikawa: China's net material product		(2) Liu and Yeh's reconstruction of col. 1 to gross domestic product	(3) Liu and Yeh's own estimates of gross domestic product
	Version A	Version B		
1949		35.69		
1950		42.33		
1951		49.53		
1952	61.13	60.58	71.73	74.67
1953	70.04	69.08	76.94	78.99
1954	73.88	73.05	81.87	83.31
1955	78.80	77.80	87.69	86.57
1956	88.75	88.70	101.89	97.28
1957	93.53	92.78	110.15	100.82
1958		124.03	153.94	114.73
1959		151.06	188.48	132.43

Sources: Col. 1: Ishikawa, p. 45. (The 1958–1959 data given by Ishikawa are 127.3 and 154.7, respectively, but in 1957 prices. I have converted these figures to 1952 prices.) Col. 2: Liu and Yeh, pp. 213, 660. Col. 3: Liu and Yeh, pp. 66, 660.

value added by the "non-material-producing" sector—that is, excluding the service and administrative sectors. This distinction, as Ishikawa explains, follows the Marxian distinction between "productive" and "nonproductive" labor. The excluded portion generally comprises between 10 and 30 percent of countries' net domestic products; underdeveloped countries are typically at the lower end of this range, while the richer nations are at the upper end.

Two sets of estimates for net material product are presented in the table: Versions A and B. Version A is based on official

Chinese data published from 1957 to late 1958. Version B is based on data published from 1958 through 1960 that, according to Ishikawa, are "much of an improvement over Version A" (up to 1957) (p. 45). However, Ishikawa relies primarily on Version A estimates because they are presented in much more detail and so can be arranged in several ways—valued added, expenditures, income; moreover, he feels that the 1958 and 1959 estimates in Version B must be used with great caution (p. 48). Although he does not issue a similar warning about the 1949–1951 estimates in Version B, these are generally considered by other experts to be less reliable than the 1952–1957 figures. It is worthwhile, however, to investigate a bit more carefully the estimates which flank both sides of the core figures of 1952–1957.

Although Ishikawa, as well as Liu and Yeh, has something to say about these estimates, Li Choh-ming's study *The Statistical System of China* presents the most thorough background on the subject. Li shows that the 1949–1951 estimates are inferior to the later ones principally because the Communists did not establish an *efficient* nationwide statistical system until 1954 or later. Before 1949, only a rudimentary statistical system existed. The Communists took this system over in 1949 and began to make some improvements in it during the next few years. In early 1950, a national survey was made of state and joint industrial enterprises, and Soviet statisticians began to help. They

> were enlisted to map the national survey, to help train statistical personnel, and to set up statistical services in the Ministries of Railways (1950) and Health (1951–52). In 1950, upon Soviet advice, the system of regular reporting with uniform statistical schedules was introduced for all major state and joint enterprises in industry and construction. During the next two years this system was extended to agriculture and internal trade. (p. 8)

The First National Statistical Conference was held in 1951, and many statistical surveys were called for. Finally, in October 1952, the State Statistical Bureau was established—a unified statistical system.

Although a nationwide statistical reporting system was not

begun until late 1952, much progress was made in the early years, and a basis existed for making estimates of national output for those years. Moreover, in 1956 some basic data

> were made available for the first time to the state statistical organization, so that the early official statistics might be properly adjusted. Clearly it was due to the increased reliability of data and the widening of statistical coverage that the work program of the state statistical services for 1956 and 1957 called for processing all statistical materials for important indicators since 1949 as well as those of 1936 in order to make them comparable year to year. (p. 63)

As Ishikawa points out (p. 46), although no national-output data have been published for 1949–1951, the Chinese have published annual growth rates of net material product for the period 1950–1959. Hence, given the 1952 figure, the absolute figures for 1949–1951 can be easily computed. The growth rates of the early years are no doubt subject to wider margins of error than are those for 1952–1957, but, from what has already been said, there is no reason to doubt that some basis existed for these early estimates.

Let us now turn to the output estimates of 1958 and beyond. In 1958, during the Great Leap Forward, the decentralization of decision-making along with the campaign against "experts" led to a deterioration in statistical reporting. Criticism was directed against unified statistical control, and the charge was made that the State Statistical Bureau tended "to ignore local party and political leadership" (Li, p. 73). The result was that many statistical units were eliminated or reduced in size; the state statistical system was badly weakened.

In 1958 and early 1959, exaggerated claims were made regarding increases in agricultural output during 1958. In August 1959, the government had to lower many of these estimates, some by substantial amounts.[4] In addition, although the "backyard furnace movement" in 1958 led to a large increase in the output of pig iron and steel, most of this "native" output was of very low quality. In August 1959, the government divided the total output figure into two parts, "factory" and "indigenous."

Although the national-output estimate for 1958 in Table 3.2, column 1, was published after the downward revisions of the original claims, it is understandable why Ishikawa and others still view this estimate with suspicion. The statistical reporting system was straightened out in 1959, so that the national-output estimate for that year is presumably better. After that, the Chinese suspended publication of national-output data, so Ishikawa's figures end with 1959.

Liu and Yeh take as their starting point the official Version A estimates for the period 1952–1957 in 1952 prices. Later on, they make estimates for 1958 and 1959 based on the official data mentioned above, but they do not estimate national output for the period 1949–1951, despite the fact that official data are available (which they fail to note). Their reason for the omission is that during those years "the economy was dislocated and the statistical coverage was meager and even less reliable than for the later years" (p. v).

Starting, then, with the Version A data for net material product, Liu and Yeh first reconstruct them to Western definitions of net and gross domestic product; the GDP series is in Table 3.2, column 2. To obtain these figures, the authors added to the official estimates the following: (1) income originating in the non-material-producing sectors, "such as passenger transportation, government services, finance, personal services, and imputed rent" (p. 224); (2) depreciation of capital in the material sectors; and (3) other adjustments.

To obtain the 1958 and 1959 figures (in column 2), Liu and Yeh derived the net value added of agricultural output from physical quantities and prices, costs of production, and depreciation allowances; derived net value added by factories in essentially the same way; and obtained value added in other sectors—handicrafts, mining utilities, and so on—in various ways (see their Appendix K).

Having obtained their reconstruction estimates of net and gross domestic product, based on Chinese claims, the authors then proceeded to "adjust" these estimates to take account of what they contend are errors, omissions, and underreporting in Chinese data. Their resulting adjusted estimates for GDP, in 1952 prices, are recorded in Table 3.2, column 3.

It is useful to group Liu and Yeh's adjustments of the Chinese data into two main categories: those involving agriculture and those involving other sectors. Table 3.3 shows the magnitude of these two sets of adjustments. It may be seen that in the agricultural sector the adjustments raise the Chinese (reconstructed) data substantially in the early years, but that this upward shift diminishes until it becomes a downward shift in 1957. The adjustments in "other sectors" lead to progressively larger downward revisions over time.

The combined result of both sets of adjustments is that Liu and Yeh's own estimates of GDP start out higher and end up substantially lower than the Chinese series, thus reducing the annual growth rate of GDP from 9.0 to 6.2 percent. Their estimates start higher principally because of their higher estimates of agricultural output; they end lower principally because of their lower estimates of output from other sectors.

With regard to the agricultural adjustments, Liu and Yeh believe that food crop production was greatly underestimated by the

Table 3.3
Adjustments by Liu and Yeh in Deriving Their Own
GDP Estimates from Chinese Data
(in billions of *yuan*; 1952 prices)

	Adjustments involving:		
	Liu & Yeh's reconstructed GDP	Agricultural sector	Other sectors	Liu & Yeh's own GDP estimates
1952	71.7	+2.6	+0.3	74.7
1953	76.9	+2.8	−0.7	79.0
1954	81.9	+2.8	−1.4	83.3
1955	87.7	+1.4	−2.5	86.6
1956	101.9	+0.2	−4.8	97.3
1957	110.2	−3.0	−6.4	100.8

Source: Based on Liu and Yeh, p. 213.

Chinese in the early years of the 1950s, which, since the gross value added of food crops was around 35 percent of GDP, lowered GDP estimates in those years by significant amounts—say, 3–5 percent. But there is no reason to assume that the Liu-Yeh estimates are closer to the truth than what the Chinese have told us, since these estimates have been derived essentially from the simplistic assumption that per capita consumption of food was constant over the period. Although there may have been some underreporting of food crops in the early years, leading to some underestimates by the Chinese, it is also likely that per capita food consumption was less then than it was later in the decade. Thus the Liu-Yeh estimates of food crops almost surely rise less rapidly than the true figures.

The second group of adjustments in Table 3.3 consists largely of downward revisions in other sectors—downward revisions that increase in size during the period. The reductions are in value added by stores and restaurants, factories, modern transportation and communications, handicrafts, and finance—with importance in that order.

The downward adjustments in value added by stores and restaurants are made, according to Liu and Yeh, because "in some cases data on retail sales are actually sales by wholesale units to retail stores" (p. 166). On that basis, the Chinese data are lowered, but I have not been able to reproduce Liu-Yeh's results. In any case, the reductions are apparently based on the extent to which they reduced another, largely unrelated set of Chinese estimates, which seems a bit odd.

With regard to value added by factories, Liu and Yeh find difficulties with the output of consumer goods. They have an "identified" portion consisting of specific items. That portion is the difference between this figure and the global figure published by the Chinese. The "unidentified" portion increased from 26 percent of the total in 1952 to 42 percent in 1957, which Liu and Yeh find mysterious, for this implies an increase of 200 percent in the unidentified portion when the identified portion rose by only 45 percent. So they assume that both portions rose by the same percentage—that is, by 45 percent (pp. 56–63, 151–52). They assume that there was no "padding" in the unidentified portion in

1952, then progressively greater padding up to 1957. This assumption, of course, reduces the Chinese figures for net value added by factories by larger and larger amounts over time.

These same percentage reductions are then used by Liu and Yeh to lower the Chinese estimates of value added in modern transportation and communications! And similar arbitrary methods are used to lower the official estimates in the other sectors.

As I have already noted, the combined result of all of these adjustments is that the Liu-Yeh reconstructed GDP estimates (Table 3.3, column 1) are raised in the early years and lowered substantially in the later years (Table 3.3, column 4), reducing the average annual growth rate from 9.0 percent to 6.2 percent. In this connection, the reader should be reminded that these data are in 1952 prices. Liu and Yeh believe that the GDP series in 1952 prices overstates the rate of growth, because prices of industrial goods were especially high that year relative to prices of agricultural goods, and that the production of industrial goods increased much faster from 1952 to 1957; and there is probably some truth in this.

Liu and Yeh not only calculate net and gross domestic product from 1952 to 1959, but they also develop data on net value added by the various sectors of the economy. In Table 3.4, I have combined their data into three large "sectors." Their figures indicate that the agricultural sector had the slowest rate of growth during the period; factories, mining, and utilities had the fastest; and all other sectors together fell in between. The growth rate of value added in factories, mining, and utilities is most impressive, and this is indeed the sector in which the Communists concentrated their development efforts up to 1960.

The Liu-Yeh estimates for factories, mining, and utilities can be compared to those constructed by Chao Kang in his book, *The Rate and Pattern of Industrial Growth in Communist China.* Chao's aim is to develop index numbers for industrial production, which includes both factories and handicrafts. His definition of factory production is similar to Liu-Yeh's "factories, mining, and utilities." We can, therefore, compare the two by converting the figures in Table 3.4, column 2, to index numbers, with 1952 =

Table 3.4
Net Value Added by Three Main Sectors, 1952–1959
(in billions of *yuan*; 1952 prices)

	Agriculture	Factories, mining, and utilities	All other	Net domestic product
1952	34.2	8.2	29.0	71.4
1953	34.8	10.1	30.4	75.3
1954	35.5	11.8	32.0	79.3
1955	35.8	13.2	33.3	82.3
1956	37.0	17.5	37.6	92.1
1957	37.2	19.8	38.3	95.3
1958	40.0	24.0	44.0	108.0
1959	42.0	31.0	52.0	125.0

Source: Liu and Yeh, pp. 66, 213.

100. The results are recorded in Table 3.5, alongside Chao's index of factory production. As Chao describes this comparison:[5] "Our index numbers are almost identical with those of Liu-Yeh's for 1953, 1954 and 1959; but differ for the remaining years. In general, our index shows a slightly slower rate of growth before 1958 than that suggested by Liu-Yeh's value-added figures" (p. 89). Both indexes, however, show an annual growth rate from 1952 to 1959 of about 21 percent.[6]

There are, however, some differences between Chao's index and that of Liu and Yeh. Chao builds his up, not from net-value-added data, but from gross value of output. Commodity series in physical terms are the heart of Chao's estimates. These are then weighted for broad categories of production by average wages paid to productive workers. Within these broad categories, unit prices of products are used as weights. Furthermore, Chao's coverage is somewhat broader than that of Liu and Yeh.

Over the full period 1949–1959, Chao's index of industrial production (factories and handicrafts) shows a substantially lower rate of growth than does the official Chinese index. Using 1952 = 100, Chao's index reaches 331 in 1959, compared to the official

Table 3.5
Indexes of Factory Production, 1952–1959
(1952 = 100)

	Liu and Yeh: factories, mining, and utilities	Chao Kang: factory production*
1952	100	100
1953	123	125
1954	144	142
1955	161	147
1956	213	182
1957	241	196
1958	293	273
1959	378	371

* Chao, p. 89. "Factory production" is roughly similar to Liu and Yeh's sector.

index of 529. Chao is certain that three main biases in the official index account for this difference. The first was due to the counting not only of final output but also of intermediate goods by the "factory-reporting method." The extent of this double counting depends on the degree of vertical integration of industrial enterprise. However, Chao feels that, because the number of establishments declined rapidly from 1953 to 1956, this factor imparted a *downward* bias to the official index.

> But the situation became quite different after 1958. In that year a huge number of small plants and factories were formed. . . . It is beyond doubt that this development tremendously reduced the average degree of vertical integration in the industrial structure, and hence significantly exaggerated rates of growth, as shown by official indices, of industrial output for the years since 1958. (pp. 14–15).

The second main bias, according to Chao, arose from peculiarities of the price system. As I have already noted, investment goods seem to have been overvalued in 1952 prices, which tended to raise the index at least up to 1957; also, many new products were introduced after 1952 at initially high prices, which again imparted an upward bias to the index.

Finally, Chao believes that the Chinese have broadened their definition of the industrial sector without correcting previous figures, thereby injecting another upward bias into their series.

It is difficult to say what the net result of these biases is. It is likely, however, that the official indexes were biased upward after 1957; but for prior years the situation is much less clear, though Chao apparently feels that some net upward bias was present even during these earlier years. However, one fairly settled point, as Chao reveals, is that during the 1950s China probably had the highest growth rate of industrial production in the world, far ahead of Japan, West Germany, and the U.S.S.R.—a comparison that is based, it should be noted, on Chao's adjusted index and not on the official Chinese one.

What can we conclude from these studies? First, there is little doubt that the official Chinese estimates of net domestic material product have some statistical weaknesses, especially in the early years of the period and in 1958 and 1959. The point is fairly well documented in Li's study, and it would be astonishing if this were not the case for any underdeveloped country.

Second, Liu and Yeh seem to have used correct procedures in "blowing up" these official estimates to arrive at estimates of net and gross domestic product in accordance with Western accounting practices. Ishikawa has a most helpful discussion of the differences between Communist and non-Communist concepts and theories of national product. But while he outlines the problems beautifully, he does not attempt to make the actual adjustments; these are made by Liu and Yeh.

Third, many of Liu and Yeh's adjustments of these reconstructed estimates seem highly arbitrary. Although it is very likely that some upward revision in food crop output for the early years of the period is called for, the major upward revisions by these authors seem to be fanciful and unsupported. Furthermore, Liu-Yeh's reductions of official Chinese national-output estimates—based on their contention that the Chinese overestimated hog production in 1957 as well as value added by stores and restaurants, factories, and other sectors—are all suspect to some high degree. And, it should be noted, all of the Liu-Yeh adjustments, whether up or down, serve the single end of reducing the output growth rate. Table 3.6 shows the annual growth rates reported by the Chinese and those calculated by Liu and Yeh. If one ignores the tremendous efforts made by the Chinese in 1958–1959 *and* does not calculate the 1949–1951 output estimates *and* adjusts for overestimates near the end of the period *and* for underestimates at the beginning—if one does all that, a growth rate for "most" of the 1950s of as low as 6.2 percent can be obtained. Though I do not believe Liu and Yeh mention it, their own figures show a growth rate of 8.5 percent over the longer period 1952–1959. But both of these rates are far below what the Chinese reported for the same periods. From all the evidence I have seen, I would say that the Chinese probably achieved an average annual growth rate during the 1950s of *at least* 10 percent. In any case, in considering this period, one should think of the growth rate as 10 percent, and not as the Liu-Yeh 6 percent, for too many capricious calculations are embodied in the latter figure.

Finally, while agricultural output probably did not grow rapidly during the period, industrial output growth in the 1950s was nothing short of spectacular—the highest in the world. This is clearly shown in Chao's study, a competent job which reflects a great deal of hard digging. However, while Chao's index series up to 1957 shows a somewhat lower rate of growth of industrial production than does the official one, Chao does not convinc-

Table 3.6
A Comparison of Growth Rates of National Output
(in percent)

	Annual average growth rate of:	
Period	Net material product as reported by the Chinese	Net domestic product as calculated by Liu and Yeh
1952–1957	9.0	6.2
1952–1959	14.0	8.5
1949–1959	15.6	

ingly demonstrate that this can be attributed to biases in the official index—for these biases push in both directions, leaving the net result rather uncertain.

Financing Growth during the 1950s

George N. Ecklund, *Financing the Chinese Government Budget: Mainland China, 1950–1959* (Chicago: Aldine, 1966).

The high rate of growth achieved by the Chinese during the 1950s, especially in the industrial sector, was based in part on very heavy investment outlays. It appears that gross domestic investment, starting at around 10–15 percent of gross domestic product, reached 20 percent by 1952 and went beyond 30 percent in 1958 and 1959. These are exceptionally fast-rising and high investment ratios for an underdeveloped country, and they certainly help to explain the high output growth rates of those years.[7] A large portion of investment expenditure was financed through the government budget. We can examine Ecklund's study for some background on this subject.

The aims of Ecklund's short book are limited: it contains a description and an evaluation of Communist China's revenue system only up to 1960, but does not consider the expenditure side of the budget and does not take up the role of government revenue in the economy's saving-investment process. The book is based on the author's unpublished Ph.D. dissertation, his 1961 monograph for the Central Intelligence Agency (why isn't this or his CIA connection mentioned?), and other papers he has written more recently on this topic. The data are almost entirely from translated Chinese sources, and, though the author feels that these are internally consistent and reasonably good, Professor Walter Galenson, in his foreword to the book, seems to disagree. Galenson warns the reader that "since [the] data are subject to serious deficiencies, the results must be viewed with caution."

The components of the state budget revenues as Ecklund has developed them are recorded in Table 3.7. These revenues rose very rapidly during the 1950s, from around 6½ billion *yuan* in 1950 to 54 billion *yuan* in 1959. If we use the Liu-Yeh estimates of

Table 3.7
Composition of State Budget Revenues
in China, 1950–1959
(in billions of current *yuan*)

	Total state budget revenues	Agricultural taxes	Industrial and commercial taxes	State enterprise profits and depreciation allowances	Other
1950	6.5	1.9	2.4	0.9	1.4
1951	13.0	2.2	4.7	3.1	3.0
1952	17.6	2.7	6.1	5.7	3.0
1953	21.8	2.7	8.3	7.7	3.2
1954	26.2	3.3	9.0	10.0	4.1
1955	27.2	3.1	8.7	11.2	4.4
1956	28.7	3.0	10.1	13.4	2.2
1957	31.0	3.0	11.3	14.4	2.4
1958	41.9	3.3	14.2	22.0	2.4
1959	54.2	3.3	15.7	33.4	1.8

Source: Ecklund, p. 20.

China's GDP (Table 3.2), then the state budget revenues were probably around 20 percent of GDP in the early years of the decade and 30–35 percent of GDP at the end of the decade. From other information, it is also apparent that these revenues financed an increasing proportion of total investment throughout the decade; that is to say, capital formation became increasingly dependent on government saving, the excess of government budget revenues over government consumption expenditures.

The main source of state revenue gains was the profits and depreciation allowances of state enterprises. Table 3.7 shows that these rose from less than 1 billion *yuan* to over 33 billion *yuan*—from 1½ percent of total revenues to over 60 percent. Agricultural taxes rose only slightly until 1954 and thereafter showed no tendency to increase. Industrial and commercial taxes made large absolute gains, but they too fell as a percentage of total revenues, from 37 percent to 30 percent. Finally, there were such miscellaneous sources of revenue as stamp taxes, the salt tax, and so on.

The bulk of Ecklund's book is a description of the state revenue system, with little attempt to link it to the saving-investment flows of the economy as a whole. Ecklund shows that the agricultural tax was levied on the "normal" or "set" yield of the land rather than its actual yield. About 90 percent of the tax was paid in farm products, mainly grain, and the rest in cash. The tax rates were progressive in most areas of the country before 1958, although the extent of progression varied with the degree to which land reform had been completed in a given area. In mid-1958, proportional rates were established throughout China, but the rate levels were different in different parts of the country. Proportional rates replaced the progressive tax structure because private ownership was largely eliminated; instead there existed cooperatives—and, a little later, communes—in which property was held in common. Since the progressive rates were largely for income redistribution purposes, there was little reason to retain them once advanced producers' cooperatives were widely established. The national average tax rate on agriculture's normal output was about 15.5 percent, and the normal output itself was 78 percent of actual 1957 farm output. So the tax rate on actual output was about 12 percent.

Taxes on industry and commerce, though numerous and complex at first, were slightly simplified in 1953 and greatly simplified in 1958. From 1950 to 1958, most types of business firms were subject to a net-income tax and a gross-receipts tax. Net income was taxed at progressive rates up to 30 percent, though tax credits were given to certain firms pursuing activities that the government wished to encourage. The tax rates on gross receipts ranged from 1 to 3 percent on sales of merchandise and from 1½ to 15 percent on sales of services, and once again lower rates were given to enterprises favored by the government. A third tax within the industrial and commercial category was the commodity tax on wholesale values. Here, the rates varied from 3 percent to 120 percent (cigarettes), and the revenues were collected at the plant or, for imported goods, at customs.

The commodities subject to the commodity tax and the schedule of rates reinforced the discriminatory objectives of the [other two business taxes]. Many commodities taxed at the lowest rate under the gross receipts tax and given the highest reduction under the net income tax . . . were not subject to the commodity tax—for example, products of the machine-building industries, iron and steel, liquid fuels, and many basic chemicals. (p. 63)

In January 1953, the business tax system was altered somewhat. (1) Tax rates were raised ½ percentage point (except for the top rate) on gross receipts. (2) The number of items subject to the commodity tax was reduced from 358 to 173. (3) A new tax, the commodity circulation tax, was applied to 22 items, on which the gross-receipts, net-income, and commodity taxes were eliminated. The base of the new tax was the state price of the commodity, and the tax rates ranged from 7 to 66 percent.

A major tax change occurred in 1958: the state abolished the commodity tax, the commodity circulation tax, the gross-receipts tax, the net-income tax, and the stamp tax. "Private enterprise in China had been eliminated by 1958, with a few unimportant exceptions, and practically all industrial and commercial activity was in the hands of state enterprises, joint public-private firms, and cooperatives" (p. 68). There was, therefore, little need for the multiplicity of taxes on enterprises. The new consolidated tax on industrial and commercial products, replacing the five mentioned above, was a turnover tax (Soviet style) imposed on end products from the production process, the rates varying from 1½ to 69 percent, plus a 3 percent retail-sales tax if a commodity reached that stage of distribution.

As Table 3.7 reveals, the most rapidly growing revenue source was state enterprise profits and depreciation reserves. This increase arose from the extension of state control over industrial enterprises, relatively high prices on industrial products, low wages, and the growth of depreciation allowances based on enlargement of the capital stock. State enterprises turned over almost all of their gross profits to the state, retaining only small bonus funds and, in 1957, small amounts given to departments administering industrial enterprises.

Other revenues included income from insurance operations,

customs duties, a 1 percent payroll tax, and an amusement tax. Ecklund also includes revenues from domestic bond sales and from foreign loans, but in most years these amounts were not large enough to matter.

So, by the close of the decade (and, in fact, continuing to the present), state budget revenues came almost entirely from three sources: state enterprise profits, indirect industrial-commodity taxes, and direct taxes on "normal" gross agricultural income. Was this a good revenue system? Ecklund thinks it was. By producing ample revenues, the system aided greatly in restraining inflation during the investment boom; by taxing consumer and luxury goods heavily, it facilitated the transfer of resources to investment; by stressing indirect taxes, it did not erode work incentives; and as state enterprise profits became increasingly important and indirect taxes were simplified, it became less and less costly to administer. Also, though the overall tax structure may or may not have been progressive, for most of the period this hardly mattered, because a "proper" income distribution was achieved through the establishment by the state of the basic urban and rural wage structure. Thus Ecklund gives a glowing account of the Communists' success with this revenue system.

His evaluation, however, is based too much on notions of how a tax system should perform under capitalism, when in fact its role may be quite different under socialism. After all, in a socialist economy, if real resources are allocated by direct state controls, no help is required from taxes. Moreover, if the desired income distribution is achieved through the basic wage structure to begin with, taxes for redistribution purposes are unnecessary. And if the state controls aggregate spending, largely by setting the level of real wages and thus the level of consumption, taxes are unnecessary. In capitalist economies, a main purpose of taxation is to reduce incomes; but socialist economies can always achieve this result directly by lowering real-wage levels (and thus increasing state enterprise profits, which revert to the budget). Consequently, if economic authorities have control over the real-wage level (and thus over profits that become budget revenues), over the structure of wages, and over resource allocation, what is the purpose of taxation? Why not collect all budget revenues from state enterprise profits and let it go at that?

One answer may be that the main purpose of taxation in a socialist economy is to stimulate incentives—workers', peasants', and managers' incentives toward greater effort and efficiency— and to do this at a reasonable cost in terms of the real resources used in the tax system. Thus the "set" agricultural tax, which is akin to a lump-sum tax, might well raise incentives above what they would otherwise be, for greater production above set yields would accrue entirely to the producing unit. Also, the higher urban money wages plus indirect commodity taxes could have the same effect if workers have money wage illusions. Moreover, this combination, by lowering the profits of state enterprises, could make managers more cost-conscious. Such tax measures would make tax administration more costly than it would be if all budget revenues came from profits, but these marginal costs would have to be compared to the marginal gains in the economy's productivity.

It may well be that the closer a socialist society comes to realizing the egalitarian, classless vision, the more its budget revenues can come from state enterprise and commune profits, and the less it need rely on taxes. A "family" transfers funds among its members; it does not "tax" them. The Chinese accusation that the Soviets are rebuilding privileged classes and promoting wide disparities in incomes ("taking the capitalist road") can be rephrased in these terms to say that their budget revenues are heavy with taxes because their "family" has split apart. Increasing taxes imply increasing class conflicts.

Some of this may be wide of the mark, and there are surely other considerations too, but I wish that Ecklund had speculated a bit more along these lines instead of relying so heavily on Adam Smith's maxims of taxation for a predatory society.

A *Quarter-Century of Chinese Development*

Joint Economic Committee, *An Economic Profile of Mainland China*, 2 vols. (Washington, D.C.: U.S. Government Printing Office, 1967).

Joint Economic Committee, *The People's Republic of China: An Economic Assessment* (Washington, D.C.: U.S. Government Printing Office, 1972).
Joint Economic Committee, *China: A Reassessment of the Economy* (Washington, D.C.: U.S. Government Printing Office, 1975).
Chu-yuan Cheng, *The Machine-Building Industry in Communist China* (Chicago: Aldine Atherton, 1971).
Nai-ruenn Chen and Walter Galenson, *The Chinese Economy under Communism* (Chicago: Aldine, 1969).

Each of the three works issued by the Joint Economic Committee of the U.S Congress is a compendium of papers by economic experts on China. The first appeared in 1967, when the cold war between the United States and China was still near its apogee; the second in 1972, shortly after Nixon's spectacular visit to China; and the third in 1975, when much progress had been made in the normalization of relations between the two countries. The assessments of China's economy in these volumes reflect these political realities almost as much as China's actual economic progress. Clearly, China's prospects depend partly on how friendly we think it is!

Consider the cold war document of 1967. This compendium came to rather pessimistic conclusions about China's future and was, in addition, full of snide and patronizing remarks about the Chinese Communists. Their economic prospects were considered dreary, but it was suggested that modest gains could still be made if private enterprise were allowed greater freedom. Both the tone and the conclusions had changed by 1972—witness, if nothing else, the simple alteration in the title from "Mainland China" to the "People's Republic of China." Indeed, by 1972 the gloom that was China had been miraculously swept away and replaced by a country on the verge of becoming a world power:

> The People's Republic of China has become an economically strong, unified nation. Its capability simultaneously to meet requirements of feeding its population, modernizing its military forces, and expanding its civilian economic base must now be as-

sumed from its record to date. Moreover, its expanding economy and military establishment provide a base for projecting increasing power in consonance with its enormous human resources. Chinese influence may also be felt both through direct use of economic and military aid and the indirect example of its model of development. Thus China may in the next decade or two join the United States, the Soviet Union, Japan, and the Western European community in a pentagon of world powers. (p. xiv)

This encomium is simply astonishing to anyone who remembers the broadsides from the same committee five years earlier:

The economic prospects facing China still remain rather bleak. . . . Food supplies are now in a more precarious position than they were in 1958. . . . there is . . . a huge amount of excess capacity in heavy industry. . . . [The] plethora of newly trained personnel . . . is known to have produced a depressing effect on social morale.

And on and on. At that time, China was presumably on the rocks; now it had become a model of development worthy of emulation! This transformation, it is true, came partly from new perspectives gained after the Cultural Revolution, but it was also stimulated by the green light from the White House.

In its most recent offering, the Joint Economic Committee has again found much to marvel at in the Middle Kingdom:

It seems clear after a quarter of a century of power that Chinese leaders aim to develop a modern, powerful, industrial state capable of joining the superpowers on equal terms and providing adequately for its citizens' needs. . . . it has become clearer in each successive economic assessment that the PRC economy has attained a firmer base for claims of meeting not only domestic but the major international goals of the leadership. In spite of many current and likely future problems, we should not assume that the People's Republic of China will not be able to meet its priority economic needs. (pp. 16–17)

So in a few brief years, during which China developed nuclear weapons and the United States rediscovered a potentially large Chinese market for its technology and other commodities, the Chinese became, in our eyes, almost human once again.

The successive reassessments of Chinese economic perfor-

mance are clearly revealed in Table 3.8, which compares estimates of the growth rates of China's national product contained
in the committee's 1967, 1972, and 1975 reports. In the first report
the contributors' general consensus was reflected in T. C. Liu's
estimates; in the other two, in Arthur Ashbrook's estimates. It
may be seen that, while Liu estimated an annual growth rate of
3.2 percent from 1952 to 1965, Ashbrook raised the figure to 3.9
percent in his 1972 study and to 5.5 percent three years later.
Similarly, Ashbrook's estimates for the longer periods 1949–1971
and 1952–1971 were substantially higher in his 1975 study than in
his 1972 study. The table also records his latest calculations for
the still longer periods 1949–1974 and 1952–1974.

The most recent estimate for the full period 1949–1974 shows
an annual growth rate of over 7 percent—or about 5½ percent if
one begins with 1952. These overall gains were made up of
unusually large gains in industrial output—between 10½ and 13
percent per annum—and of lesser gains (2½ to 4 percent per

Table 3.8
Annual Growth Rates of China's National Product in
the Joint Economic Committee's Studies of
1967, 1972, and 1975
(in percent)

	T. C. Liu	Arthur Ashbrook	
	1967*	1972†	1975‡
1952–1958	7.1	8.3	9.1
1958–1965	0	0.3	2.5
1952–1965	3.2	3.9	5.5
1949–1971		6.0	7.4
1952–1971		4.2	5.7
1949–1974			7.1
1952–1974			5.6

* Net domestic product in 1952 *yuan*; p. 50 in 1967 volume.
† Gross national product in 1970 dollars; p. 5 in 1972 volume.
‡ Gross national product in 1973 dollars; p. 23 in 1975 volume.

annum) in agricultural output. While the growth of agricultural output, therefore, has lagged behind that of industrial output, it has nevertheless remained ahead of population growth, which has probably been a bit greater than 2 percent per year. Per capita national output, then, has been growing about 5 percent a year since 1949. This has resulted in a tripling of per capita income since 1949 or a doubling since 1952.

It cannot be mentioned too often that what is especially noteworthy about China's performance is not such growth rates, which, however, have been equaled or surpassed by only a few other poor countries during the postwar period, but rather the fairness with which both the burdens and the fruits of economic development have been distributed among the population. In these respects, China has had no equals.

Cheng Chu-yuan's book on the Chinese machine-building industry analyzes an important component of the modern industrial sector, a sector that, as we have just seen, was largely responsible for the substantial growth rates of China's national output. Cheng begins by examining the composition of the machine-building industry in China and its relative importance to the economy as a whole. He then attempts to measure the growth rate of the industry during the two periods 1952–1957 and 1958–1966, the first, of course, proving much easier to measure than the second. Inasmuch as such stark quantities alone do not catch the full significance of machine building in China, Cheng discusses the qualitative changes and technical development of the industry and their impact on other sectors of the economy. Next, he analyzes the factors affecting the growth of machine building, and, finally, he specifies the contributions of this industry to the national goals.

How important was the machine-building industry in the total economy? Table 3.9, which contains official Chinese data, gives some indication of this for 1956. The table shows that machine building, the largest component of metal processing, contributed about 10 percent of the gross value of the output of modern industry, while modern industry contributed about 35 percent of the gross value of total output. Consequently, though machine building was an important part of industrial production, and

Table 3.9
Gross Values of Output in 1956*
(in billions of *yuan*; 1952 prices)

Gross value of total output		167.5
Agriculture		58.3
Handicrafts, trade, construction, transportation, and communications		50.5
Modern industry		58.7
Textile	13.0	
Food	12.0	
Iron and steel, electric power, coal, and petroleum		7.2
Other		17.2
Metal processing		9.3
Metal fabricating Machine repairing	3.6	
Machine building	5.7	

* Gross-value output includes double-counting of material outlays and so is substantially larger than net material product in Table 3.2.

Source: Nai-ruenn Chen, *Chinese Economic Statistics* (Chicago: Aldine, 1967), pp. 139, 210, 212–13, and 222–23.

though it had vital forward and backward linkages to many crucial areas of the economy, it still constituted only 3½ percent of the gross value of output. This figure, however, probably understates the industry's true relative importance, for the official data exclude machinery produced by nonmachinery departments (for example, textile machinery produced within the Ministry of Textile Industry), though they include output for military purposes, some of which might not be producer goods. In any case, Cheng tries to take all civilian machinery production into account, omitting only machine building for defense because of the lack of good data.

What civilian "machines" are included in his study? From the standpoint of output value, the most important are: merchant ships, spindles, AC generators, internal-combustion engines, freight cars, power machinery, AC electric motors, and bicycles.

But the list also includes locomotives, automobiles, turbines and boilers, clocks and radios, and ball bearings.

To measure the growth rate of the machine-building industry, Cheng builds up series for twenty-three major civilian products, most of them specified above, for the years 1952–1957, with 1952 wholesale prices as weights. But he also develops a value-added index for the entire machine-building industry, including both civilian and military output. For the years 1958–1966, he constructs an output index for eleven civilian machinery products; at the same time, he provides rougher estimates of the annual growth rates for the machine-building industry as a whole. Finally, he furnishes some sketchy information for 1967 and 1968. I have recorded his main conclusions in Table 3.10.

Thus the industry grew by about 18–20 percent per annum during the 1952–1966 period, though its performance during the 1950s was substantially better than that of the 1960s. If we consider the longer period 1949–1971, taking account of the Chinese data for the years before 1952 and Chinese claims regarding industrial production since 1968, it would seem that machine building grew by around 23 percent per annum on the average.

These are high growth rates. Cheng finds that they were due principally to the substantial capital investment in the industry and to Soviet aid, although increases in labor inputs and steel products and improvements in technology also helped. The machine-building industry, he concludes, contributed much to industry in general and to national defense, aided agriculture only marginally, and rapidly attained a high degree of self-sufficiency.

Cheng's overall appraisal of machine building in China is at first in glowing terms:

> During the first eighteen years of Communist control, the machine-building industry achieved an impressive record of development. In terms of gross output value, the industry grew from a minor position to become a significant branch in the modern sector. . . . The industry also experienced technological progress. There was a constant evolution in the product mix; the output composition in the 1960's differed significantly from that of the 1950's. The industry in 1966 was no longer merely a repair or assembling busi-

Table 3.10
Growth Rates in the Machine-Building Industry,
1949–1968
(in percent)

	Average annual growth rates		
	Civilian	Military	Total
1949–1952			
Official Chinese index			69.0
1952–1957			
Official Chinese index			34.6
Derived official index	32.4		
23-item index	28.7		
Value-added index			31.1
Derived military index		33.6	
1957–1966			
Gross-output-value index			12.3
11-item index	14.9		
Derived military index		13.0	
1952–1966			
23-item and 11-item indexes (adjusted)	17.8		
Value-added and gross-output-value indexes			18.6
Derived military index		19.8	
1966–1968			
Rough indicators			0.0

Source: Cheng, pp. 8, 69, 81, 89, 122–23, 128–29, and 207.

ness, but a major manufacturing sector, embracing more than twenty branches, which could turn out fairly sophisticated machinery and equipment. The fact that China can now supply more than 80 percent of her domestic demand for machinery indicates the advances made in both quantity and variety of products. Today, the machine-building industry is a vital buttress of China's program for industrialization and the main material basis for her military strength. . . . Being a key industry, machine-building demonstrated high "linkage effects" to other industries. Its expansion created demand pressures on certain input industries, such as metallurgy, rubber, glass, and plastics. The increases in the supply of new machinery also stimulated the rapid growth of several new industries, such as chemical fertilizers and petroleum. (pp. 225–26; 230–31)

That isn't bad for a country that only a few decades ago was almost hopelessly sick and the victim of virtually every preying-praying imperialist power.

However, Cheng cannot leave it at that, for he immediately explains that Chinese industry is technologically far behind the USSR, the United States, and Japan. "While the Soviet industry turned out 800 types of machine tools in 1958, China could turn out only 400 types in 1959." Imagine! What is really remarkable he does not mention: that China is worthy enough these days to be compared to the wealthiest and most powerful countries in the world. That sixteen years ago it was still four hundred tools behind is hardly the right headline for this story.

Cheng then goes on to point out some serious shortcomings of China's machine-building industry: suboptimal small plants, outdated machinery, an absence of quality control, inefficient verticalization, weak management, waste caused by government meddling.

While some of these shortcomings can be traced to the backwardness of the inherited economy, in part these defects can be ascribed to the nature of the new economic system. The central planning system, which exploits unutilized savings to facilitate a high rate of capital formation, at the same time becomes the source of suboptimal resource use due to market imperfections, the growing bureaucracy, and misplanning. (p. 227)

Aside from the fact that Cheng could not possibly prove "suboptimal resource use" in China, where social costs and benefits are so complex and so pervasive as to defy the specification of socially optimal prices and quantities, and aside from the obvious bias, shown here and elsewhere in his book, against any system that isn't capitalist- and market-inspired—aside from all this, in his discussions of weak management, the small size of plants, and the need for rationalization and modernization, Cheng misses just about the most important aspect of Chinese development.

What Cheng has missed is that, as Stephen Andors has succinctly put it, "contemporary China is both a modernizing and a revolutionary nation."[8] This means that the Chinese are striving not only for a high level of efficiency but also for human relationships within the work process that are in harmony with their revolutionary goals of eliminating social divisions of labor, promoting enthusiasm for work based on collective and moral incentives, reducing the hierarchical structures that subordinate workers and peasants to "bosses" and humble them before experts and technicians, encouraging self-sufficiency at all levels, and fashioning working and living environments that are nonalienating, warm, and cooperative, and in general worthy of human beings.

If Cheng would consider what Andors and others have to say about these Maoist goals, he would soon find that the problems are not as easy as he makes them out to be. Given these goals, just what *is* the optimal size of a firm? Just what *is* a good structure of management? Exactly when is outdated machinery "inefficient," if it is assembled and maintained by the workers themselves out of materials found in their locality? Cheng makes short work of such questions because he is confident that the answers lie in the capitalist model of development, which pays much more attention to commodity relationships than to human relationships. His study deals with commodity relationships admirably; in neglecting human relationships, it misses what is most admirable about China these days.

Chen and Galenson's volume is strange in that, despite the great industrial gains made by China and analyzed by Cheng and others, its authors recommend that China stick to agriculture. Nevertheless, their book is a good, concise economic survey of China. The factual material is presented fairly, clearly, and without excessive detail. Here and there, however, the analysis is colorfully wrapped in capitalist-imperialist ideology.

Chen and Galenson present, first, a sketch of the economy during the several decades prior to 1959. Then they turn to the alternative economic-development paths that faced the Communists at the outset, and they go on from there to explain the development policies that were actually adopted in industry, agriculture, and international trade, and to describe the economic and social reorganizations that supported those policies. Finally, they discuss the conditions of life and labor in China since 1949, and the prospects for the economy over the next few decades.

This is probably the best book now available for anyone who wants to learn about the general pattern of economic development in Communist China without spending too much time at it. The book can be read with great understanding by noneconomists.

Chen and Galenson are quite critical of many aspects of China's economic-development efforts and recommend some rather drastic revisions in its present policies. Their main advice is that China should concentrate much more on increasing agricultural output and holding back population growth. At the same time, it should postpone heavy industrialization, emphasizing instead light, labor-intensive industries, such as textiles. Chen and Galenson believe that it would be best if China turned itself into "the world's supplier of labor-intensive agricultural commodities" and imported, not heavy capital equipment, but wheat, chemical fertilizers (not fertilizer plants), and some capital goods for light industry.

Some readers will recognize this as a neat prescription for economic subservience, for the return of China to its "rightful place" in the expoitative hierarchy of international capitalism, in which underdeveloped countries are advised to go slow and to maintain their comparative advantage in supplying the rich nations with raw materials, agricultural products, minerals, and oil. China is one of the few countries, and certainly the most important country, that has escaped this exploitative system in recent years, and the escape has been precisely through rapid and complete industrialization, without the "help" of foreign investment and, in the last fifteen years, without the "help" of foreign aid.

Throughout their book, Chen and Galenson point to Japan, India, and Taiwan as worthy examples for China. No doubt, China could learn many things from all three, and some of these are ably discussed in the book. But the authors do not note that the Chinese leaders have very good reasons to avoid the awful human costs that accompanied Japanese development,[9] the fawning subservience and pathetic dependence that characterized Taiwan's growth, and the gross inequalities in India, where fabulous fortunes, however high they are piled, cannot hide the widespread starvation, the beggars, the homeless, and the millions who are still hardly conscious of being human. In sum, this book, technically very good and ideologically capitalist, should appeal to a wide audience.

Agricultural Policies

Kuo-chun Chao, *Agrarian Policy of the Chinese Communist Party, 1921–1959* (Bombay: Asia Publishing House, 1960).
Kenneth R. Walker, *Planning in Chinese Agriculture: Socialisation and the Private Sector, 1956–1962* (London: Frank Cass, 1965).

Kuo-chun Chao has written a dull book that contains a lot of information, arranged one, two, three . . . one, two, three. It also contains a solidly based evaluation of the Communists' agrarian programs, much sympathy for their cause, and unquestioning reliance on their data. If Liu and Yeh are the skeptics and manipulators par excellence, Chao is the positive supporter.

Chao first presents a historical survey of the Communists' agrarian policies during the period 1921–1949, from the founding of the party to its final victory over the Kuomintang. The party had no land until Mao Tse-tung established a soviet in late 1927 in Hunan province; later soviets were set up in Kiangsi and Fukien. Until the Communists were driven out of these areas, they confiscated land and redistributed it to the poor, sometimes with "great force and bloodshed"; abolished rent contracts and usurious loans; and carried out various political and social programs. The Long March, which began in October 1934, led the Communists to Northern Shensi, where a new soviet had been established and a land reform program enforced.

During the Sino-Japanese war period, 1937–1945, the Communists ceased land confiscation in order to create a common front against Japan and to expand production. The reduction of rent and interest and the cancellation of some debts constituted the crux of their land policies during the war years. These policies were continued for more than a year after the war, but from December 1946 to October 1947, there were compulsory sales by landlords of their "excess lands," and then in the next six months a swing to the left set in motion "a series of radical measures in the form of 'struggle meetings' and 'settle account' mass gatherings which often resulted in harsh treatment of the landlords and rich peasants" (p. 78). However, the Communists followed a much more moderate policy from spring 1948 to June 1950, "with the reduction of rent and interest again becoming the order of the day in the new liberated areas" (p. 74).

Chao then takes up the land reform program of 1950–1953, which he considers to have been an indispensable step in the process leading from individual ownership to mutual-aid teams, to agricultural producers' cooperatives, and finally to the communes. The program broke the hold of the landed gentry and made later reforms possible. Land was taken from landlords and rich peasants and redistributed to poor peasants and farm laborers to such an extent that, by the spring of 1953, almost the entire rural population of China had been affected and around 46 million hectares had been redistributed.

This, however, left landholdings fragmented, precluding the advantages of efficient large-scale production methods. The next step, therefore, taken in late 1955, was the organization of agricultural producers' cooperatives (APCs), composed of a few hundred families which contributed their land, draft animals, and large farm implements to the common pool. The peasants received payments for both their labor and their capital contributions. The cooperatives were quickly transformed into higher-stage APCs, in which land and capital goods were both centrally managed and centrally owned, and the peasants received compensation only for their labor.

The communes came next, in mid-1958. The first few were probably developed spontaneously by local cadres and perhaps by the peasants, but Peking soon gave them firm support—and then the movement spread like wild fire. At the end of 1958, 99 percent of some 120 million peasant households were communized. Instead of 740,000 APCs with an average of about 160 households, there were in September 1959 about 24,000 people's communes, averaging over 5,000 households in each. (p. 162)

Chao's book has a great deal of information on both the APCs, especially the higher-stage ones, and the communes. It covers the Communists' agrotechnical, rural-finance, and market control programs as well as many other aspects of their agrarian policies in the period 1955–1959. The final chapters contain an evaluation of those policies. Chao feels that the Communists went about agricultural reform in almost exactly the right way and that they have been quite successful in raising labor productivity in agriculture and in effectively utilizing rural manpower for large-scale projects, such as irrigation, reforestation, and conservation. However, his main point here and throughout the book is that the Communists' investment in human capital—in the education, social welfare, and health of the peasants—has been one of the most important aspects of their agrarian policies.

Chao describes the miserable condition of the Chinese peasants down through the centuries. Progress was retarded by

superstitious beliefs and practices, such as the worship of spirits and idols, the complete resignation to fate, blind following of witch doctors, fortune tellers and ignorant midwives, membership in mystic and secret cults and societies, and frequent sacrifices to temples or idols. . . . When there was either drought or flood, many peasants went to the temples to appease the "Dragon King," instead of taking preventive or remedial measures. When insect pests became inordinately destructive, farmers burned incense at the temple of "Great Deity Chang" or, as in some Kiangsu villages, beat up a "bewitching woman." The gambling houses and opium dens indirectly contributed their share to the retardation of important improvement in agriculture. (pp. 5, 11)

To superstition, gambling, and opium may be added widespread diseases; mass illiteracy; perpetual indebtedness to landlords and moneylenders, growing out of wasteful spending on "general good fortune" and on births, weddings, and funerals; exploitation by the landed gentry through exorbitant rents and by warlords through heavy taxes for military ventures; the denigration of labor. It was a vicious circle: the political and social system robbed the peasants and inculcated an attitude of resignation which perpetuated the power of their exploiters.

Chao feels that the crucial element in what seemed to be the irremediable misery of the Chinese peasants was the lack of "efficient, devoted leadership at the grass-roots level, in addition to direction and systematic planning from the Central Government" (p. 283). This type of leadership was provided by the Communists, who in short order profoundly altered the political and social structure of the villages under their control and on that new basis began to lift the peasant from the muck.

Referring to the 1927–1937 period, Chao states:

> The political and social features of Chinese Communist land policy in the Soviet period—the mobilization of the masses, indoctrination of cadres, betterment of the status of women and the elimination of superstitious practices—achieved far more than the purely economic platforms. (pp. 37–38)

In later years, these programs were carried out all over China. They included public-health campaigns, universal opportunity for education and medical help, newspapers and journals especially designed for rural readers, the creation of rural film teams and other entertainment, mass participation in athletics, and equality of the sexes.

In Chao's eyes, the result has been

> the coming into being of a new type of Chinese peasant freed from traditional superstitious beliefs and inferiority complex. Liberated from landlord-gentry dominance as well as magico-religious inhibitions, a positive, communal and enterprising spirit is becoming increasingly evident among the Chinese villages. . . . Instead of the toilers' former despondence and resignation, they are now proud and forward-looking. (p. 254)

It is by now a well-known story that during the 1950s the Chinese Communists sought rapid economic development through a heavy investment program in the industrial sector, and that they attempted to raise agricultural output more by reorganization techniques than by investment. To this, Chao reminds us, should be added the investment in the peasant himself—the impressive gains achieved in his standards of health and education and in his general welfare and outlook. In the long run, these are the gains that may well count the most.

In the introduction to his book *Planning in Chinese Agriculture*, Kenneth Walker notes that some economists have concluded that China's socialization of agriculture went more smoothly than the Soviet Union's partly because Chinese pigs retained their freedom—that is, were not socialized. Walker considers this an oversimplification, and his small book, rich in pig manure and private plots, tells why.

The problem, as Walker sees it, is this: The Communists would collectivize all of agriculture and thus eliminate the peasants' private plots if the costs of doing so were reasonable. However, the private plots produce mainly vegetables and pigs, and the pigs produce manure, the dominant fertilizer of the collective sector. If the government eliminated the private plots, would the peasants rebel by slaughtering the pigs? Even if the pigs survived, could they prosper under socialization? Could the collective sector get along with less pig manure?

In answering these three questions, Walker begins by running through the history of Communist agricultural policy—from the land reforms of 1949–1952 to the communes of 1958–1959, and beyond. Almost all of the land was privately held until mid-1955, though much of it was worked by mutual-aid teams. From mid-1955 until spring 1956, the land continued under private ownership but was managed centrally by agriculture producers' cooperatives (APCs). Private plots—that is, land privately owned and privately managed—were allotted to peasants by the 5 percent rule: the area given per head could not exceed 5 percent of the arable land per head in the village. Despite the authorities' initial intention, during 1956 cadres in the villages "squeezed" the private plots. Some private plots were done away with, land of very poor quality was assigned for other plots, manure was not paid for, "excessive" work on private plots was subject to fines, and so on.

From spring 1956 to August 1958, land—and major capital goods—was collectivized under the higher-stage APCs. But the private plots were retained, although there was a second drive against them in early 1958. From August 1958 to spring 1959, communes were established which eliminated the private owner-ship of land and capital goods (with minor exceptions). After 1960, however, the private plots were reopened, and since that time they have continued to exist side by side with the collective sector.

How did the peasants behave during the two drives against their private plots and during the time when the plots were actually eliminated? In 1956, the "peasants responded by continu-ing to kill pigs and poultry, while allowing their draught animals to die through neglect, so exacerbating the decline which had begun in 1954 in anticipation of the cooperativisation campaign and the uncertainty it brought regarding ownership" (p. 62).

The harassment was stopped, and the private plots were once again honored. In June 1957, the limit of private plots was raised from 5 to 10 percent, pig prices were increased, and village trade and private sideline production were encouraged.

This liberal attitude toward private plots ended in the spring of 1958, when a second drive against them began. Later in the year, private plots were said to be inconsistent with the communes, the labor brigades, the free supply of food, and so on. Pigs were socialized and reared by the common mess halls. Walker believes that the peasants were quite unhappy with this turn of events. "One article reported that peasants had destroyed tools rather than give them over to the communes. . . . The land formerly worked as private plots had fallen out of use. Without such plots peasants had no opportunity to use their leisure time produc-tively" (p. 80).

Turning to the second question—could the pigs prosper under socialization—Walker claims that the pigs fared badly when they were reared by the APCs and socialized under the communes. This was because the APCs and the communes were wasteful of the capital resources going into pig rearing. The "collectives built pig sties of lavish dimensions . . . luxurious buildings" (pp. 66–67); were badly managed ("[It was] openly conceded that poor management, giving rise to disease, was the main cause [of the high death rate of pigs in 1960]" (pp. 84, 90); used skilled labor for other work, leaving little or none for pig rearing; did not allocate sufficient fodder for pigs; and wasted large quantities of animal fertilizer.

As to the third question—is pig manure really needed?— Walker says yes, for many years to come. He estimated that (in 1965) China was producing only a small fraction of the chemical fertilizers required for good performance and that it would be many years before chemical-fertilizer production was at the necessary levels. This is also the conclusion of Owen L. Dawson's chapter on "Fertilizer Supply and Food Requirements," in J. L. Buck et al., *Food and Agriculture in Communist China* (New York: Praeger, 1965). Dawson is extremely pessimistic (if that is the right word!) about China's ability to produce enough chemical fertilizer to ward off famines by the mid-1970s.[10]

Summing up, Walker's findings are that the peasants have jealously guarded their private possessions, including pigs; that pig rearing by collectives is inefficient; and that the collective sector badly needed and would continue to need pig manure. He therefore concluded that a private sector was a necessary adjunct to the collective sector. Later on, when the collective sector had greatly increased its use of chemical fertilizers and its output had responded, there would be less need for the private sector, and the peasants, their fears allayed by ample output in the collective sector, would more willingly give up their private possessions.

It is apparent that Walker's book has a much narrower focus than Chao's. It also reflects a mild obsession with the supposed virtues of private property, a disposition to see no good in any collective effort, even in the attempt to socialize the pigs. But the book does contain the best account I have seen of the undulations in the status of the peasants' private plots, and that may be enough to justify it.

Foreign Trade and Aid

Alexander Eckstein, *Communist China's Economic Growth and Foreign Trade* (New York: McGraw-Hill, 1966).
Sidney Klein, *The Road Divides* (Hong Kong: International Studies Group, 1966).

Feng-hwa Mah, *The Foreign Trade of Mainland China* (Chicago: Aldine, 1971).

During the time that China was "isolated from the rest of the world"—before Nixon's visit—it was trading with more than 90 countries. In the 1950s, its trade was mostly with the Soviet Union and other Communist countries, although Hong Kong received large volumes of Chinese exports from the beginning, and other non-Communist countries became more attentive to this trade as the United States-led embargo against China weakened. After the Sino-Soviet split in 1960, China's trade with non-Communist countries rapidly replaced its previous economic transactions with the USSR; Japan, Western Europe, Australia, and Canada were increasingly drawn into China's orbit. By the early 1970s, China's main trading partners were Japan, Hong Kong, Canada, and West Germany. However, throughout the 1950s and 1960s, China traded briskly with many African, South American, and, of course, Asian nations.

China's imports in the 1950s were predominantly machinery, equipment, and industrial materials; these included 150–200 complete industrial plants from the Soviet Union. To pay for these imports, China exported minerals and textiles, processed foods, and other consumer goods. During the 1960s, the composition of its imports changed markedly, though its exports were more or less the same, except that during the early years of the decade less food was shipped out. In this decade, China's imports consisted mostly of wheat, chemical fertilizers, iron and steel products, and continued shipments of machinery and equipment.

Despite its extensive activity in international markets, China's total trade, in keeping with its large geographic size, has been a rather small percentage of its national output. This is shown in Table 3.11, which contains data on China's exports, imports, and GNP for certain subperiods. These figures reveal that China's exports plus imports have consistently been around 4 percent of its GNP. They also disclose that China had an import surplus during much of the 1950s and an export surplus or balanced trade for most of the time after that. This swing in the trade balance was a result of the economic and military aid extended by the

Table 3.11

China's Exports, Imports, and GNP for Selected Subperiods
(in millions of U.S. dollars)

	Annual Averages				Total trade as percent of GNP
	Exports	*Imports*	*Surplus (+) Deficit (−)*	*GNP**	
1950–1957	1,125	1,233	−108	64,000	3.7
1958–1959	2,085	1,943	+142	93,000	4.3
1960–1966	1,796	1,603	+193	88,000	3.9
1967–1974	3,084	3,171	− 87	180,000	3.5

* The first three figures in this column are in 1970 dollars, and the last is in 1973 dollars.

Sources: Nai-ruenn Chen, "China's Foreign Trade, 1950–74," in Joint Economic Committee, *China: A Reassessment of the Economy* (Washington, D.C.: U.S. Gov't. Printing Office, 1975), p. 645; Ashbrook's articles in Joint Economic Committee, *People's Republic of China: An Economic Assessment* (Washington, D.C.: U.S. Gov't. Printing Office, 1972), p. 5, and *China*, p. 23.

USSR to China in the 1950s and of China's obligation to repay the debt later on. The initial import surpluses were borrowed from the Soviet Union, and some of the later export surpluses were used to repay the loans.

The relative importance of Soviet aid to China can be evaluated on the basis of the data in Table 3.12. Of all the exports to China during the period 1950–1961, the Soviet Union's comprised 45 percent. Of these Soviet exports, almost a quarter were in the form of complete industrial plants, including 63 machine-tool and engineering plants, 24 electric power plants, 3 plants producing iron and steel, and others in nonferrous metals, chemicals, aviation, electronics, and so on. In addition, during the 1950s 10,800 Soviet technicians and scientists were sent to China as part of the aid program, while over 13,000 Chinese students were given advanced training in the USSR. China paid for most of the Soviet exports of goods and services within the year in which they were received, the payment being in textiles, foods, minerals, and other goods. But over a quarter of the Soviet

Table 3.12
Soviet Exports and Loans to China, 1950–1961
(in millions of U.S. dollars)

Total exports to China	$16,720
Total Soviet exports to China of which:	7,672
complete industrial plants	1,800
other machinery and equipment	1,200
Soviet loans to China	2,064
Soviet loans as a percentage of Soviet exports	27

Sources: Joint Economic Committee, *An Economic Profile of Mainland China* (Washington, D.C.: U.S. Gov't. Printing Office, 1967); *People's Republic*; Eckstein.

exports came as loans that China was obligated to repay, with interest, in goods, services, and foreign exchange before 1965. Table 3.13 records these repayments. Not all of the Soviet loans were for economic purposes: substantial amounts were negotiated in connection with the Korean War. Consequently, China paid on the spot for the great bulk of the strictly economic goods it received from the Soviet Union. Still, whether paid for immediately or not, China received a few billion dollars in investment and industrial goods from the USSR that it would otherwise have been unable to obtain.

Table 3.13
China's Repayments of Soviet Loans, 1950–1965
(in millions of U.S. dollars)

	Repayments of principal and interest	China's export surplus with USSR	Net foreign exchange payments to USSR
1950–1954	66	0	66
1955–1959	1,045	648	397
1960–1965	1,183	906	277
	2,294	1,554	740

Sources: Joint Economic Committee, *Economic Profile* and *People's Republic*.

In *Communist China's Economic Growth and Foreign Trade*, Alexander Eckstein concludes that China's growth would have been markedly reduced without foreign help. It is generally accepted that foreign trade may enable a country to increase its domestic investment in two principal ways. First, if foreign saving is available, the resulting import surplus releases real resources, at a given consumption level, for investment purposes. Second, even if no foreign saving is tapped (that is, imports equal exports), a country's domestic investment might still be enlarged if it has net imports of investment goods. Suppose a country imports investment goods and exports an equivalent amount of consumption goods. Then, its domestic investment is higher to the extent that it could not have produced the investment goods at home with the real resources that went into the exported consumption goods.

Eckstein's conclusion, therefore, rests on an examination of these two matters, and I shall consider each in turn. To what extent did China have access to foreign saving? While the figures in Table 3.11 seem clear-cut, Eckstein shows that the answer is uncertain because China's exports and imports can be built up only from the trade data of the countries trading with it; thus the data are in terms of foreign currencies. This means that the *yuan* amounts of imports and exports can be obtained only by converting dollars, rubles, and so on into *yuan* at an appropriate exchange rate. Ideally, one would want to value China's exports at *yuan* prices that reflect the·worth of the real resources going into producing them, and to value its imports at *yuan* prices that reflect the worth of the real resources that would have been used to produce them domestically. These calculations would give the true magnitude of China's trade balance in terms of its own resources.

I will not follow Eckstein through his analysis of this problem, for there is no golden way to divine the correct rates. The best we can say is that the figures in Table 3.11 probably approximate the truth: China did not tap foreign saving over the period as a whole to any significant extent; instead, on balance, it may have exported capital to other developing nations. Over the entire quarter-century, China probably financed its investment program from its own saving and used a small part of this saving to help other countries.

Now to the second question, To what extent did China further its economic development by importing capital goods? Again, one cannot be certain about the answer, but it is fairly clear that China imported capital equipment, chemicals, and metals in heavy volume up to 1960, including complete plants from the USSR, with technicians and advisers, but that it imported mostly food products in the 1960s. China exported some investment goods—to North Korea, North Vietnam, and other countries—but mainly food products and textiles, after 1960 the latter especially. Data in Eckstein's study and elsewhere suggest that for the years 1952–1963 China's net imports of investment goods amounted to 10–15 billion *yuan*, or about 3–5 percent of its total domestic investment.

Eckstein, attacking the problem differently (because the above estimates are based on some rather shaky figures), computes the extent to which net fixed-capital investment would have fallen if China had not imported machinery and equipment (a component of fixed-capital investment). For the period 1952–1956, this estimated decline is about 10 billion *yuan*, from approximately 43 billion *yuan* to 33 billion *yuan*. The higher (or actual) figure was associated with a 27 billion *yuan* increase in net national product; so the lower figure, it is assumed, would have yielded an increase in net output of 20 billion *yuan*—7 billion *yuan* below the actual increment. For the period 1953–1957, this signifies a reduction in the annual growth rate from 6.3 percent to something less than 5 percent.[11]

It should be noted that these calculations apply to the 1953–1957 period, when net imports of machinery and equipment were at their peak. Moreover, Eckstein assumes that the ratio of equipment investment to total fixed-capital investment is constant (40 percent); hence, a decline in the numerator, owing to a decrease in imports, would reduce the denominator by a multiple of the decline in equipment investment. If one assumed, instead, that the other components of fixed-capital investment would not be affected by the reduction in equipment imports, the importance of the imports would of course be much smaller. Also, Eckstein assumes that if equipment imports decline, capital goods could not be domestically produced with the real resources released from the counterpart exports. To the extent that such substitution could occur, the output growth rate would be less affected by a decline in imports. On the other hand, the actual *yuan* value of machinery and equipment imports may have been higher than the level suggested by the exchange rate Eckstein used in his calculations, namely 2.62 *yuan* = $1. If so, the elimination of those larger imports, everything else remaining the same, would have a larger impact on the output growth rate.

So the matter is pretty much up in the air. But there is little doubt that, at least up to 1957, China's growth rate was boosted by its import surpluses and by the large capital-equipment component of those imports. Thereafter, and especially after 1960, its growth rate probably suffered, as it ran export surpluses to repay debts and extend aid to other countries, and as its own capital-goods exports probably surpassed its imports of such goods—at least until the late 1960s. Thus it is quite likely that the higher growth rates of the earlier years and the lower ones of the later years were significantly influenced by foreign trade and aid.

Sidney Klein's book *The Road Divides* is mainly concerned with the economic aspects of the Sino-Soviet dispute. Klein outlines the long history of Sino-Soviet relations and disputes, starting with the Mongol invasion of European Russia, and describes the recent events before and after the latest split between the two countries. He then presents detailed information on the extent to which the Soviet Union aided China during the 1950s, and on the size and composition of trade between the two countries. (This presentation contains much more detail than does Eckstein's work.) Next, Klein turns to the issues dividing China and Russia and to the prospects for rapprochement.

Although China received much Soviet aid during the 1950s, and no doubt, as I have argued, profited from it, Klein thinks that *"the bulk* of China's economic progress prior to 1960 is directly attributable to Soviet Russia" (p. 131, my italics). However, he makes no attempt to quantify or prove this, and he seems to be unaware that the aid extended by China to other countries was to some degree an offsetting factor. Eckstein's analysis of this problem goes far beyond Klein's.

Klein also seems to feel that China has been quite ungrateful for the aid it received from the Soviet Union. But, as he points out, China got nothing free; everything had to be paid for, in a short period of time, with interest. Furthermore, China had some reason to be annoyed that on a per capita basis the Soviet aid it received was not as large as Soviet aid to almost all of the other Communist countries and to many non-Communist countries. China also had some cause for complaint about the inadequate extent of Soviet aid during the Korean War, the sudden withdrawal of Soviet technicians just when it was suffering its first severe economic setback, and the high prices set by the Russians on some goods.

Although both sides undoubtedly contributed to the fight, China did have economic reasons for being quite unhappy with its partner. In addition, as Klein points out, China felt that it had other—political and military—reasons for its acrimonious behavior. Given all this, Klein saw little prospect for an end to the dispute, and, in fact, at one point he more or less predicted "that by the mid-1970's one or more full-scale battles will have been fought between Russia and China" (p. 156), a prediction that came partly true in the form of a small-scale war only three years after this book was published.

Klein's little book can be used as a supplement to Eckstein's work, since it fills out many of Eckstein's tables with useful additional information and offers a better, fuller discussion of the economic basis for the Sino-Soviet split and of the split's possible consequences. Moreover, the book contains interesting photographs and amusing typographic and binding errors.

The four noteworthy topics of Mah Feng-hwa's book are: (1) its analysis of China's export of rice and import of wheat; (2) its analysis of China's exchange rates; (3) its inquiry into Sino-Soviet trade prices; and (4) its construction of China's international balance of payments.

On the first topic, Mah examines the argument that in the 1960s China gained by selling rice and importing wheat because, while the calorie values of rice and wheat are about the same for equal weights, rice sells for substantially more than wheat. Mah claims however, that the "gain" was not in foreign-exchange earnings because the value of wheat imports greatly exceeded the value of rice exports—by $1.8 billion from 1960 to 1967. Mah's contribution to this subject is this dollar estimate of China's loss of foreign-exchange reserves on these particular transactions. He concludes that so much wheat was imported in the 1960s primarily to relieve food shortages. However, there are many other reasons for the continuing wheat imports, only a few of which Mah considers.

Mah contends that at the official or effective exchange rates the *yuan* is undervalued with respect to the Soviet ruble and overvalued with respect to the U.S. dollar. He establishes that the operative exchange rates between the *yuan* and the ruble were 0.975 *yuan* = 1 ruble from 1950 to 1957, 2 *yuan* = 1 ruble from 1958 to 1960, and 0.45 *yuan* = 1 new ruble from 1961 on. But he has no direct proof that these rates undervalued the yuan, though he does show from indirect evidence that this is probably so. Mah next works out the effective *yuan*-dollar rates: 3.26 *yuan* = $1 (in 1950), 2.26 *yuan* = $1 (from 1951 to 1952), 2.46 *yuan* = $1 (from 1953 to April 1955), 2.36 *yuan* = $1 (after April 1955). Using direct analysis of commodity price data, based on earlier work of Kang Chao, Mah supports the contention that at these rates the *yuan* was overvalued. He finds that the weighted average price ratio for China's imports is 7.823 *yuan* per dollar; for China's exports, 3.372 *yuan* per dollar. Considering the relative importance of imports and exports, he estimates the exchange rate to be 5.418 *yuan* per dollar, an estimate that seems to be roughly supported by other, indirect evidence.

Mah therefore concludes: "When conversion is accomplished by way of more realistic foreign exchange rates, then the total volume, the regional distribution, and other related aspects . . . of Communist China's foreign trade all appear different from what one can read in the official Communist claims" (p. 91). In particular, the extent of Sino-Soviet trade is exaggerated, while that of Sino-Western trade is understated. However, Mah has so many reservations about his calculations that he tells us: "The conversions . . . are presented purely for the purpose of illustration. . . . No accuracy is claimed" (p. 92). Mah implies that even if he could find "equilibrium" rates, they would have little meaning, since in China domestic prices do not reflect relative scarcities as they do in capitalist countries. But when one considers all of the benefits and costs excluded from market demand and supply curves in capitalist countries, the induced "utilities" in demand curves, the extent of monopoly and oligopoly market powers, the innumerable governmental interferences with markets, and a host of other factors, it is clear that Mah's distinction rests on faith and on faith alone.

Next Mah analyzes whether the Soviets exploited the Chinese in their trade during the periods 1955–1959 and 1960–1964. He does this for the first period by computing and comparing the "actual payments and receipts for the covered Chinese imports from and exports to the USSR with the hypothetical payments and receipts if the same trade had been carried on at the unit values in Soviet trade with Western Europe" (p. 142). He finds a comparative price disadvantage for China in its imports from the USSR for each of the five years 1955–1959. On the other hand, during those years China probably had no price disadvantage in exports. Mah believes that these results can be explained by the higher costs of transporting Soviet exports to China than to European countries. For the years 1960–1964, he finds that China apparently paid increasing prices for Soviet imports compared to the import prices paid by Asian countries in general. The Chinese claimed that this was because the Soviets acted like "bourgeois merchants." In the end, however, there is little evidence that China suffered any significant loss from this trade.

Finally, Mah turns to the construction of China's international balance of payments from 1950 to 1967. After making many estimates based on scanty information, he concludes that China had a net surplus in its international accounts in the periods 1950–1952, 1953–1957, and 1961–1967, and a net deficit only during the period 1958–1960. Much of the overall surplus, however, was paid, not in foreign exchange or gold, but in IOUs, as part of China's own foreign-aid program.

Large parts of Mah's book have previously been published,

most of it deals with rather trivial problems, and the combination of triviality and inadequate data shows up much too frequently. In his short, final chapter, Mah turns for the first time to an important issue—the extent to which the volume and pattern of Soviet aid and trade helped China's economic development. Here is a problem worthy of his many talents, but it is brushed off in a few pages. The liberal's attitude is that authors should work on whatever they consider to be "interesting," but I commend the radical's attitude to Mah: work on something that is really important.

I have briefly touched on China's own foreign-aid program. In the already discussed 1972 and 1975 Joint Economic Committee volumes, Leo Tansky and Carol Fogarty present some interesting data and viewpoints on this effort. The principal data are shown in Table 3.14, where it may be seen that from 1953 to 1974, China's economic aid totaled $6.0 billion and its military aid $1.8

Table 3.14
China's Extensions of Economic and Military Aid,
1953–1974
(in billions of U.S. dollars)

	1953–1969	1970–1974
*Economic aid**		
To non-Communist underdeveloped countries	1.0	2.4
To Communist countries	1.8	0.8†
Military aid		
To non-Communist underdeveloped countries	0.3	0.3
To Communist countries	0.6	0.6†
Total aid	3.7	4.1

* These data exclude $1 billion of grants in the form of free technical services to development projects.
† These figures are partly guesses.

Sources: Leo Tansky, "Chinese Foreign Aid," in Joint Economic Committee, *Economic Profile*; Carol H. Fogarty, "China's Economic Relations with the Third World," in Joint Economic Committee, *China*.

billion. In addition, China granted $1.0 billion in the form of free technical services to development projects. Thus the total is something close to $9 billion, although probably only 60 percent of this amount has been drawn on by recipient countries.

China's economic aid has risen rapidly in recent years, especially that to African countries. Much of China's economic aid to non-Communist countries has been for the construction of transportation networks, such as the Tanzania-Zambia railroad project and roads in Nepal, Pakistan, and elsewhere. Other portions of that aid have enabled recipient countries to obtain textile mills, plywood and paper factories, food processing plants, and the like. A heavy machine-building complex was constructed in Pakistan.

A small part of China's economic aid has been in the form of grants, and all of China's credits have been extended without interest and with repayment stipulated over ten to thirty years after grace periods of ten to twenty years and even longer. The countries receiving aid are

> required to pay only the local costs to maintain Chinese technicians, and these are covered by the Chinese credit. Since Peking requires that its technicians live at a standard comparable to that of their local counterparts, these expenditures are kept to a minimum. Local cost outlays for Chinese technicians [of whom there were 18,700 abroad in 1971] are estimated at an average of $55 per month per man. (Joint Economic Committee, *Economic Profile*, pp. 375, 377)

Most of China's economic aid to Communist countries has gone to North Vietnam, Albania, North Korea, and Rumania. Much of this has been for transportation, foodstuffs, machinery and equipment, and light industrial projects.

China's military aid has been given largely to North Vietnam, but Albania and North Korea have also received some. A few non-Communist countries have been given small amounts of military supplies. The bulk of this military aid to non-Communist countries has gone to Pakistan, in the form of aircraft, tanks, and other arms.

Tansky believes that China will continue to emphasize labor-intensive projects in its aid programs, contributing much of its aid in the services of technicians sent to the recipient countries. He also believes that Black Africa will continue to get the bulk of Chinese aid. The Chinese themselves currently see the countries of the world as divided into three groups: the two superpowers—the United States and the USSR; the "first intermediate zone," consisting of the underdeveloped countries of Latin America, Africa, and Asia; and the "second intermediate zone," consisting of the advanced countries of Europe, along with Canada, Japan, and others. The superpowers, in Chinese eyes, vie for domination of as much of the two intermediate zones as possible. The intent of China's economic and military aid is to help the countries of the first intermediate zone break loose from both the superpowers and dominating countries in the second intermediate zone. The amount of aid China has given for this purpose has been extraordinarily large for such a poor country.

Money and Banking

Katherine Huang Hsiao, *Money and Monetary Policy in Communist China* (New York: Columbia University Press, 1971).

This book, covering some new ground, deals with banking institutions, the money supply, and monetary policy in the People's Republic of China during the 1950s, for which fairly good data are available. The author first discusses the banking system, which quickly came to be dominated by the People's Bank—the central bank, monopoly commercial bank, and leading savings bank all rolled into one, with 20,000 branches around the country. This bank issued the country's currency, sold deposits of several types (principally settlement or current accounts, budgetary deposits, and personal-savings deposits), and made short-term loans, mainly to commercial enterprises (the state trading network) but also to industrial and agricultural units. In addition, urban savings units and rural credit cooperatives were established in every nook and cranny, the latter for the purpose of selling savings deposits to peasants' and producers' cooperatives, making loans for agricultural purposes, and selling extra currency to the People's Bank for deposits.

This, essentially, was (and still is) the monetary system, ubiquitous and unisonous. However, an Agricultural Bank relieved the People's Bank of some of its agricultural-credit responsibilities for a time, and other financial institutions served temporarily as intermediaries between the state budget and economic units engaged in capital-investment projects—that is, as fiscal agents dealing with budget grants rather than as banking institutions involved in loans and deposits. Still other financial institutions briefly saw the light of day before being eliminated.

Next, the author discusses the operation of the monetary system, its loans, and its resulting liabilities in the form of currency and deposits. In general, currency was used by state enterprises to pay workers' wages, by the state to purchase agricultural commodities from the agricultural producers' cooperatives, by the APCs to pay part of the incomes earned by peasants, and by individuals to purchase consumer goods and services. Currency held by state enterprises and cooperatives above some minimum transaction requirement usually had to be sold to the People's Bank for deposits. Similarly, individuals were encouraged, and at times pressured, to deposit their extra currency in the People's Bank or in other savings units.

Within the state sector, all transactions above small amounts had to be made with demand deposits rather than currency. Such transactions included purchases by one state enterprise from another, payments between state enterprises and government administrative organs, and some payments from the state to the APCs. These current accounts and settlement deposits could be checked only according to the First Five-Year Plan, and so were not completely liquid.

Despite the various degrees of illiquidity associated with current and savings deposits, the author includes these financial assets as well as currency in the money supply, an aggregate comparable to Friedman's M_3. It appears, though the author does not make the calculations, that during the 1950s (and perhaps the 1960s) this money supply was only 12–15 percent of China's gross domestic material product. It must be noted that the financial assets making up the author's money supply included almost all of the financial assets in the economy, for interfirm indebtedness was not permitted, the state had very little outstanding debt to the public, and individuals probably had few debts among themselves. Thus total financial claims in China must have been an unusually small percentage of the nation's real wealth, and the public's liquidity must have been pushed to unusually low levels.

While the current claim by the Chinese that theirs is a country with neither domestic nor foreign debts is not strictly true, it is true that large deficit or surplus budgets are quite rare in China; that, consequently, most investment expenditures are self-financed so that little external financing is necessary; and that whatever deficits do exist are largely covered by state grants rather than loans, while the small remainder is indirectly financed through the monetary system rather than directly through nonfinancial economic units. Furthermore, China has had close to a balanced overall foreign account too, though in the first several years after liberation it was a borrower, and in the last few years it has been a relatively large lender.

Finally, the author analyzes monetary policy, which she regards as rather liberal in granting loans and creating deposits and currency. However, the People's Bank was subsequently covetous of the liquidity thus created. The bank's initial generosity was simply an accommodation to the requirements of the Five-Year Plan—if such financing was needed, it was available, and what was "needed" was judged along the lines of the real-bills doctrine—while its subsequent covetousness led to the recapture of currency by the bank through its promotion of personal-savings deposits, through its requirement that excess currency holdings of enterprises be deposited, and through its extension of transactions requiring settlement by transfers of deposits. In addition, some excess liquidity was captured in budget surpluses (largely owing to the increasing profits of state enterprises), which became budgetary deposits at the People's Bank and were then partly transferred from liabilities of the bank to its net-worth accounts (called the credit fund); a similar process took place in earlier years through bond sales to the public. So, as the author sees it, money gushed forth but was recaptured in more or less adequate amounts, though at times there was some inflation, open and repressed.

On the whole, Professor Hsiao has made a worthwhile contribution to our understanding of China's financial institutions and monetary policy. Her writing is clear, her analysis is generally good, and her detective work in obtaining a series for currency outstanding is outstanding. The study, however, is disappointing in a few ways: it does not adequately relate the financial sector to the development effort as a whole; it concentrates much too much on the monetary system's role as a stabilizer of prices to the relative neglect of its role as an integral part of the planning mechanism; and its discussion of the relation between the monetary and banking theories of the Chinese and their actual policies is inadequate. Moreover, I think that the author made a mistake when she decided to confine her study to domestic finance, for China's international financial transactions during the 1950s were very important to its overall planning effort. But this failure is related to the author's aim of concentrating on price stability rather than the planning mechanism, and here international transactions were not so important or interesting.

National Planning and Markets

Dwight H. Perkins, *Market Control and Planning in Communist China* (Cambridge, Mass.: Harvard University Press, 1966).

Joan Robinson, *Economic Management in China*, 1972 (London: Anglo-Chinese Educational Institute, 1973).

Stuart R. Schram, ed., *Authority, Participation, and Cultural Change in China* (Cambridge, England: Cambridge University Press, 1973).

Dwight Perkins' study, which carries us only to 1964, is most interesting, but the material is so poorly organized that the reader is continually struggling to put the various pieces together. It is hard to tell what the basic trouble is, but it may be that organizing the book around sectors and markets—agriculture, industry, labor, consumer goods—leads to a multiplicity of partial views of the economy, preventing the reader from ever seeing the whole picture.

Perkins pursues two problems. The first is a stabilization-growth problem: Given the huge investment program, how could the required saving with fairly stable prices be obtained? The second concerns resource allocation: What role did "the market" or planning play in allocating resources and goods? Although the analysis of the second problem is at times served fairly well by the sector-by-sector approach, the analysis of the first, to which I now turn, decidedly is not.

Perkins shows that the Communists successfully rejected inflation (and forced saving) as a method of financing their investment expenditures. The official retail price indexes record an annual increase of only 1 percent from 1951 to 1958, and there are no indications of a prolonged serious inflation after that. These indexes, however, probably have a downward bias, as Perkins explains, since they are based largely on controlled prices which were at times below equilibrium levels. Black-market prices apparently exceeded official prices in 1953, 1957, and 1960–1962. However, as Perkins states: "None of these qualifications . . . negates the basic contention that price increases in Communist China have in fact been quite modest" (p. 158). The potential excess demand was largely eliminated by other means.

Perkins describes well the state's attempts to raise agricultural output. Land reform, although primarily a redistribution measure and a means of destroying the landlords as a class, was also meant to increase incentives toward land improvements. The regime also used advance-purchase contracts containing state-guaranteed purchase prices, eliminating some of the risks to individual farmers. Later, in November 1953, the state began to use compulsory quotas for major crops, principally for the purpose of controlling the marketed portions of the crops. In 1955–1956, the peasants were organized into agricultural producers' cooperatives, whose income was distributed according to the amounts of labor and land contributed; later, in the advanced cooperatives, only the labor contribution counted. In the summer of 1958, communes were established. These expanded the basic unit from around a few hundred·families to several thousand. Subsequently, the communes were reorganized: their center of control was located in lower-level units, and the peasants were encouraged to devote some of their time to small private plots. Finally, the government has in recent years stepped up its investment spending in agriculture.

Perkins feels that land reforms, although raising peasant incentives, removed many rich peasants "who had more capital and better knowledge of advanced techniques of farming than poor peasants"; that centralization in the form of cooperatives and communes was on the whole a failure. He concludes that "there appears to be little that centralization accomplishes that cannot be done better through extension services, taxes, and market and price controls in the context of a free peasant economy" (p. 97).

The lack of success, as Perkins sees it, on the supply side made it much more urgent for the government to restrain demand for consumer goods and services. The required saving came largely from tax receipts and profits of state enterprises—very little came from foreign saving. Perkins believes that individual saving did not contribute much, that the drives to elicit such saving were "makeshift measures" whose "negative effect on incentives [outweighed] their usefulness in controlling inflation or in accomplishing other objectives" (p. 176). In my judgment, some of this is correct and some incorrect; but in no instance does Perkins offer adequate support for his contentions.

For example, although government saving through the state budget grew remarkably from 1950 to 1960, owing to the rapid growth of budget revenues relative to government consumption and transfer payments, Perkins gives only the budget revenue figures. Furthermore, he does not relate these figures to anything at all—to investment, GNP, and so on. In fact, the book contains no GNP figures, though good estimates exist. Worse yet, despite the fact that the investment program is so vital a part of Perkins' story, nowhere does he present aggregate investment data—and they, too, exist. Consequently, it is not possible for the reader to judge how important budget receipts were in financing the total investment program.

In fact, budget revenues rose from around 10 percent of gross product in 1950 to more than 30 percent in 1958 and an even higher proportion in the following year; government saving probably financed about half of aggregate investment in the early years and more than three-quarters later on. Perkins' description of the tax system that largely produced this impressive record is fragmented, but it shows clearly that the most rapidly growing revenue source was the profits of state enterprises. In the earlier years, large revenues were also provided by taxes on the net income and gross receipts of business firms and on commodities. All of these taxes were replaced in 1958 by the turnover tax. Throughout the period, the agricultural tax, imposed on the gross yield of output and based on "normal" rather than actual yield, declined steadily relative to total revenues. Agricultural tax revenues were about one-third of budget revenues in 1950, but only 5 percent in 1960.

Perkins' views on individual saving are unsupported. Although he emphasizes the unimportance of this saving, his figures—once again, unrelated to anything else—show fairly sizable increases in deposits and bond holdings. Apparently, because Perkins feels (correctly) that coercion was used in the savings drives, he is quick to ascribe large disincentive effects (work?) to the resulting saving. His only evidence for this view is the statement that such saving would be akin to a tax—an observation that raises more questions than it answers.

In fact, there must have been very large increases in the real demand for financial assets during the early years of development—not only for the savings deposits and bonds discussed by Perkins but also for money balances and other financial assets. The cessation of hyperinflation would in itself have renewed real demands for financial assets, and the rapid increase in national income would have added to these demands. Furthermore, several key financial assets were provided with purchasing power clauses or lottery features; mobile banks were sent to rural areas; new types of savings deposits were introduced; new financial institutions were established; saving through insurance contracts was pushed vigorously. Moreover, the land reforms, by decentralizing ownership and decision-making, probably raised both the demand for and the supply of loanable funds in the rural areas, as many poor and middle peasants, owning land for the first time, had to finance expenditures, and many acquired savings for the first time from sales of grain to the state. In addition, the demand for money was probably raised by the increasing efficiency of the payments mechanism: the early consolidations of currency issues, the establishment of clearinghouses, the reduction of remittance charges. Finally, there were forced-saving schemes and patriotic savings drives.

The combined force of these factors in the early years of the period must have raised real demands for financial assets far above the growth of income. But it is likely that later on, as the economy was socialized—private businesses eliminated, cooperatives and communes established—the real demand for financial assets lagged behind the growth of national income. This is suggested by estimates which show that nonstate net domestic saving grew very rapidly from practically nothing in 1950 to 4–7 percent of GNP in 1955 and then remained within this range. These estimates signify that such saving financed a negligible part of aggregate investment in the initial years, 15 to 20 percent of aggregate investment by 1955–1956, and probably a declining portion thereafter.

Perkins' second and major theme concerns the comparative roles of the market and national planning in resource allocation. For Perkins, "market controls are decentralized controls that tend to encourage plant managers and rural cadres to operate in an economically efficient manner" (p. 208); they promote decisions in response to prices, which in turn are determined by demand and supply forces in open markets. Planning means centrally determined controls over resource allocation, decisions which supersede market forces. The Chinese Communist Party, in Marxian fashion, attempted at the earliest moment to replace "the anarchy" of the market by national planning.

The move toward this goal began almost immediately, when the banking system, most transportation, and nearly half of industry were either nationalized or state-run. The nationalization of finance and industry was largely completed at the end of 1955. A year later, agriculture was collectivized, eliminating individual family farming and thus helping to bring the agricultural sector more fully into the national plans. As early as 1950, however, the government had unified the distribution of certain key raw materials or major equipment to industrial firms. In late 1953, it began to develop centrally determined compulsory quotas for major agricultural crops, starting with grain and later adding cotton and edible oil-producing materials. In 1953, too, the First Five-Year Plan began, though a detailed document was forthcoming only in 1955. Urban wage rates, wage bills, and prices of major commodities also came under national control rather quickly. The profits, cash balances, working capital, and investment funds of enterprises were subjected to financial controls.

Perkins shows that over the 1949–1963 period he analyzed, market forces were much more significant in agriculture than in industrial production and construction. In the early years, the authorities used varying purchase prices to influence the output of certain crops, and even with the advent of cooperatives "a free market was still the major determinant of a wide range of subsidiary [agricultural] products" (p. 199). In industry and construction, prices played only a marginal role, the major allocating device being the physical plan targets and the rationed allocation of most key inputs. Perkins finds that the market was an important factor in the distribution of consumer goods, though some of the principal commodities were rationed in both rural and urban areas as early as 1953–1954, but that there was also a high degree of physical control over the labor market, the main object here being to control the growth of the urban population. He concludes that the market has played "an important role in directing the Chinese economy, but a role subordinate to that of centrally determined physical controls" (p. 200), an assessment that seems obvious and correct.

A thesis Perkins' book expresses several times is that central planning may be easier in an underdeveloped economy like China's than in a more developed economy because of the smaller number of commodities produced, the simpler interdependencies in the production and allocation of these commodities, a relatively simple labor market, and the economy's ability to borrow technology from highly developed nations, which obviates the need to stimulate technical advance through market forces.

However, Perkins also sees important drawbacks to centralized controls in China, among them the lack of adequate data, insufficient numbers of trained people, the sheer size of the country, and the large number and diversity of farms. Although these pros and cons are mostly left hanging in midair, Perkins seems to feel that the net advantages lie with the market. Still, he believes that such economic considerations were unimportant in China's decision to impose central planning; much more significant were ideological and political factors. In other words, since it seems obvious to him that the economic advantages are clearly with "the market" as against national planning, any country choosing the latter must have done so because it was hung up on ideology.

What is obvious to Perkins, however, is far from evident to Joan Robinson, the Cambridge economist, who visited China (for the sixth time) in the spring of 1972 to study the country's system of planning and management. Robinson defines the issue between planning and the market as a struggle between production for use and production for profit, and she firmly believes that the former is the superior system, if done the Chinese way.

The basic characteristic of the Chinese economy, according to Robinson, is that 80 percent of the population work in communes and feed and house themselves. The surplus produced by the communes feeds the rest of the population, who are mainly in the urban areas, and provides raw materials (for example, cotton, tobacco, sugarcane, timber) to industry, whose major enterprises are state-owned and whose other enterprises are collectively owned by smaller groups. The surplus of the communes flows to the nonagricultural sectors by four means: the agricultural tax, compulsory quota sales to the state, above-quota sales to the state, and the free market. The communes are paid for the surplus (except for the small part taxed away) and spend most of the funds for manufactured consumer goods and capital investment, the remainder being saved. The state-owned enterprises turn over their profits and sales taxes to the state budget, while the smaller, collectively owned industries retain about half their profits, the rest going to provincial and local governments. The state-owned enterprises are allocated investment funds from the state budget and obtain their extra working funds from People's Bank loans.

The commune members earn workpoints. Each member's income depends on the number of workpoints he or she accumulates and on the value of the workpoint, which in turn depends on the production of his or her group. Industrial workers earn wages, the wage scale being in eight grades, with the highest generally around three-to-five times the lowest, though wages of some highly trained technicians are outside this range. There is a nationwide system of wage grades: wages are highest in Shanghai, higher in heavy than in light industry, lower in collectively owned firms than in state enterprises, and higher than rural incomes. Managers of enterprises earn wages too, and do not receive bonuses. Workers in commune factories are paid wages, but those in brigade workshops earn workpoints, as do the peasants in the communes.

The national government directly controls not only the major agricultural crops but also main-line transportation, foreign trade, and defense industries and the other major manufacturing and extractive enterprises, which are mainly urban-based. The prices of all outputs and inputs are given to these firms, and their production plans are worked out with the central planning authorities. "The general principle of this system," Professor Robinson explains,

> is that the workers and the management of an enterprise are concerned with efficiency and quality of production, but have nothing to do with sales. . . . as long as income or bonuses [of production workers] depend on sales, there is an irresistible temptation for the producer and the retailer to fix up schemes to exploit the public and share the swag. (pp. 6–7)

Furthermore, production workers and managers do not take it upon themselves to fix or change prices, which Robinson believes leads to greater rationality and efficiency.

> When the enterprise has the right to fix the prices of its own products, much of the waste and irrationality, such as is only too familiar to us in a market economy, is bound to follow— monopolistic pricing, advertisement, catering to the tastes of the higher income families and neglecting the needs of the poorer ones. (p. 4)

In addition, a socialist enterprise does not have a board of directors, an account with an advertising agency, or financial experts on stock and bond markets, and "it has no need for legal advice on tax dodging" (p. 18).

The rest of industry, most of which is collectively owned, is under provincial and local control and planning. Such enterprises are found increasingly in rural areas and towns. They sell their products to communes, large factories, or the local ministry of commerce. Through contracts, this ministry purchases from the communes manufactured consumer goods as well as such agricultural output as vegetables, fruits, eggs, and meat. It provides the services of wholesalers by distributing the products to retail outlets. The commune members may sell extra agricultural produce on free markets where demand and supply determine prices up to the price ceilings set by the authorities.

The rationale of the price-wage structure, Robinson points out in a simplified illustration, is as follows: (1) The price of grain is set. (2) The lowest wage rate in industry is established at a level that enables such workers as apprentices and unskilled workers to have sufficient food. (3) From this wage rate, other wage rates are scaled upward according to skill and seniority. (a) The extent of the wage differentials depends on the degree of proletarian values in industry. (b) The wage structure determines the prices of industrial goods. (c) However, necessities are priced on the low side, and the most important necessities are rationed at those prices; luxuries are priced on the high side. (4) The gross value of grain less taxes, welfare funds, and accumulation funds equals the net income of peasants, which is broken down to the level of production teams. This, together with the total workpoints accumulated by the peasants, determines the value of each workpoint. Each peasant family earns an income equal to the value of a workpoint times its total workpoints. (a) Some of the net income may be distributed according to the need of the families, depending on the degree of social consciousness. (b) The range of workpoints over the various tasks may be great or small, depending on social consciousness within the communes. (c) Accumulation funds are used to replace seed, fertilizer, agricultural machinery, and so on, and for net additions to the capital stock, including small industries. (5) The state collects agricultural taxes, sales taxes, and the profits of state enterprises. (6) The wage incomes of industrial workers plus the cash incomes of peasants should equal the value of commodities put on the market by industry and handicraft cooperatives, thus determining the prices of handicraft goods and services.

Most of the planning decisions regarding production, distribution, and prices are made at the lower levels. Increasingly, production plans are being made in terms of local areas, the two thousand counties being focal points for the development goal of local self-sufficiency. In a way, this is guerrilla warfare applied to economic planning, in which Peking, the center, sets the national goals, the overall strategy, and the ideology—the general developmental framework—while "commanders" at the scene of action exercise independent, imaginative judgment in making local decisions (Perkins, pp. 18, 83). The theory and practice of guerrilla warfare have apparently guided Mao in fashioning a congenial mode of economic development, a mode that encourages struggle and self-reliance in making the highly productive communist worker.

For these and other reasons, Robinson admires the Chinese planning system, and she deeply suspects that the profit motive and free markets would work to the disadvantage of large numbers of Chinese. Perkins, on the other hand, has faith in individualism and markets, but his attitude has grown out of efficiency criteria rather than considerations of fairness or class struggles.

I have included a third book in this section because it contains a good pertinent article, "Levels of Economic Decision-Making," by Marianne Bastid, chargée de recherche at the Centre National de la Recherche Scientifique in Paris. This article offers some information that supplements what has been presented.

The economic decision-making structure, according to Bastid, consists, first, of the "center"—Mao, the Central Committee of the Chinese Communist Party, the State Council, the State Planning Commission, and a few dozen "economic" ministries and special agencies, including the Committee on National Prices. The center sets quantitative targets for the basic products and "mainly for the provincial level but not below it." However, general and qualitative directives from the center go to all levels. The provinces now have a high degree of autonomy: they are the highest authority regarding education, planning, and most job assignments; they manage factories which probably turn out over half of the nation's industrial production. The counties, below the provinces, run smaller factories; are responsible for such things as water control, electrification, roads, and some small railways; and direct the operations of the communes. The communes manage still smaller factories, assign production quotas to the brigades, and convey directives from above. The brigades are now "taking over the organization of collective side-line activities," manage workshops, and supervise the production teams. Each team decides "on the sowing plan according to local conditions" and is responsible for devising its own measures for increasing production and "for counting work-points and allocating income to its members."

Decisions at each level are formally made by the revolutionary (government) and party committees. The party committees set the direction and lay down general policies, while the revolutionary committees focus on the concrete measures to implement the policies.

Bastid neatly summarizes the development strategy and structure as of 1969:

> The development strategy of 1969 bore similarities to that of the Great Leap; it also relied heavily on the mass line; on the mobilization of the whole population and of all available resources; on efforts to improve the agricultural infrastructure; and on industrialization through small-scale labour-intensive rural enterprises. But there are also differences. New industries are primarily those which support agriculture. The industrial network is much more clearly laid out, with a hierarchy of responsibility from the province down to the brigade, according to the scale of the projects. Management of economic operations is concentrated at the brigade level (small-scale projects in both industry and agriculture), the county level (medium-scale projects in both agriculture and industry) and the provincial level (large-scale projects); the alternative administrative levels—communes or special districts—mostly supervise the operations of the level immediately below them. (pp. 191–92)

By 1972, she tells us, there had been some backtracking from the advanced positions attained during the Cultural Revolution. "Less emphasis has since been put on the creativity of the masses, or on mass representation and participation, with more emphasis on technical experience, on the responsibility of the cadres and on their function as leaders." Nevertheless, much of the greater participation of the masses in decision-making and in the "deconcentration" of decisions has remained. On this last point, Bastid's view is that decision power has not been transferred from the center to local units, in the fashion of decentralization, but that local units have been encouraged to exercise their own initiative along with that of the higher authorities, to apply imaginatively the directives from above to local conditions. Not decentralization of power but the motto "Two initiatives are better than only one" reflects what Bastid calls "deconcentration."

Workers and Wages

Christopher Howe, *Wage Patterns and Wage Policy in Modern China, 1919–1972* (Cambridge, England: Cambridge University Press, 1973).

Charles Hoffmann, *The Chinese Worker* (Albany: State University of New York Press, 1974).

Christopher Howe, head of the Contemporary China Institute at the University of London, states that his book "is an attempt to provide a statistical analysis of changes in the level and structure of Chinese wages from the 1920s to the early 1970s. It also seeks to elucidate both the mechanisms responsible for these changes and their economic significance" (p. xi).[12]

With regard to pre-1949 China, Howe found that wage differentials (by skill and by occupation) were higher in light than in heavy industry; that, over time, these differentials declined; that the Chinese differentials were low relative to those in other underdeveloped countries; and that China's interindustry wage structure (that is, the ranking of specific industries by their average monthly earnings) was about the same as those elsewhere. Each of these findings, however, rests on weak statistical foundations and is subject to serious qualification; all are based largely on

Shanghai and Manchuria, which produced five-eighths of China's industrial output in 1933.

Proceeding to the post-1949 period, Howe's story is essentially the following. During most of the 1950s, the Chinese used sharp wage differentials as an allocating device, as the Soviets were doing at the time. They found, however, that periodic revisions of the structure were required and that these revisions tended to raise the general level of urban wages. This widened urban-rural income differentials and led to increased migration into the cities. Consequently, the system of using wage rates and the market to allocate labor was gradually replaced by more direct controls over labor allocation, which included a policy of holding real wages fairly constant in the urban areas while attempting to raise real incomes in the countryside. At the same time, there was a swing away from the incentive systems of the 1950s—which emphasized material rewards for individual performances—and toward internal incentives and collective work stimulants.

Howe calculated that the average real wage rose by only 1.9 percent per year from 1952 to 1972. This information and other relevant data are in Table 3.15. Aside from the initial spurt of wages—for which the data are shaky—the most rapid rise of real wages occurred during the First Five-Year Plan, especially as a result of the wage reform of 1956. This reform altered the wage structure to make occupational differentials more rational and in the process raised the general level of wages. Since that time, real wages, on balance, have not changed, although in the last few years there have been further increases. Howe stresses that it would be wrong to conclude that urban workers have gained little during the Communist period, for substantial advances during the 1950s boosted the living standards of workers and staff to fairly high levels, "and the total welfare implications of wage levels and changes thereof cannot be evaluated without analysis of supplementary benefits, income security and other factors outside the scope of this analysis" (pp. 33–34).

Wage policy during the years 1949–1957 reflected "a willingness to use both the level and structure of wages as instruments to stimulate work-effort and allocate labour resources," along the lines of the Soviet system (p. 153). Wage differences were in-

Table 3.15
Wages of Workers and Staff, 1949–1972

	Annual average money wages of:		Retail prices in 8 cities (1952 = 100)	Annual growth rate of real wages of:	
	Workers and staff*	Industrial workers and staff†		Workers and staff	Industrial workers and staff
1949	262 yuan	350 yuan			
1952	446	525	100	{21.2%	{17.0%
1957	637	694	109	{ 6.0 ⎫	{ 4.0
1963	607		118	{−2.1 ⎬ 1.9	
1972	715		118‡	{ 1.9 ⎭	

* *Workers and staff* are "all persons employed in public administration, economic enterprises, education, health and Mass Organizations, in rural and urban areas, who have a regular wage or salary" (p. 30). The term excludes capitalists, cooperative members, and others in occupations where incomes are variable.

† *Industrial workers and staff*, a component of workers and staff, comprised about 20–25 percent of the urban employed during the 1950s.

‡ Howe assumes no rise in retail prices from 1963 to 1972.

Source: Howe, pp. 31–34.

tended to induce workers to transfer to where their marginal products were higher, to acquire new skills, and to work harder; they were also intended to impel rational use of labor by managers. For a time, the Chinese accepted the Soviet piece rate system, which by 1956 covered 42 percent of the Chinese industrial labor force, but piece rates were eased out after 1957. However, premium payments to individual workers for extra efficiency and innovative efforts, to some extent a substitute for piecework, were widespread up to 1966, declining only after that as they were consolidated into automatic monthly bonuses. Emulation heroes and model workers have also been used to stimulate work performance. Since 1957–1958, as I indicated above, wage policy has swung toward direct controls over labor allocation and toward attempts to keep urban wages from rising very much, the purposes being to stabilize aggregate demand for consumer goods and to reduce the income differences between urban and rural areas. Among the Maoists, there has been growing sentiment for more egalitarian wage structures and for more emphasis on group rewards and collective incentives.

Howe ends by predicting that, as the modern industrial sector grows, the Chinese will have to apply "incentive systems appropriate to large scale, specialised organisations" (p. 149), by which he means "external incentives" consisting of significant wage differentials and hierarchical forms of organization in which rewards are "allocated by persons external to the recipient, usually on the basis of objective criteria of performance." On the other hand, he concludes that "internal incentives"—"rewards and penalties that arise within a person as a result of his work experience" (pp. 136–37)—are more appropriate to smaller organizations, where initiative and innovative activity by individual workers are important. Howe's analysis of these different incentive systems is excellent, and he shows engagingly why Chinese tradition reinforces the case for internal incentives. However, his discussion of "variations in the efficiency of different incentive instruments in different situations," while suggestive, is not at all persuasive. Although the discussion ranges across sociology, psychology, and economics, the prescription in the end boils down to this generality: avoid extremes and find a judicious mixture of external- and internal-incentive systems. Howe appears to believe, that, as time goes by, such a mixture will include relatively more external incentives, an outlook that is based on the assumption that Chinese society's predominant movement is toward industrialism rather than communism. The weakness of Howe's outlook, in other words, is that he takes Western experience much more seriously than he takes Chinese avowals of their determination to depart from that experience.

This mistake is not made by Charles Hoffmann, whose book *The Chinese Worker* thoughtfully considers Mao's dictum that rapid industrial progress is not possible unless it is accompanied by movement toward communism. For Hoffmann's purposes, the latter goal is summed up in terms of the elimination of "the three great differences"—the differences between town and country, between industry (the worker) and agriculture (the peasant), and between mental and manual labor—that is, in terms of the development of a classless society. The heart of Hoffmann's work is his analysis of Mao's rejection of the Soviet model of industrialization and of what that rejection has meant for the workers of China—and for the peasants too. Hoffmann's keen awareness of the importance of the communist vision to the Maoists distinguishes his work from Howe's. While Howe searches for an optimal mixture of external and internal incentives, Hoffmann perceptively delineates the Maoist vision of the future society. This proves immeasurably more helpful for an understanding of what has happened than does Howe's detailed empirical work, which seldom gets below the surface of facts.

The Soviet model, which was pressed on the Chinese and accepted by them for most of the 1950s, consisted of an urban-centered industrial effort that utilized capital-intensive operations in large-scale, hierarchical enterprises. Workers and technicians were recruited into this modern sector by the inducements of high and rising wages and the promise of other benefits, by the advantages of advanced training in a rather elitist technical-school system, and by the attractions of urban life. These industrial workers were stimulated to work hard by sharp wage differentials, an expanding system of piecework rates, bonuses, and other material rewards for outstanding individual performance. The bulk of state investment was directed to the industrial sector, while the agricultural and consumer goods sectors received lower priorities, which were ultimately reflected in their retarded growth rates.

Hoffmann shows that this system led to thriving inequalities at many levels: between managers and workers, skilled and unskilled, trade-union members and nonmembers, workers and peasants, employed and unemployed, permanent and temporary workers. The Soviet model magnified "the three great differences"; industrialization was pursued at the onerous expense of exalting bourgeois values, attitudes, and practices. By 1957, it was clear that technicians and managers were forming into a separate class and that the workers themselves were being stratified into at least three layers: the secure and favored permanent workers, the exploited temporary workers, and the masses of urban unemployed (numbering in the millions), many of whom had left precarious lives in the countryside only to find blank walls and misery in the cities. Furthermore, the employed urban workers had clearly improved their living standards more swiftly than had the masses of peasants, so that the gap between the cities and the rural areas was now menacing any alliance that had been formed between the two classes. Modern technology in the urban centers was beginning to make a joke of the crude implements of the countryside.

Hoffmann expresses incisively the dilemma confronting the Chinese:

> To the extent that modernization-industrialization along Soviet lines conflicted with the socialization of the means of production and of the consciousness of the work force, and to the extent that that conflict was resolved in favor of industrialization, or "production in command," effective socialization and building of socialist consciousness was frustrated, and the ultimate Communist goals were put in doubt. Thus the Maoist realization matured to the view that modernization-industrialization and socialization had to be molded in an opposite way to the Soviet practice, and socialization took priority for the time. The [Cultural Revolution] meant that until a socialist superstructure was firmly established, to proceed single-mindedly to modernize-industrialize would be to wind up on the return voyage to capitalism. (p. 180)

Mao's solutions to these problems were worked out by degrees. Some were introduced in 1957–1958, others subsequently. All of the solutions were modified, extended, and applied whenever a favorable opportunity existed. Mao set out to industrialize the countryside with labor-intensive, small-scale enterprises, and to promote massive rural work projects that would engage tens of millions of otherwise idle peasants. As Mao's program unfolded, further increases in urban real-wage rates were delayed, the prices of some of the commodities sold by the peasants were raised, and the prices of some of the goods they bought were lowered, so that the terms of trade were eventually turned in favor of the countryside as against the cities. The labor force was allocated less by market forces and more by direct controls, the most dramatic illustration of this shift being the tens of millions of young people, professionals, and unemployed who were sent out of the cities to aid the countryside. Over time, wage differentials were reduced, material incentives softened, piece rates largely eliminated, and personal bonuses phased out. To supplement and ultimately to replace these bourgeois stimulants, the Maoists pressed for collective incentives, nonmaterial rewards, and social goals rather than the individual pursuit of material wealth. The planning system was decentralized, and the development and self-sufficiency of smaller areas throughout China, county by county, became the strategy to replace the highly centralized and bureaucratic system fostered on China by the Soviet Union. Within the factories, the workers were placed on a more equal footing with the managers.

"For the Maoists," Hoffmann concludes,

> the new society, if it is to fulfill Marxist-Leninist ideals, must put technology in the service of man and woman rather than cast them in the roles of alienated actors directed and used by a bureaucratic technocracy. . . . For the worker, the Maoist vision predicts, alienation is erased by group identification, development of self-reliance and creativity of individuals and groups, and personal fulfillment and satisfaction through functional participation in numerous facets of daily economic, social, and political life. (p. 191)

And that, Mao has repeated over and over, is the path not only to leaps in productivity but to genuinely human relationships, unsullied by craft or stratagem for personal gain.

Concluding Remarks

Although I have reviewed a large number of volumes in this survey, there are many others that I had hoped to include. Let me end by setting down what I would have liked to have done, if I had had the time and space. This will provide the reader with additional information about books on the Chinese economy as well as assuage my feelings of guilt.

I wanted very much to begin the survey with a discussion of Mark Elvin's provocative study *The Pattern of the Chinese Past* (Stanford, Calif.: Stanford University Press, 1973), which offers a two-thousand-year perspective on Mao's economy and also advances many fascinating insights and judgments, as well as a theory, on the long sweep of Chinese economic development. But this would have opened up too many new paths for investigation and too many arguments with the author, and so I had to be satisfied with a few brief references.

Another fine effort that moves across centuries is Dwight Perkins' *Agricultural Development in China, 1368–1968* (Chicago: Aldine, 1969), the theses of which could have been compared in many interesting ways to Elvin's propositions. To this group, I might have also added Albert Feuerwerker, *China's Early Industrialization* (Cambridge, Mass.: Harvard University Press, 1958), a more specialized treatment which is confined to the much shorter period of the late Ch'ing. Finally, Alexander Eckstein's "The Economic Heritage," an excellent chapter in A. Eckstein, W. Galenson, and T. C. Liu, eds., *Economic Trends in Communist China* (Chicago: Aldine, 1968), could have been worked in profitably. These four studies would have provided a worthy introduction and a wealth of material for debate.

In my discussion of the Kuomintang economy, I had hoped to introduce the reader to R. H. Tawney, *Land and Labor in China* (Boston: Beacon Press, 1966), originally published in 1932. This is a beautifully written and highly perceptive book by the late British economic historian, who at that time could forecast:

> The revolution of 1911 was a bourgeois affair. The revolution of the peasants has still to come. If their rulers continue to exploit them, or to permit them to be exploited, as remorselessly as hitherto, it is likely to be unpleasant. It will not, perhaps, be undeserved. (p. 74)

There are three books on China's economic geography that I intended to include, perhaps at the very beginning of the survey. They are: Keith Buchanan, *The Transformation of the Chinese Earth* (New York: Praeger, 1970); T. R. Tregear, *A Geography of China* (Chicago: Aldine, 1965); and Theodore Shabad, *China's Changing Map* (New York: Praeger, 1972). They are interesting, informative, and set forth the geographic framework, and hence the limitations, within which development has had to proceed. I especially like Buchanan's sympathetic approach to what the Chinese have been doing to improve the earth.

I have learned much from four studies that cover the development of Mao's economy in an expansive way. I tried several times to find a good spot for these four books: Jan S. Prybyla, *The Political Economy of Communist China* (Scranton, Pa.: International Textbook, 1970); Audrey Donnithorne, *China's Economic System* (New York: Praeger, 1967); E. L. Wheelwright and Bruce McFarlane, *The Chinese Road to Socialism* (New York: Monthly Review Press, 1970); and Leo Goodstadt, *China's Search for Plenty: The Economics of Mao Tse-tung* (Tokyo and New York: Weatherhill, 1973).

The Prybyla and Donnithorne books are encyclopedic, the former more analytic, biased, and lively, the latter more institutional, evenhanded, and deadly. Prybyla starts the adrenalin flowing; Donnithorne stupefies. Wheelwright and McFarlane's work is a Maoist account, and a very good one, of the economics of the Cultural Revolution. Of Goodstadt's book, I recently wrote the following opening paragraph in reviewing it for a journal:

> In 249 pages of pedestrian and, what seems to the reader to be, almost endless prose, there are only ten breaks in the narrative by headings of any kind. All of these are chapter headings, none of which gives the reader any good idea of the content of the chapter (*e.g.*, "Poor and Blank," "Ghosts and Monsters," and "Preserve Oneself and Destroy the Enemy"). The reader is on his own from the first page to the last in search of Mao's economics. What he finds is, in fact, plenty—hundreds of pieces to the puzzle, all strung together in only God knows what sort of pattern; what he cannot discover is any guide from the author on how to put the pieces together to form a consistent and coherent statement of the topic. This is very disappointing. But there are compensations, for each of the pieces is fashioned with expert hands and so tells us something important about the economic theories and policies of Mao.

To this I must now add that, on fourth reading, the book revealed more compensations than I previously allowed for: it presents some critical theses about Mao's economics that are well worth pondering.

I really should have found time to review Barry Richman's

massive study *Industrial Society in Communist China* (New York: Random House, 1969). Richman, a Canadian, was one of the first economists teaching in the United States to visit the People's Republic, and his written response is a weighty one. One virtue of the book is his comparisons of China with India and the Soviet Union. That topic alone would have kept me busy for a good while.

Well, there are dozens more. Aside from books, the interested reader should consult *The China Quarterly*, which first began publication in 1960 and contains some of the best pieces on Chinese economics. *The Far Eastern Economic Review*, a weekly from Hongkong, enables one to keep up-to-date. The English-language Chinese publications *Peking Review* and *China Reconstructs* serve the same purpose.

Notes

1. This is contained in his "External Trade, Foreign Investment, and Domestic Development: The Chinese Experience, 1840–1937," *Economic Development and Cultural Change*, October 1961, pp. 26–27. I could not find a similar conjecture in his book.
2. While this is especially true of the later years of the Ch'ing dynasty, to its fall in 1911, and even of the subsequent period, there is some evidence of industrial development from 1912 to 1949. That evidence is presented below in the review of John Chang's study.
3. John K. Chang, "Industrial Development of Mainland China, 1912–1949," *Journal of Economic History*, March 1967, pp. 73–81.
4. For data on original claims and subsequent revisions during that period, see Choh-ming Li, *The Statistical System of Communist China* (Berkeley: University of California Press, 1962), p. 90; Alexander Eckstein, *Communist China's Economic Growth and Foreign Trade* (New York: McGraw-Hill, 1966), p. 63; and Jan S. Prybyla, *The Political Economy of Communist China* (Scranton, Pa.: International Textbook, 1970), chap. 8.
5. The Liu-Yeh estimates in Chao's comparison are almost the same as those in my Table 3.5. Those used by Chao come from his earlier RAND publication.
6. It will be remembered that John Chang's study of industrial growth

from 1912 to 1949 found an annual growth rate of only 2.3 percent for combined modern industry and handicrafts (Table 3.1). The Communists exceeded this growth rate by almost ten times during the 1950s.

7. In a more recent publication, Yeh has computed the gross investment ratio as only 24 percent in 1958–1959, but this seems to include only fixed investments by the state. See K. C. Yeh, "Capital Formation," in A. Eckstein, W. Galenson, and T. C. Liu, *Economic Trends in Communist China* (Chicago: Aldine, 1968), pp. 510–11.

8. Stephen Andors, "Revolution and Modernization: Man and Machine in Industrializing Society, the Chinese Case," in Edward Friedman and Mark Selden, eds., *America's Asia* (New York: Vintage Books, 1971).

9. William Lockwood, in *The Economic Development of Japan* (Princeton, N.J.: Princeton University Press, 1954), writes:

> The entire system rested on a grossly unequal distribution of wealth and power which was itself technologically inefficient in some respects and wholly opposed to human and democratic values. One may hope that elsewhere the potential contradictions in these objectives may be reconciled more successfully than in prewar Japan. And indeed it may be doubted whether most Oriental peoples will so patiently tolerate a similar concentration of economic privilege, where it does not carry with it a more direct responsibility to the nation. For Japanese capitalism displayed an all too callous disregard for the immediate well-being of the worker in the factory and the field. (p. 303)

10. Jung-chao Liu, in "Fertiliser Application in Communist China," *The China Quarterly*, October–December 1965, forecasts somewhat higher levels of chemical-fertilizer production and seems less gloomy about the prospects. In fact, China has in the past decade made notable gains in this area.

11. The 6.3 percent growth rate is that of Liu and Yeh, which Eckstein accepts. The main point, however, is the reduction of the growth rate by about 20 percent.

12. See also Howe's article, "Labour Organization and Incentives in Industry, before and after the Cultural Revolution," in Stuart Schram, *Authority, Participation, and Cultural Change in China* (Cambridge, England: Cambridge University Press, 1973).

4

Mao and the Building
of Socialism

Mao Tse-tung has been a Marxist revolutionary his entire adult life. But, unlike Marx, Mao has not pursued the economic theory of exploitation and capitalist processes. And, unlike Lenin, he has applied his talent over long periods of time not only to revolution but also to the task of building a socialist society. For almost half a century—ever since he first took to the hills in 1927 to found a revolutionary base area—Mao has combined revolution against an old society with the construction of a new one. His base areas in the years 1927–1949 contained not only guerrilla armies but also economic-development programs to improve the lives of the people residing in them. Thus, before gaining national power in 1949, Mao and his party, unlike Lenin and his, accumulated a wealth of experience in the design and implementation of economic policies, such as land reforms and agricultural development. Since becoming the guiding spirit of his nation, Mao has continued his search for a Chinese model of economic development—a Chinese path to communism.

Today, China is a rapidly developing country whose people have been freed of the worst afflictions suffered by them over the centuries. This transformation in a few decades from the old to the new China has been noticed by many of the world's poor and in time is likely to change their own lives too. What Marx and Engels started and Lenin continued, Mao has carried forward.

It required a few centuries and several revolutions for

capitalism to establish itself on the ashes of feudalism in Western Europe. Socialism has had an equally difficult time in the world at large. The Russians and Chinese have carried out the two largest proletarian revolutions to date, and several smaller nations have followed in their wakes. It is likely that some of these socialist buds will die out or be crushed—a few already have—and some will no doubt flower. The ultimate outcome of these attempts to fashion socialist societies depends on too many factors to be easily handled here. However, it is useful, before turning to China's efforts at socialist development, to compare the starting points from which the two socialist giants—the USSR and China—set out to establish socialism. These starting points were so dissimilar that this fact alone offers valuable insights into why the two countries subsequently took such divergent paths in their pursuit of, presumably, the same end.

Starting Points: Russia and China

The Chinese Communists contend that the USSR has failed to achieve socialism and has in fact retrogressed to a form of state capitalism. Whatever one's judgment about this, facts confirm that during their first few years in power the Bolsheviks encountered enormous problems in their efforts to establish a transition between capitalism and socialism. Their early difficulties may have proved so redoubtable as to subvert, for a very long time, any attempt by them to produce socialism in their land. What were these difficulties?

The Lack of Socialist Theory and Practice

First, in contrast to the Chinese Communist Party (CCP), the Bolsheviks had no experience and very little theory to assist them in the building of a socialist society. They had carried out no land reforms, no programs of income redistribution, no development policies. Indeed, most of the Russian Marxist leaders had lived in European cities much of the time prior to the revolution, a background totally different from Mao's life in the mountains among the peasants of his own country. Lenin and the other Bolsheviks gave little systematic thought to what things would be like after the revolution, so that when the time came to move forward they did not have a clear conception of the path that should be followed. Lenin in 1923 virtually admitted that the party, with its attention riveted on the revolution, had followed Napoleon's dictum: "First engage in a serious battle and then see what happens." Furthermore, Bolshevik ideas about economic policies were often mutually contradictory, for the party was seriously split on these issues. In this respect, the CCP was ideologically more unified by the time it assumed power in 1949, and by then it knew a great deal about peasants' miseries and how to alleviate them, though it had inadequate knowledge about urban, industrial problems.

The Added Difficulty of Being First

Second, in addition to their lack of theory and practice in this area of building a socialist society, the tasks before the Bolsheviks were exceedingly difficult. Lenin pointed this out in early 1918:

> The more backward the country which, owing to the zigzags of history, has proved to be the one to start the socialist revolution, the more difficult is it for that country to pass from the old capitalist relations to socialist relations. New incredibly difficult tasks, organizational tasks, are added to the tasks of destruction. [1]

These "incredibly difficult tasks" included the major one of mobilizing the people to raise the country's productive forces quickly—without at the same time nourishing bourgeois values, incentives, and institutions that in time would transform the society back into a capitalist one. The building of bourgeois societies in the past, Lenin said, was a relatively easy job, for much had been formed within the womb of the previous societies, as the resistance of workers and peasants to the rising bourgeoisie had been weak and the spontaneously growing national and international markets had been enormous aids to the new class. But the task of the proletariat was now much harder, as Lenin explained:

The principal task of the proletariat, and of the poor peasants which it leads, is the positive or constructive work of setting up an extremely intricate and delicate system of new organizational relationships extending to the planned production and distribution of goods required for the existence of tens of millions of people. Such a revolution can be successfully carried out only if the majority of the population, and primarily the majority of working people, engage in independent creative work as makers of history. Only if the proletariat and the poor peasants display sufficient class-consciousness, devotion to principle, self-sacrifice and perseverance, will the victory of the socialist revolution be assured. By creating a new, Soviet type of state, which gives the working and oppressed people the chance to take an active part in the independent building up of a new society, we solved only a small part of this difficult problem. The principal difficulty lies in the economic sphere, namely, the introduction of the strictest and universal accounting and control of the production and distribution of goods, raising the productivity of labor and *socializing* production *in practice*.[2]

Of course, the Chinese faced much the same problem from equally depressed economic conditions, but they did have the experience of the USSR to draw upon. They had learned from the mistakes made and the economic victories won by the Soviets. They knew, or could quickly learn, about five-year plans, investment programs, and other economic operations.

The Narrow Political Base

Third, the Bolsheviks' strength was narrowly confined to the cities. They came to power not on the basis of having organized the peasants, not on the wings of socialist demands by this numerous class, but because of the support of the poorer industrial workers of Petrograd and Moscow plus spontaneous uprisings of peasants who called for land to the tillers, a petty-bourgeois demand. The party was city-based and hardly knew the countryside. Even as late as 1924, G. E. Zinoviev, a prominent Bolshevik leader, could admit that "the party is still too much an urban party, we know the country too little." To cover up this weakness, symbolic appointments of "peasants" were made, an example being Kalinin as president of the All-Russian Central

Executive Committee, who, as Lenin explained (with perhaps some irony), "still keeps up his connection with the country . . . and visits it every year." Thus the Bolsheviks did not have roots among the great majority of the people who, consequently, were largely ignorant of anything approaching socialist ideology or goals. It was this gluey mass of rural petty bourgeoisie that quickly enveloped and then immobilized the Bolsheviks.

By contrast, Mao and the CCP worked with and mobilized increasing numbers of peasants for at least twenty years before they captured power. By 1949, millions of peasants had had firsthand experience with struggles against landlords and moneylenders, and millions of other peasants knew of these exploits. Mao's party was implanted in his country's most numerous class; it sowed seeds of socialism everywhere, and thus, after 1949, could move forward into collectivization and other socialist programs with more facility than the Soviets had mustered.

The Disruption Caused by Civil War

Fourth, several months after assuming control, the Bolsheviks were plunged into a civil war supported by foreign powers, which lasted for two and a half years and brought the Bolsheviks to their knees—in the end to the point of bare survival. At the close of this holocaust, tens of thousands had been killed and the economic machinery of the country had come almost to a standstill. But for the Bolsheviks as a party, the most damaging blow was the dissipation of the industrial proletariat, the very base of party support. The fighting not only damaged and disrupted production, not only led to the deaths of significant numbers of former industrial workers who had been mobilized into the armies, but brought about a mass flight of urban workers and their families to the countryside in search of food. The number of industrial workers declined from around 2.5 to 3 million in 1917 to 1.2 million in 1921–1922. Petrograd lost almost 60 percent of its population in three years, and Moscow lost about 45 percent. The population of forty provincial capitals fell by a third. At the termination of the civil war, which, in conjunction with World War I, involved almost six years of combat for the Russian people, industrial production was only about 20 percent of its 1913 level, and the proletariat had all but disappeared from the face of Russia. With no base in the countryside, the decimation of the proletariat was a shattering blow to Lenin's party. Lenin later noted that while the imperialists had failed to dislodge Bolshevism, they did solve half their problem by seriously retarding any forward movement to socialism.

While the Chinese Communists suffered similarly from the decade of anti-Japanese and civil wars, they had the advantage of winning their civil war *before* gaining national control. The corruption and ineptness of the Kuomintang (Chiang Kai-shek's Nationalist government, in power from 1927 to 1949) in its last years had alienated growing numbers of its erstwhile supporters. This enabled the Communists to ride to power on waves of goodwill and enthusiasm. By comparison, Lenin's party, after having already won power, bore the discontent and sufferings of the populace, and received the blame for the human misery that spread with the civil war.

The Isolation of Bolshevism

Fifth, Lenin, Trotsky, and others claimed that socialism could not be built in a single country that was surrounded by class enemies and that did not receive help from foreign proletarian governments. Lenin stated this frankly on several occasions, and Trotsky gnawed on the issue to the end of his life. Isaac Deutscher, in his book *The Prophet Armed*, has expressed Trotsky's position on this point most poignantly:

> But to Trotsky the isolation of Bolshevism was already a nightmare too terrible to contemplate, for it meant that the first and so far only attempt to build socialism would have to be undertaken in the worst possible conditions, without the advantages of an intensive international division of labor, without the fertilizing influence of old and complex cultural traditions, in an environment of such staggering material and cultural poverty, primitiveness, and crudity as would tend to mar or warp the very striving for socialism.[3]

The disadvantages of the isolation were that it would compel Russia to devote precious scarce resources to defense, deny it the industrial aid of more advanced countries, all but eliminate potential gains from trade with these countries, and shut it off from opportunities to raise its cultural level. The very striving for socialism was bound to be warped in such an environment of deprivation.

In this respect, too, the Chinese were in a superior position. For one thing, they received valuable industrial and technical help, as well as protection, from the USSR during the early, crucial years of their industrialization. For another, despite hostile actions by the United States, implacable foes were not poised for the kill around China's borders. During most of the 1950s, the Communist countries North Vietnam, North Korea, and Mongolia, as well as such non-Communist countries as India and Pakistan, were tolerant neighbors. The Bolsheviks were in a much less comfortable position during their first decade.

The Inadequate Cadre Base

Sixth, the ranks of the Bolsheviks were too thin to allow them to replace the bureaucracies of the tsar, to provide industry with the specialists and technicians required for industrial leadership, to supply the needed manpower for the planning agencies, and to fill the top positions in the Red Army. Consequently, as time went by, in E. H. Carr's apt metaphor, "more and more of the bricks and foundation-stones of the old dilapidated edifice were used in the construction of the new." This meant that the Bolsheviks had to work through thickening walls of hostility, or at least of evasion, in order to reach the people. "Down below," Lenin complained in 1922, "there are hundreds of thousands of old officials whom we got from the tsar and from bourgeois society and who, partly deliberately and partly unwittingly, work against us."[4]

By contrast, the Chinese Communists had large numbers of trained, dedicated cadres to implement policies at the village level and to carry out other necessary functions. In short, Mao's party had not only a much broader base of support but also a sizable body of experienced party workers to make contact with the masses of workers and peasants.

The Early Loss of Continuity

Finally, what significance should be assigned to Lenin's disability and death only a few years after the cessation of hostilities, while Mao has lived on to guide his country for more than a quarter of a century? It is, naturally, impossible to say what would have happened in the USSR if Lenin had lived another 20 years, but, as already noted, in his last years he was acutely aware of the serious, growing problems facing the party and so might have dealt with them effectively. In any case, the USSR quickly lost its premier leader and with him the continuity of its philosophical outlook. In contrast, Mao, despite some serious errors, which he has admitted, has provided his party and country with a consistent, continuing philosophical framework within which to judge and decide policy actions.

Much has happened in the Soviet Union since Lenin's death in 1924. While these later years are not strictly speaking part of our story, according to the most plausible interpretation, Stalin, in subordinating almost everything else to the rapid buildup of his country's productive forces (which he narrowly interpreted to exclude human agents), fostered growing inequalities in wealth and status, and allowed the erection of a huge bureaucracy and the fashioning of a labor aristocracy and a managerial elite. Stalin failed to rely on the working classes and the masses generally in the struggle against the forces of capitalism, and in effect depoliticized the masses. As a consequence, workers' and peasants' concerns and motivations were turned inward, and private affairs came to rule the daily lives of the people. Without a high level of political and class consciousness among the workers, without their continuing participation in the building of a socialist society, the planning mechanism went awry and work incentives increasingly had to take compensating capitalist forms. In the process, the working class lost political power, and the new ruling class became an expanding state bourgeoisie. The Soviet Union has, therefore, it would seem, restored a bourgeois society—but of a new kind. The bourgeoisie owns and manages the means of production through the state bureaucracies. This capitalist restoration largely emanated from Stalin's policy of overstressing the growth of the productive forces, thereby postponing real (as opposed to superficial, juridical) socialist transformations of the relations of production and of the superstructure. Still, this policy itself can be explained only by considering the historical conditions from which it arose. The Bolsheviks started out in a hole, the hole was deepened by subsequent events, and, to crawl out, the party had to choose from a restricted set of programs, none of which led easily to socialism.

The Strategy to Achieve Chinese Socialism

Although Mao and the Communist Party accumulated rich experiences in rural development prior to 1949, when they assumed national control, they were not prepared to unfurl a complete economic development plan for the country as a whole. They had definite notions regarding land reforms and rural improvement, but they were much less certain about urban and industrial development. Indeed, Mao was apprehensive about entering the cities:

> The centre of gravity of the party's work has shifted from the village to the city. . . . We must do our utmost to learn how to administer and build the cities. . . . If we do not pay attention to these problems . . . we shall be unable to maintain our political power, we shall be unable to stand on our own feet, we shall fail.[5]

The Strategy of Economic Development

Only twenty-five years after Mao and his party captured national power, China had more than doubled agricultural production, raised industrial output by twenty times, kept population growth to about 60 percent, become a formidable military power, greatly reduced illiteracy, and virtually eliminated the threat of famine and most pestilence. The people of China had tripled their per capita income, achieved high employment levels without inflation. They could look forward with assurance to the education and good health of their children.

Of course, Mao alone did not fashion the policies to attain these results. Nevertheless, the strategy that evolved in the quarter-century after 1949, even though built on much trial and error, has turned out to bear a remarkably close resemblance to what he thought and did during his guerrilla days. In the 1950s, Mao restated his broad strategy almost exactly as he had worked it out in the mountains three decades earlier: "Historical experience has proved that only by first creating revolutionary public opinion and seizing political power, and then changing the relations of production, is it possible to greatly develop the productive forces."[6] And, as he added at another time, ideological revolutions are also necessary to lower further the barriers to continued economic progress.

This strategy for economic development was revealed in practice. First, the Communists seized political power from the Kuomintang in 1949. They then set out to consolidate this power through land reforms which aimed to eliminate the old ruling classes (the economic power behind the political force of the Kuomintang) and to fix power in the hands of the millions of peasants and workers. Second, the party radically changed the social relations of production in both the countryside and the cities. The initial change in the rural areas was land reform itself, which, aside from consolidating the party's political power, removed semifeudal institutions in favor of private ownership mixed with cooperative efforts. In the next stage, the party initiated a series of collectivization measures. In urban areas, private enterprise was controlled and then gradually nationalized. Thus, socialist institutions and practices *preceded* the modernization of the country's productive forces, which means that industrialization and agricultural modernization have since taken place largely through socialist and not capitalist institutions.

Third, despite the priority given to socialism, the party did not wait for its completion before embarking on an enormous industrialization effort. Indeed, it was felt that, aside from its important military implications, heavy industry would be required if agriculture was to be transformed into a modern sector. Socialism in the rural areas clearly came first, but eventually it had to be followed by the infusion of modern inputs, such as electric power, machinery and tractors, chemical fertilizers, and the like.

Fourth, the party carried out ideological campaigns, such as those in the 1950s which were directed against bourgeois values, corruption, waste, bureaucracy, and antisocial behavior. But the major ideological campaign came as a cultural revolution in the late 1960s, after the other elements of the strategy had been established. This timing accorded with Mao's belief that socialist values could be firmly implanted only in an environment that already contained rising output levels and socialist institutions. Only then could socialist ideas be reinforced by daily experience, and only then could these ideas react back on the economic base in a vigorous way. "The transformation of ideology into a system," Mao explained in the early 1960s, "invariably occurs at the end of the movement of things in general, because ideological understanding is a reflection of the movement of matters."[7]

The Strategy and Economic Policies

That was the grand strategy. The economic policies that served as vehicles for the strategy occurred in six distinct waves:

1. Economic reconstruction and land reforms 1949–1952
2. Industrialization, nationalization, and collectivization: the First Five-Year Plan 1953–1957
3. The Great Leap Forward 1958–1959
4. Readjustment and recovery; priority to agriculture . . 1960–1965
5. The Great Proletarian Cultural Revolution 1966–1969
6. Balanced growth 1970–

After the Communist takeover, the party immediately undertook the repair and reconstruction of the country's basic capital, which had been severely damaged during the twelve years of war. By 1952, China had more or less recovered its pre-1949 peak of economic activity. During this initial period, the party also carried out land reforms. The second period, 1953–1957, saw the start and completion of a successful five-year plan, which was greatly aided by the USSR and was accompanied by socialization measures in town and country.

From 1949 to 1956, however, the party considered the nation to be in the transition phase of new democracy. Accordingly, the land reforms in the countryside led to private ownership of land, which the party also encouraged in other ways. Capitalist enterprises in urban areas, while controlled, were sometimes encouraged too, at other times only tolerated. In any event, there were at first no concerted drives toward socialism, although some decisive moves in that direction were made immediately. Still, the new democracy stage proved to be of much shorter duration than Mao had suggested it would be. By the mid-1950s, collectivization and nationalization were in full swing, and China, according to Mao, moved from new democracy to socialism at that time.

In the third development phase, 1958–1959, the Great Leap Forward was a reflection of Mao's dissatisfaction with Soviet methods and his attempt to find a Chinese way to economic growth. The Great Leap was a bold program to achieve phenomenal progress on all fronts through the mobilization of peasants and workers, men and women, civilians and soldiers, for heroic tasks, and, from the crest of these efforts, to "enter communism." The Great Leap aimed for the sky on the basis of traditional rural labor methods and the inspiration generated by collective goals and action. Although the upsurge was astonishing for a year or so, it was soon brought to a halt by overambitious plans, miserable weather conditions, and the sudden departure from China of the Soviet technicians in mid-1960 after Khrushchev's break with Mao. As a consequence, economic activity declined precipitously during the first few years of the 1960s, the most serious setback being the sharp decline in the output of agricultural crops, especially grain. In the fourth phase, therefore, the party desperately shifted its priorities to favor agriculture, including added emphasis on rural industries, agricultural machinery, and chemical fertilizers.

The economy rebounded from its low point in 1961–1962 and gained momentum until the advent of the Great Proletarian Cultural Revolution (1966–1969). This unprecedented campaign was Mao's attempt to rid the party and the rest of the superstructure of bourgeois values and institutions. It was his effort to speed up economic development the socialist way, but the resulting turmoil did interfere temporarily with economic progress. Since 1969, the economy has made large gains on a broad front. The countryside has benefited from the rapid development of thousands of rural industries and from the repeated infusion of educators, doctors, technicians, young people from the cities, and cultural workers. Substantial progress has also been made in the urban areas in both heavy and light industry. In fact, industry and agriculture have grown together since 1962 and have supported each other in a mutual relationship that was largely missing during the 1950s under the Soviet model that overstressed heavy industry and neglected agriculture.

Mao's strategy for economic development can now be better understood if it is examined more closely within the context of some of the key economic policies just discussed.

Land Reforms

The primary objectives of the Agrarian Reform Law of 1950—Mao's basic land reform program—were to eliminate the feudal-landlord system in the countryside, improve the lives of the poor, and develop agricultural production as a precondition for the country's industrialization. Land reform not only took land from the landlords and some rich peasants but also confiscated their draft animals, farm implements, houses, and grain—and redistributed all of this to the middle and poor peasants. The landlords, as a class, were wiped out by mass peasant struggles, confiscation, and execution. The Communist Party encouraged and guided the peasants' struggles against their former oppressors, but the peasants themselves often took the law into their own hands, without the party's sanction, in deciding how to settle accounts with these people. Theoretically, the power of the landlords could have been nullified without killing any of them, but in fact the peasants' confrontations with their oppressors awakened grievances that ran much too deep to allow for that idyllic outcome. Mao knew that the long-suppressed rage of the rural poor could not be entirely controlled when the revolutionary turn came. "A revolution," he said early in his career,

> is not a dinner party, or writing an essay, or painting a picture, or doing embroidery; it cannot be so refined, so leisurely and gentle, so temperate, kind, courteous, restrained and magnanimous. A revolution is an insurrection, an act of violence by which one class overthrows another.[8]

In keeping with Mao's contention that the peasants had to liberate themselves, land reform was not simply legislated, passed, and carried out from above. It was a revolutionary movement involving millions of peasants struggling against their former tormentors, gaining confidence and understanding in the process, and acting in ways that committed them to new lives and made the entire movement irreversible. This revolutionary movement was the prerequisite for later socialist development in the countryside, for without it the old class structures and wealth ownership patterns would have been regenerated by the persistence of old attitudes and of institutions favorable to the rich. During part of the Yenan period, for example, when the party's policy was to lower the rents that peasants had to pay in grain to their landlords (generally from their previous level of 50 percent to around 30 percent of the crop), some peasants surreptitiously continued to pay the old amounts because they feared landlord reprisals and, presumably, because they felt that the former arrangement was part of the natural order of things.

The land reform helped to raise the ratio of gross investment to GNP from the 6–7 percent level that prevailed in the 1930s to over 20 percent by 1953. It did this by redistributing wealth and hence income from the rich to the poor, thereby eliminating the luxury consumption of the rich, raising by lesser amounts the essential consumption of the poor, and making the rest available to the state for capital construction.

Nationalization and Collectivization

Once the peasants and the workers had gained political power, the Communist Party began changing the relations of production, at first in ways that preserved some capitalism in industry and widened private ownership in rural areas, later in ways that eliminated industrial private enterprise and led to agricultural collectives.

Despite the lip service paid to the transition stage of new democracy, the party, almost immediately after gaining power, nationalized a substantial portion of heavy industry, including iron and steel, cement, electric power, petroleum, railroads and highways, and air transport—all of which had been owned by the Nationalist government. Foreign-owned firms were soon taken over, as were all banks and other major financial institutions. Foreign trade was also brought under central control. By 1952, over half of the output of modern industry was produced by socialist enterprises. The privately owned industries (mostly smaller firms, such as textiles, food processing, and consumer durables) were increasingly controlled: they were supplied with raw materials by the state trading companies, their output was often purchased by the socialist sector, and prices and other terms were frequently set by the state. Some industries were placed under joint state-private control, which meant that the state invested in the enterprises and assigned personnel to share in management with the capitalists. By 1956, almost all industries were either completely or largely socialized. In addition, wholesale and retail trade, along with handicrafts, were formed, step by step, into cooperatives and thus brought into the socialist sector. New democracy, the transition stage envisioned by Mao between the old society and socialism, lasted only a few years. Mao was eager to change the relations of production into socialist forms.

Today, the largest industrial enterprises, especially the urban enterprises turning out producer goods, along with the major transportation and communications facilities and mining operations, are owned and managed by the state. Many industries, however, are owned and managed at lower administrative levels or are state-owned and locally managed. Counties, for example, engage in the manufacture of numerous consumer goods as well as iron and steel. Communes own and manage small enterprises producing cement, chemical fertilizers, agricultural tools, processed food, and so forth. Increasingly, locally administered rural industries have become important sources of major products. While all of these industrial firms are owned by "the people," this term often refers to collective ownership at local levels. To that extent, industrial decision-making has also become decentralized, although the most important decisions, including those in the military area, are made at the top, as part of the national plan.

In the mid-1950s, the party also undertook rural collectivization. After land reform, the Chinese leaders, in four stages, transformed small private holdings into large-scale communes. In the first stage, the party encouraged the development of mutual-aid teams, units of several households whose function was to pool privately owned resources in order to compensate for shortages of labor and other inputs during the rush seasons of planting and harvesting. Initially, this was done on a temporary, seasonal basis, the teams being dissolved at the end of the planting or harvesting period, but later some of the teams were organized on a permanent basis. The permanent teams were somewhat larger than the temporary ones and often held some capital goods and animals as common property. By 1954, there were almost 10 million mutual-aid teams, about half of them seasonal and half permanent, comprising 58 percent of all peasant households.

In the second stage, the party founded elementary agricultural producers' cooperatives, some of which were organized as early as 1950 but most of which were formed in the second half of 1955. Each APC comprised several mutual-aid teams, or around thirty to forty households, that is, a village. Land and other capital goods continued to be privately owned, but these assets were now pooled in the APCs for use according to annual plans prepared by cooperative management. Peasants were compensated according to their labor and their contributions of land, implements, and animals; labor, however, was usually the basis for claims on most of the output. By early 1956, almost all peasant families had joined APCs.

In the third stage, 1956–1957, the party consolidated the elementary APCs into larger, advanced APCs, comprising several small villages or perhaps one large village and from one hundred to three hundred households. In the advanced APCs, the peasants held title to a share of the collective equity and no longer had any private claim on their former holdings of land and other capital goods. Accordingly, net earnings were distributed to the peasants only on the basis of work done. The earnings withheld, including those contributed by capital goods, were collectively owned, and they were generally larger than the withheld earnings under the previous organization. Similarly, the payment of the agricultural tax became a collective obligation in the advanced APCs, whereas in the elementary APCs it had been an individual responsibility.

In the final stage, 1958–1959, the party established people's communes during the Great Leap Forward. The commune, as the Chinese have explained, "is the basic unit of the social structure of our country, combining industry, agriculture, trade, education, and the military. At the same time, it is the basic organization of social power." The communes were organized to provide larger, more efficient units for carrying out large-scale water control projects and for building factories and workshops throughout the countryside. They were organized, moreover, to provide additional labor through the establishment of mess halls and other communal services that released many women from household tasks. The communes also became the basic governmental unit; they ran factories, schools, and·banks and controlled their own militia. They weakened the patriarchal family unit and in general the peasants' exclusive identification with very small groups. Furthermore, they introduced a "half-wage, half-supply system" which provided free supplies of some necessities to peasants whether they worked or not, the remaining commune income being distributed according to work done.

The party encouraged the rapid organization of communes during the Great Leap Forward, beginning in May 1958. During the following year and a half, the Chinese made an all-out effort to industrialize the rural areas, to build a large iron and steel industry, to grow record agricultural crops, to raise the education, health, and cultural levels of the peasants, and to catch up with the leading industrial nations of the world within fifteen years.

The enlargement of rural units and the accompanying collectivization during the 1950s enabled the peasants, especially the women, to work longer hours at useful tasks. The communes employed the increased labor not only in traditional farm work and subsidiary occupations but also in large-scale water control projects, basic construction, and rural industrial work. Much labor was also used for communal services—administration, cultural activities, medical care, and education. So that peasants would not waste their time during off-seasons, the communes organized them into large units for community and area projects.

During the 1950s, then, the basic organizational unit in the countryside grew from individual peasant households to mutual-aid teams (at first temporary and later permanent), to elementary APCs (which became production teams in the communes), to advanced APCs (which became production brigades in the communes), and finally to communes. The basis for the distribution of income also changed from distribution according to work and asset ownership, to distribution according to work only, to distribution according to work and needs; and, at the same time, the value of a peasant's workpoints came to depend on the work done by increasingly larger groups.

The downturn of economic activity in the early 1960s, however, led to the reversal of some of these advances. During those years, when Maoist ideology waned, the party reduced the average size of the communes, thus greatly increasing their number. It also transferred much decision-making authority from the communes to production brigades and teams, thereby forging closer links between individual effort and compensation. In addition, it de-emphasized income payments according to need, reduced the level of communal services, and restored private plots on which peasants could grow crops for their private use or for sale on private markets.

Thus, in the early 1960s, the party admitted in effect that it had pushed communization so rapidly as to reduce seriously the peasants' work incentives. Compensation according to need, work within huge, impersonal armies of laborers, and demanded overtime all tended to separate the peasants' rewards from their individual efforts. During the 1950s, the peasants did identify themselves with increasingly larger groups—from mutual-aid teams to APCs—but the communes, as highly centralized decision-making units, were several steps beyond the feasible front line of advance. The commune structure, however, with its commune-brigade-team-family levels, in which the team and to a lesser extent the larger brigade are directly responsible for the daily work and income of the peasants, has remained intact to the present day and has prospered.

Today, there are about 50,000 communes. The average commune has 5,000 acres of land and 15,000 members, but there is much variation around the average. Within the communes, there are 750,000 brigades, about 5 million teams, and 170 million families. Functions requiring large-scale management—such as water control projects, agricultural extension programs, hydroelectric generating stations, hospital and higher-school administration, military operations, rural industrialization, reforestation—are performed at the commune level. The communes are also responsible for procuring grain for the state, collecting taxes, and coordinating production plans. The brigades (on the average comprising about one thousand people) operate orchards, some small industry (such as farm equipment repair shops and food processing), health stations, primary schools, and supply, marketing, and credit cooperatives. They also oversee the work done by the teams. The teams (with an average of 140 members who cultivate an average of fifty acres) control the work actually done in the fields, distribute income to their members, own their tools, and decide on the use of some of the surplus they generate. Most households also have private land—about 5 percent of the total area—on which they raise vegetables, grow fruit, keep poultry and hogs, and so on.

The two thousand counties of China (which on the average contain twenty-five communes), the communes, and the brigades coordinate their activities in various ways. For example, a county factory may produce farm machinery which receives major repairs at the commune level and minor ones in a brigade workshop. Or, the county may have a hospital, the commune a clinic, and the brigade a smaller health station. Similarly, education, marketing services, and community projects are coordinated, sometimes down to the team level.

The commune structure, therefore, although introduced too hurriedly in 1958–1959, in its reorganized form is today the basic rural institution, comprising 80 to 85 percent of the country's population. The Maoists hope that it will gradually assume a more socialist character in that the peasants will come to identify their interests with the activities of ever-larger groups—from their own families, to their teams, then to brigades and beyond. The Maoists expect the communes' land and capital goods to be transformed in time from narrow collective ownership into ownership by all the people in the full socialist form.

Planning and Industrialization

The party captured political power for the peasants and the workers, transformed their work institutions and practices into socialist forms, and began building up the country's productive forces. The Communists wanted to transform China quickly from an agricultural and largely defenseless nation into a major industrial economic power capable of defending its national borders militarily.

An industrial program required a national planning system, which in any case the party considered to be an integral component of any socialist society. The obvious place to look for help in this regard was the Soviet Union, which had had two decades of experience with such planning. This "socialist" neighbor was willing to show the Chinese how to establish a national plan and, at the same time, to extend economic aid for China's industrialization effort. Accordingly, with Soviet assistance, the Chinese set up a State Planning Committee in 1952. This committee was the forerunner of a series of planning commissions designated for short-run, long-run, and special purposes. Below these national commissions was erected an entire network of economic planning agencies, which eventually extended into the country's two thousand counties and from there into the cities and communes.

The First Five-Year Plan started in 1953, the second in 1958.

But the second plan was interrupted by the Great Leap Forward and was never completed. The first plan, fashioned in Soviet style insofar as its investment allocations were concerned, accentuated capital formation over consumption, heavy industry over light industry, industry over agriculture, and urban development over rural development. Thus the plan stressed such industries as iron and steel, petroleum, electric power, machine building, mining, chemicals, and electronics. Consumer goods industries grew too, but at a slower pace. Finally, most of the investment in agriculture came from that sector's own saving, not from the national budget. In fact, the rural areas, as we have seen, were mainly reorganized along socialist lines, not modernized with new equipment.

The USSR extended loans to the Chinese which enabled them to buy, on deferred payment, around two hundred complete industrial plants as well as military equipment and other commodities. In addition, more than ten thousand Soviet experts went to China during the 1950s to train the Chinese in industrial techniques, and China in turn sent more than thirteen thousand students to the Soviet Union for advanced training. Although the Chinese had to repay the Soviet loans with interest, by exporting ferrous metals, handicrafts, food products, tea, and tobacco to the USSR, the loans greatly helped China to establish a solid industrial base. By the end of the decade, the Chinese were able, for the first time, to produce motor vehicles; jet aircraft; metallurgical, mining, and power-generating equipment; and high-grade steel alloys. At that time, industrial production was almost nine times greater than it had been in 1949.

However, toward the end of the First Five-Year Plan (1953–1957), Mao grew restless under the Soviet-imposed development policies that stressed tight centralization and heavy industry to the neglect of local initiative and agriculture. Moreover, the relative neglect of agriculture resulted by 1956–1957 in a retardation of its growth rate, threatening to reduce China's exports (and hence its imports) and basic food supplies, especially those of the urban-industrial population. Mao's reaction was to search for a way to replace the Soviet model with one more in keeping with

China's and the Chinese party's traditions. The outcome of this search was the Great Leap Forward.

The Primacy of Agriculture

While the Great Leap applied to urban-industrial areas, it was principally an effort to apply to economic development in the countryside the "guerrilla tactics" that had worked so well for Mao prior to 1949 in the military field. These tactics emphasized man over the machine, heroic deeds, local initiative, nonmaterial incentives, and collective aims, spirit, and discipline. Paradoxically, the failures of the Great Leap served to place even more emphasis on the primacy of rural economic development, though the guerrilla tactics for getting the job done were depreciated. Thus Mao's peasants remained in the spotlight, but "Maoism" was pushed into the wings.

By late 1960 and early 1961, not only had agriculture and light industry been badly hit, but heavy industrial growth had fallen to virtually zero. The Chinese leadership, no longer dominated by Mao, altered its economic priorities to place agriculture first, light industry second, and heavy industry last. These new rankings, however, did not reflect a sharp diminution of interest in industrialization. Rather, they served notice that the top priority would go to industrial pursuits that directly aided agriculture, either by producing modern inputs (raw materials and capital equipment) for that sector or by processing output (food and industrial crops) coming from it. Industries at one remove from agriculture would be emphasized to the extent that they directly served these inner, top-priority firms, and so on. Increasingly, as the 1960s advanced, the party expected the countryside to establish not only small industries that directly assisted agriculture but also, whenever possible, small basic industries, such as iron and steel, cement, coal mining, and so on. By the end of the decade, the economy was better able to support agriculture with both the output of large-scale urban industry and of tens of thousands of small, indigenous plants throughout the countryside. Thus the effort of the 1950s that stressed the mobilization of traditional inputs (labor, natural fertilizers, draft animals, traditional tools) was redirected in the 1960s to the production of modern inputs, such as chemical fertilizers, insecticides and pesticides, small hydroelectric plants, electric motors, rice transplanters, tractors, trucks, and seed-improvement stations. This redirection was made possible by the industrial effort of the 1950s.

By 1965, the economy was growing rapidly in a balanced way, reaching in that year a national-output level that was over 60 percent higher than that of 1961 and almost 20 percent above the peak of 1958–1959. However, in the following year, the Cultural Revolution burst in the skies above Peking and Shanghai.

The Cultural Revolution

The downturn of the economy during the years 1959–1961 presented Mao's opponents, including Liu Shao-ch'i, the head of state, with an opportunity to reinvigorate the economy and at the same time to downgrade Mao's stress on class struggles and collective goals. Thus individual and material incentives were restored, rural markets reestablished, and productive forces emphasized over class and ideological contradictions. These and other policies, as Mao saw them, promoted bourgeois values which were permeating the entire society. Mao, having lost some power in the early 1960s as a result of Great Leap failures, looked from the sidelines in dismay at these developments, for it was his conviction that China could not progress toward communism if the superstructure of society reflected bourgeois ideas at variance with the socialist economic base. The superstructure, according to Mao, did not automatically change to socialist forms; this transformation required recurrent campaigns and continual reinforcement. Otherwise, a strengthening bourgeois superstructure would in time restore the bourgeoisie to political power and thus restore the capitalist mode of production. The struggle between the proletariat and the bourgeoisie, Mao proclaimed, was still going on:

> In China, although in the main socialist transformation has been completed with respect to the system of ownership, and although the large-scale and turbulent class struggles of the masses character-

istic of the previous revolutionary periods have in the main come to an end, there are still remnants of the overthrown landlord and comprador classes, there is still a bourgeoisie, and the remolding of the petty-bourgeoisie has only just started. The class struggle is by no means over. . . . The proletariat seeks to transform the world according to its own world outlook, and so does the bourgeoisie. In this respect, the question of which will win out, socialism or capitalism, is still not really settled.[9]

The Great Proletarian Cultural Revolution, which ran its course during the years 1966–1969, was Mao's supreme effort to cleanse the superstructure of bourgeois values that had crept back into drama, literature, party work, education, medicine, and in fact into all phases of Chinese life. Mao's mission was to root out the old values, replace them with proletarian values, and in the process rebuild some of the key institutions in ways that would advance socialism and lead to the restoration of his authority. Thus the Cultural Revolution was a power struggle, but it was a struggle over which course China should follow, the path back to capitalism or the one ahead to socialism. "At present," Mao said, "our objective is to struggle against and overthrow those persons in authority who are taking the capitalist road." The task, as he saw it, was to repudiate bourgeois ideology wherever it might be found.

At the same time, the Cultural Revolution was a response to two acute problems: the danger of an armed invasion by the United States or the Soviet Union, or both, and the danger of reactionary successors to Mao and the other Maoist leaders. The first danger was touched off by the growing involvement of the United States in Southeast Asia and the worsening relations between China and the USSR. The second was intensified by the results of the Stalin succession in the USSR, which Mao interpreted negatively. In both cases, as Mao saw the situation, bourgeois tendencies in China heightened the threats, and proletarian ideological unification provided a solution.

To combat the Chinese bourgeois currents, Mao called on millions of students to form themselves into Red Guards, who in turn were backed by the People's Liberation Army, which strongly supported Mao and reflected his real locus of power—the peasants in the socialist countryside. The targets for attack, Mao advised the Red Guards, were the cultural and educational units and leading organs of the party and government in the large and medium cities. His directive to the Red Guards revealed another aspect of the Cultural Revolution—Mao's repeated attempt to capture the cities from the bourgeoisie. His peasant-based movement had implanted socialism with some success throughout the countryside, but, although industries had been nationalized, the urban areas had still not been fully incorporated into the socialist movement. The Communist Party itself, Mao believed, had become increasingly city-based and bureaucratic, and as such had become impregnated with the bourgeois ideas of individualism, material incentives, privileges, and soft living. He called upon the peasants in the socialist countryside and young people everywhere to transform the cities from capitalist into socialist centers. Mao expected that in the process the young people would also be transformed themselves as they absorbed the party's true revolutionary traditions and engaged in revolution.

It was Mao's contention that the Cultural Revolution would lead to increases in economic productivity. In his mind, ideology and economics were closely related:

> The aim of the Great Proletarian Cultural Revolution is to revolutionize people's ideology and as a consequence to achieve greater, faster, better and more economical results in all fields of work. If the masses are fully aroused and proper arrangements are made, it is possible to carry on both the Cultural Revolution and production without one hampering the other, while guaranteeing high quality in all our work. The Great Proletarian Cultural Revolution is a powerful motive force for the development of the social productive forces in our country. Any idea of counterposing the Great Cultural Revolution to the development of production is incorrect.[10]

The Cultural Revolution was meant to achieve a revolution in ideas—in ideas that, because they conformed to the socialist economic base, would act powerfully on that base through the release of human energy and ingenuity. The development of the productive forces, Mao asserted, was being impeded by an outmoded superstructure that had to be swept away.

It is an essential part of Mao's thinking that progress is made through struggle, when new talents emerge and knowledge advances by leaps. Thus, Mao pressed, progress depends mainly on the human factor, not on machines.

> In building up the . . . country, we—unlike the modern revisionists who one-sidedly stress the material factor, mechanization, and modernization—pay chief attention to the revolutionization of man's thinking and through this, command, guide, and promote the work of mechanization and modernization.[11]

There is much evidence, therefore, that Mao saw the Cultural Revolution as largely a struggle within the superstructure—within the ideological realm. Yet the danger to China was more than that the growing bourgeois ideas might in time restore capitalist relations of production. In fact, the bourgeoisie was being generated and regenerated, in hothouse style, by the capitalist relations of production fostered after the Great Leap faltered in 1959. The Cultural Revolution attacked not only the resulting growth of bourgeois values but the social institutions and practices that bore capitalist imprints and spawned such values. Although Mao saw the bourgeoisie as "a remnant," it was in fact being continually recreated by social relations not yet fully transformed into socialist forms. The real success of the Cultural Revolution, therefore, should be measured by the extent to which it elevated the economic base into a socialist one—and by this measure it attained some success.

Economic Policies in the 1970s

Since the windup of the Cultural Revolution in 1969, the Chinese have pursued a balanced development program that emphasizes both agriculture and industry, large and small enterprises, self-reliance ("keeping the initiative in our hands") and the import of foreign technology, individual and collective incentives, and so on. The results have been good—better, however, in industry and mining than in agriculture. The country experienced no recession, inflation, or energy crisis in the first half of the 1970s.

China's most notable achievement since the Cultural Revolution has been the marked growth of small industries and mining operations throughout the countryside, a movement that was initiated during the Great Leap Forward. The communes are now dotted with enterprises that produce many of the inputs needed by agriculture—cement, steel, fertilizers, and so on—and process the agricultural sector's output of food, cotton, sugar, tobacco, and other commercial crops. There may now be half a million of these rural industrial units. Despite their presence, however, the growth rate of grain output since 1969 has not been high, and in fact it has shown some signs of slowing down. This has recently induced the planning authorities to contract for thirteen huge chemical fertilizer plants from Western Europe, the United States, and Japan, which will be in full operation toward the end of this decade. At the same time, the authorities have promoted greater intensity of land use, further mechanization, and other measures to keep food supplies ahead of population, including a nationwide effort to limit birthrates.

Perhaps the most dramatic single economic achievement in the past several years has been the surge of crude oil production, which rose by 300 percent from 1969 to 1975. It is estimated that China will be producing at least 200 million tons of crude oil by 1980—ten times the level of 1969—and exporting a fourth of it. China has also made notable gains in industry generally since 1969, although iron and steel production lagged during 1973–1975. An interesting development in the mid-1970s was the 25 percent decline in China's military expenditures from their level of the late 1960s, a fact that has not been adequately explained by Western observers.

From 1970 to 1975, China's international trade grew by a third (in real terms). China imports not only complete industrial plants from major capitalist countries but large amounts of high-quality and specialty steel products from Japan; grain from the United States, Canada, Australia, and elsewhere; and copper, nickel, and lead from several countries. It exports crude oil to Japan and the Philippines, and it exports textiles, foodstuffs, and other consumer goods (bicycles, sewing machines, cameras, watches, radios) to countries all around the world. Altogether, however,

China's total trade in 1974 came to only 6 percent of its national output.

Table 4.1 illustrates some of China's main economic achievements from 1949 to 1974. It includes, along with population estimates, the major agricultural crop (grain), four products from heavy industry, one from light industry (bicycles), and the overall measure of national output (GPN).

The Chinese Vision of Communism

The Maoists visualize a communist society—the higher stage of socialism—as a richly productive (though not necessarily in private goods), planned, classless, highly egalitarian, and self-reliant society in which the means of production are collectively owned and the work processes are regulated by workers. In a communist society, the people have a high level of communist consciousness and morality (selflessness, simple and frugal living, collective work incentives and goals, a desire to "serve the people," honesty, modesty, and so on), and they consider labor to be the prime necessity of life; products are distributed according to need; and the state and party (as the dictatorship and the vanguard of the proletariat), the social divisions of labor (town versus country, mental versus manual work, peasant versus worker), and commodities, markets, and money have all withered away.

In the lower stage of socialism, the party's principal task is to raise the nation's productive forces to levels that will insure security and comfort for all, but in ways that will promote progress toward the other communist goals as well—in particular, toward a classless society. Thus the Maoists have seriously sought to advance the communist goal of eliminating the social divisions of labor through several programs. They have furthered education that combines work and study, partly in order to reduce the elitism associated with mental work as opposed to manual labor. They have advanced physical work periods in the countryside for city-based administrators, teachers, and other "mental workers,"

Table 4.1
Some Economic Achievements of China, 1949–1974

Year	Grain	Crude steel	Crude oil	Chemical fertilizer	Tractors (thousands)	Bicycles (millions)	GNP (1973 dollars)	Population (millions)
		(millions of metric tons)						
1949	108	*	*	*	†	‡	40	530
1952	154	1	*	*	†	‡	67	564
1957	185	5	1	1	1	1	94	626
1959	165	13	4	2	9	1	107	651
1962	180	8	6	3	20	1	93	686
1965	210	13	11	10	33	2	134	723
1969	240	16	20	11	58	3	157	774
1974	259	24	65	25	133§	5	223	838

* Less than 500,000 tons.
† Less than 500 units.
‡ Less than 500,000 million units.
§ 1973.

Source: Joint Economic Committee, China, pp. 23, 42, 77, 165–67, 228, 276, and 351.

for the purpose of breaking down the division between town and country as well as that between mental and manual work. They have sent millions of city youth to rural areas, more or less permanently, to work with the peasants; similar programs have been put into operation for doctors, educators, and others. The party has also conducted ideological campaigns that extol manual labor, peasants' lives, "barefoot doctors," and dedicated youth in outlying areas of China.

Similar campaigns commend the communist virtue of "serving the people," a phrase that can be seen all over China these days. "Our point of departure," Mao has written,

> is to serve the people wholeheartedly and never for a moment divorce ourselves from the masses, to proceed in all cases from the interests of the people and not from one's self-interest or from the interests of a small group, and to identify our responsibility to the people with our responsibility to the leading organs of the party.[12]

Even Pope Paul VI, as reported by *Time* magazine, has taken note of this call and of other Maoist intentions. The Maoist doctrine, he stated, is "a moral socialism of thought and conduct," and China "looks toward the mystique of disinterested work for others, to inspiration to justice, to exaltation of a simple and frugal life, to rehabilitation of the rural masses, and to a mixing of social classes." While this is not a completely accurate account of Mao's goals, it does very nicely catch the spirit of Maoism.

The Maoists also see communism in terms of self-reliance—for the nation, local areas, individuals. At all levels, this refers to keeping the initiative in one's own hands by doing whatever one can do without seeking help from "the outside." Self-reliance is not autarky, for aid and trade may be welcomed if they do not subordinate the receiver to an exploitative relationship. In this sense, the Maoist vision is that of a cellular nation of self-reliant communes and counties, in which each local unit seeks to produce its needs, not only in food, clothing, and housing, but also in basic industrial products, in education and health care, in culture and recreation. At times, this vision seems to have no place for massive cities or for the ultraurban life of the present day and its suave, sophisticated veneer. It is a vision of rusticity, of social development in thousands of small but integrated units, each springing from the uncorrupted soil of the countryside.

Mao has made several estimates of the length of the lower stage of socialism in China, the stage preceding that of communism[13] "Fifty years from now," he said in 1955, "a communist China will emerge." However, Mao added, perhaps with tongue in cheek, it would not look right for China to enter communism ahead of the Soviet Union. After all, the October Revolution came first and it was Lenin's cause, which should be respected. If we hurried ahead of the Soviet Union, he said, "it would be only for the purpose of seeking credit from Marx." And it would be shameful, he added, to shove ahead only for that!

The transition to communism will not occur as a class revolution, Mao pointed out, but will be a social revolution, a transformation of collective ownership into ownership by all the people, a transformation from distribution according to work to distribution according to need. Communism itself, he thought, will go through many different phases and will have many revolutions. It will not be without contradictions, and it will certainly not be the last stage of world development. In fact, Mao prophesied, human beings themselves are not the final stage of development, for after they have died out there will be still higher forms of life. "Mankind will eventually reach its doomsday. When theologians talk about doomsday, it is pessimism used to scare people. When we speak about the destruction of mankind, we are saying that something more advanced than mankind will be produced."

Thus the dialectics of destruction-construction may be said to be Mao's beginning and his ending.

Notes

1. V. I. Lenin, "Political Report of the Central Committee, March 7," *Selected Works* (New York: International Publishers, 1967), 2: 575.
2. Lenin, "The International Position of the Russian Soviet Republic and the Fundamental Tasks of the Socialist Revolution," *Selected Works*, 2: 646, 649.

3. Isaac Deutscher, *The Prophet Armed* (New York: Vintage, 1954), p. 450.

4. Lenin, "Five Years of the Russian Revolution and the Prospects of the World Revolution," *Selected Works*, 3: 724.

5. Mao Tse-tung, "Report to the Second Plenary Session," in *Selected Works* (Peking: Foreign Languages Press, 1961), 4: 363–64.

6. This thought is expressed in Mao, "Reading Notes on the Soviet Union's 'Political Economics,' " in Joint Publications Research Service, *Miscellany of Mao Tse-tung Thought (1949–1968)* (Arlington, Va.: JPRS, 1974), pp. 259, 269.

7. Ibid., p. 303.

8. Mao, "Report on an Investigation of the Peasant Movement in Hunan," *S.W.*, 1: 28.

9. K. H. Fan, ed., *Mao Tse-tung and Lin Piao* (New York: Anchor Books, 1972), pp. 267–69.

10. "Decision of the Central Committee of the Chinese Communist Party Concerning the Great Proletarian Cultural Revolution," in Joan Robinson, *The Cultural Revolution in China* (Harmondsworth: Penguin, 1969), p. 95.

11. In *Peking Review* during the Cultural Revolution.

12. Mao, "On Coalition Government," *S.W.*, 3: 315. See also, *Quotations from Chairman Mao Tse-tung* (Peking, Foreign Languages Press, 1966), pp. 170–71.

13. The quotations that follow are from Joint Publications Research Service, *Miscellany*, pp. 26, 210–11, 394.

5

Rural Development, 1949–1972, and the Lessons to Be Learned from It

The precarious position of the Chinese peasants down through the ages and the oppressive conditions under which they labored are too well known to require much comment from me. In Han (206 B.C.–A.D. 220), T'ang (A.D. 618–906), or Sung (A.D. 960–1279) records, and indeed right down to yesterday, one can read at length about their diseases, their illiteracy, their superstitions and fatalistic attitudes, and the natural disasters and periodic famines that all but wiped them out.

Nevertheless, the records also reveal, if one examines them closely, an ingenious peasantry producing a substantial surplus during most of this long period, not, of course, for itself, but mostly for the sustenance and pleasures of the few people who made up the ruling classes—the emperor and his family and retainers, bureaucrats, landlords, moneylenders, and military officers. This small but powerful ruling group pumped the surplus out of the countryside through taxes, rents, interest, corvée labor, enslavement, extortion, and other means, fair and foul. It may well be that, on the average over the many centuries, one-third of what the peasantry produced was taken away from it for the enjoyment and support of less than 2 percent of the population. What was left to the peasants was usually just enough for their survival, but from time to time not enough even for that. Undernourishment was common, starvation not unusual.

Let R. H. Tawney, who with much acumen observed the Chinese peasants in the early 1930s, have the last word:

Exaggeration is easy. Privation is one thing, poverty to the point of wretchedness—la misère—another. A sturdy and self-reliant stock may grow in a stony soil. But, when due allowance has been made for the inevitable misconceptions, it is difficult to resist the conclusion that a large proportion of Chinese peasants are constantly on the brink of actual destitution. They are, so to say, a propertied proletariat, which is saved—when it is saved—partly by its own admirable ingenuity and fortitude, partly by the communism of the Chinese family, partly by reducing its consumption of necessaries and thus using up its physical capital. . . .

It is true, however, that, over a large area of China, the rural population suffers horribly through the insecurity of life and property. It is taxed by one ruffian who calls himself a general, by another, by a third, and, when it has bought them off, still owes taxes to the Government; in some places actually more than twenty years' taxation has been paid in advance. It is squeezed by dishonest officials. It must cut its crops at the point of the bayonet, and hand them over without payment to the local garrison, though it will starve without them. It is forced to grow opium in defiance of the law, because its military tyrants can squeeze heavier taxation from opium than from rice or wheat, and make money, in addition, out of the dens where it is smoked. It pays blackmail to the professional bandits in the neighborhood; or it resists, and, a year later, when the bandits have assumed uniform, sees its villages burned to the ground. . . .

There are districts in which the position of the rural population is that of a man standing permanently up to the neck in water, so that even a ripple is sufficient to drown him. The loss of life caused by the major disasters is less significant than the light which they throw on the conditions prevailing even in normal times over considerable regions.[1]

Explanations of Persistent Poverty Before 1949

There were, of course, reasons for the persistence of this deprivation and misery. The conventional explanation is that, even with the highest efficiency in carrying out the best-intentioned policies to alleviate rural poverty, the job would have been a most difficult one for any government. It is argued that during the past century successive Chinese governments have had to contend with rebellions, civil wars, encroachments of imperialist powers on the economy, and Japanese invasions. When all of this turmoil is considered within the context of the widespread and deeply embedded poverty in the society, the argument continues, it is no wonder that very little was accomplished.

While this argument has some validity, it represents a very narrow view of the social forces at work in this period. For the disruptive events themselves emanated in part from the failure of the Chinese authorities to alleviate poverty. It was a two-way street. The battles that went on were fed by the rural misery, but these struggles in turn contributed to further political disintegration and so to the growing inability of governments to shore up the crumbling base.

However, even the foregoing reformulation is only a part of the total story. Most of the rest has to do with the "best intentions" assumed above. Social scientists these days usually suppose that all governments really want economic development and that, if they do not achieve it, this must be because the problems are unusually difficult or because the solutions take a long time to work themselves out. Thus persistence and technical knowledge are what is required for success. These suppositions, however, do not take adequate account of the class structures of societies, of the often conflicting aims that exist among the various classes, and of the class nature of "success" and "failure." From the standpoint of the ruling classes, poverty may not be a failure but a prerequisite for their accumulation of wealth, their privileges, and their social, political, and economic domination.

This is partly because poverty is often the carcass left from the acquisition of wealth; or, at best, the stagnant backwaters of society, as yet untouched by a development process that stresses private profitmaking and hence efficiency and "building on the best." But poverty also persists because it is closely associated with peasant characteristics which are highly supportive of existing class structures and hence of the privileges and wealth of the dominant classes. I refer to such characteristics as illiteracy, passivity, obedience, and fatalism; a lack of awareness of the world at large and, therefore, a propensity for mythical and spiritual explanations of personal hardships and disasters; a lack of organization; a willingness to work hard for very little; and being setups for all sorts of manipulation by "superiors."

A widespread, thoroughgoing program of economic development, which reaches deeply into the structure of society, is a dangerous thing to ruling classes because it tends to undermine the very attributes of the masses of people that nourish the wealthy and powerful. Such a program awakens people, and for the ruling classes it is often best that they doze; it mobilizes people for gigantic economic efforts, and such mobilization can be turned to political subversion; it sweeps away people's illusions and thus may open their eyes to the causes of their oppression.

Furthermore, any serious economic-development program that involves industrialization within an agrarian and commercial society threatens existing class structures by creating new economic bases from which new social classes arise, weakening the economic foundations that support the present dominant classes. Economic development stirs up a society, establishing new classes that compete with the old order, socially, politically, and economically.

These considerations are applicable to pre-1949 China. The peasant misery of that country during the century preceding the Communist victory was due not only to the inherent difficulty of raising millions of people out of abject poverty during a century of violence but, more important, to the almost complete lack of interest by the Chinese governments and foreign investors in doing any such thing. The peasants remained poor in large part because poverty served a purpose; or, at best, because it did not prevent the wealthier classes from extracting the economic surplus of the countryside.

Changes in the Countryside Since 1949

Degrading and humiliating peasant misery is now gone from China. This is not to say, of course, that a rural paradise has miraculously arisen. The Chinese peasants are still very poor, especially by the standards of industrial countries; the struggle against nature goes on, and every now and then some Chinese peasants find themselves on the losing end; and there are still plenty of problems and some small areas of severe poverty.

However, the overriding economic fact is that for over twenty years, for the first time in China's history almost all the people have had a decent standard of living in the basic necessities— food, clothing, housing, health care, education, culture, and recreation. Starvation, infanticide, cannibalism, selling children into virtual slavery, and blank ignorance no longer exist. The Chinese now have what is in effect an insurance policy against pestilence, famine, and other disasters. They have all risen together; no one seems to have been left far behind. And the rural areas are alive with water control projects, small industries, transportation and communication networks, and plans for many other things that promise fuller lives for the peasants, who, while not prosperous, are prospering, awake, and optimistic. Some gains of the Chinese economy since 1952 are shown in Table 5.1.

How did this happen? I shall first present some social, political, and economic reasons for this rural transformation, reasons that I believe to be basic to an understanding of the change. After that, I shall take a closer look at the economic policies that have transformed the countryside.

Prerequisites for the Transition

The Chinese peasants have been able to improve their lives over the past two decades because they carried out a revolution of blood and fire, the only means that could enable them to break the bonds retarding their economic progress. This violent revolution was necessary but not sufficient to transform an agrarian society into an industrial one. The following five developments, however, established a political-social-economic framework for the transition.

1. After 1949, the Chinese Communist Party fashioned itself and the government into organs that represented the masses and

Table 5.1

Some Production Data of the People's Republic of China: Selected Years, 1952–1972
(in million metric tons unless otherwise specified)

	Grain output	Steel production	Crude oil	Chemical fertilizers	Cotton output	Industrial production index (1956 = 100)	Cement production	Coal production	Electric power (in million kwhr)
1952	154	1.4	0.4	0.2	1.3	56	2.9	67	7.3
1957	185	5.4	1.5	0.8	1.6	109	6.9	131	19.3
1959	170	10.0	3.7	2.0	1.6	182	11.0	300	42.0
1965	208	11.0	8.0	8.0	1.5	167	11.0	220	42.0
1970	240	18.0	20.0	14.0	1.7	220	13.0	300	60.0
1971	250	21.0	25.0	18.0	1.6	242	16.0	325	70.0
1972	240	23.0	29.0*	21.3	1.6		20.0		

* *Far Eastern Economic Review*, February 19, 1973, p. 5, reports 42 million tons.

Sources: These data come from the Joint Economic Committee's publications on the Chinese economy, various issues of the *Peking Review, China Reconstructs, The Far Eastern Economic Review*, and the work of United States scholars.

wanted thoroughgoing economic development in order to improve the lives of almost everyone. This, perhaps, is the most important thing that one can say about the framework for the economic transformation. The party did not represent and work on behalf of a small group of merchants and traders, or a class of landed proprietors and moneylenders, or foreign interests allied with domestic entrepreneurs. It gained victory through a nationwide revolution of the peasants against domestic oppression and foreign imperialism, and it continued to be a party representing the interests of these masses of poor people. That may not have been exactly an *economic* determinant of peasant prosperity, but nothing has proved more important.

2. The government and party were efficient, honest, and well organized in carrying out the party's development programs. Some inefficiencies occurred, some bribes were taken, and some confusion was sown, but on the whole the party and its cadres performed remarkably well in translating plans into actions.

3. The party formulated worthwhile inspiring goals that mobilized the enthusiasm and energy of the people; it enabled the people to pursue those goals by improving their education, health, and nutrition. It liberated women and youth from their previous oppression, and it liberated most people from debilitating beliefs in "ghosts and monsters."

4. Through land reform, nationalization of industry, and the cooperativization of the countryside, along with good use of monetary and fiscal powers, the government and the party generated a high volume of saving, and with a fair amount of efficiency used the saving for investment in heavy industry, light industry, and agriculture.

5. The USSR aided China substantially during the 1950s. The bulk of this "aid" was Soviet exports for Chinese goods (rather than Chinese securities), but the Soviet goods consisted of over 150 complete industrial plants accompanied by thousands of Soviet technicians. Soviet aid was designed to establish, in a short period of time, the industrial base for a full-scale economic-development effort. It remains, despite the subsequent rancor between the two countries, an outstanding example of how one country can help another if it really wants to.

Specific Policies in Rural Areas, 1949–1972

The developments just described established the general environment in which specific economic policies for rural improvement were fashioned and carried out. These economic policies, however, were not neatly laid out in the early 1950s, all ready for sequential implementation. Instead, China's rural-improvement policies have been ad hoc at times; they have been fought over at the leadership level; and some have not worked well and have had to be replaced. But even allowing for this, the policies have achieved a remarkable transformation in the rural areas.

These policies can be grouped into four categories: land reform (1949–1952), collectivization-communization (1955–1959), capital formation for agriculture (1960–1972), and the gradual alteration of the terms of trade between agriculture and industry in favor of agriculture and the peasants (1953–1972). The first redistributed wealth and income from the rich to the poor and eliminated the former ruling classes, thus raising both peasant consumption and rural savings. The second raised output in the rural areas by encouraging better utilization of the labor supply. The third further boosted agricultural output by increasing capital goods and other inputs available to the rural sector and by establishing small industries almost everywhere in the countryside. The fourth raised the prices paid by the state for agricultural products and lowered the prices of many goods purchased by the peasants. Thus, initially the masses of peasants gained control; then their labor was better utilized; next they acquired increasing agricultural inputs; and throughout the period from 1953 to 1972 they gradually gained more favorable terms of trade.

The following four sections consider these four categories of agricultural policies. To illustrate the application of some of these policies, the transformation of Tsunhua, a rural county located about 100 miles from Peking, is then described. The last section takes up the possible relevance of all this for other poor countries.

The Nature and Impact of Land Reform, 1949–1952

The primary objectives of the Agrarian Reform Law of 1950 were to eliminate the feudal-landlord system in the countryside, improve the lives of the poor, and develop agricultural production as a precondition for China's industrialization. Land reform took not only land from the landlords and some rich peasants but also draft animals, farm implements, houses, and grain—and redistributed them all to middle and poor peasants. Altogether, 300 million peasants received 700 million *mou** of land (about 45 percent of the total arable land) formerly owned by perhaps 10–12 million persons; of all the land redistributed, two-thirds was taken from landlords and one-third from rich peasants; two-thirds of the redistributed land was given to poor peasants, one-third to middle peasants. Many rich peasants retained much of their land and other assets (but not their hired laborers) and so, even after the reform, remained better off than the middle and poor peasants. Furthermore, since the land reform regulations did not forbid the subsequent resale or renting of land, some of the redistributed land gravitated back to the rich peasants. On the other hand, the landlords as a class were wiped out by mass peasant struggles, confiscation, and execution. A few results of the land reform are shown in Table 5.2, which also contains definitions of the terms used above.

Land reform was much more than legislation passed and carried out from above. It was a revolutionary movement involving millions of peasants who struggled against their former oppressors, gained confidence and understanding in the process, and took actions against the landlords which committed them to new lives and made the entire movement irreversible. Keith Buchanan quotes Liu Shao-ch'i on this as follows:

> In carrying out the land reform our Party did not take the simple and easy way of merely relying on administrative decrees and of "bestowing" land on the peasants. For three solid years after the

* One *mou* equals .167 acre or .067 hectare.

Table 5.2
Some Results of Land Reform in China, 1949–1952

	Percentage of households	Percentage of crop area owned:		Average crop area owned:	
		before reform	after reform	before reform (in mou)	after reform (in mou)
Landlords	2.6	28.7	2.1	116.10	11.98
Rich peasants	3.6	17.7	6.4	35.75	26.30
Middle peasants	35.8	30.2	44.8	15.81	18.53
Poor peasants and farm laborers	57.1	23.5	46.8	6.25	12.14
Other	0.9	0.0	0.0		

Households were classified by amounts of income and wealth, sources of income, and size.

Landlords: Owners of land not engaged in labor, whose livelihood depended on exploitation—that is, land rent, moneylending, hired labor, and so on.

Rich peasants: Similar to landlords, except that their exploitation took chiefly the form of hiring long-term laborers and contributed somewhat lesser shares of their total incomes.

Middle peasants: Owned all, a portion, or none of the land they worked; depended for a living wholly or mainly on their own labor.

Poor peasants: Rented land for cultivation and were exploited through rent and interest.

Farm laborers: Owned neither land nor farm implements; depended for a living wholly or mainly on the sale of their labor.

Source: Peter Schran, *The Development of Chinese Agriculture, 1950–1959* (Urbana: University of Illinois Press, 1969), pp. 21, 22, and 25.

establishment of the People's Republic of China, we applied ourselves to awakening the class consciousness of the peasants. . . . We consider the time spent was absolutely necessary. Because we had used such a method the peasant masses stood up on their own feet, got themselves organized, closely followed the lead of the Communist Party and the People's Government, and took the reins of government and the armed forces in the villages firmly into their hands. . . . The broad masses of the awakened peasants held that exploitation, whether by landlords or by rich peasants, was a shameful thing. Conditions were thus created which were favourable to the subsequent socialist transformation of agriculture and helped shorten to a great extent the time needed to bring about agricultural cooperation.[2]

Through its redistribution of rural assets, the land reform not only broke the domination of the landlord-gentry class and transferred power for the first time to the poor and middle peasants but also immediately raised the consumption level of most peasants and increased the rural savings available for investment. These savings were results principally of wealth redistribution, not of gains in total output flowing from land reform, for such gains were insubstantial, though output gains were generated by the cessation of civil strife and the reconstruction and repair of dikes, irrigation canals, and equipment. Much of the increased rural savings was captured by the state for investment purposes. Thus land reform contributed in a major way to the higher investment ratios of the early 1950s.

The ratio of net investment to national income rose rapidly, from perhaps 1–2 percent in 1949 to around 20 percent in 1953. After that, despite the 1955–1956 drive to cooperativize the countryside, the ratio rose very little more until 1958–1959, when the communes were introduced. Thus the initial rapid increase in saving and investment came in the early years of the period 1949–1957.

Land reform had much to do with this, for it redistributed wealth and hence income from the rich to the poor, and much of the redistributed wealth was captured by the state through taxation, the profits of state enterprises, differential pricing, and private savings. Land reform eliminated the luxury consumption of the rich, raised the basic consumption of the poor by lesser amounts, and made much of the difference available to the state for investment.

Victor Lippit has computed that the rent, interest, and farm business profits of the rural propertied classes, plus net taxes to the state, constituted as much as 19 percent of national income just a decade before land reform.[3] Land reform redirected this income, which was almost entirely consumed, to the middle and poor peasants by rural-asset redistribution. Thence it found its way into investment via several channels: self-financed investment in agriculture; increased tax payments to the state; increased profits of government and private enterprises, which reverted wholly or partly to the state; increased profits of state purchasing agencies (mostly from grain purchases); and increased financial-asset holdings of peasants, which released real resources for investment, financed by borrowed funds from the banking system. Over one-third of the total savings from land reform was probably contributed to the state investment program in 1952 (and, presumably, in later years too).

What we said earlier bears repeating. The Chinese land reform did not *give* land to the poor peasants. It encouraged them to organize themselves to *take* it, and in the process to crush their former oppressors. This was the prerequisite for later socialist development in the countryside, for, had it not been done, the old class structures and wealth ownership patterns would have been regenerated by the persistence of old attitudes and of institutions favorable to the rich.[4]

Rural Collectivization and Labor Mobilization, 1952–1959

After land reform, the Chinese leaders transformed small private holdings into large-scale communes in four stages, each of which is discussed in detail in Chapter 3. The first involved the encouragement of mutual-aid teams; the second the formation of elementary agricultural producers' cooperatives (APCs); the third the consolidation of elementary APCs into advanced APCs; and the fourth the establishment of people's communes.

The communes were quickly organized during the Great Leap Forward, the aims of which were stated in *Peking Review*:

The objective is to build China in the shortest possible time into a great socialist country with modern industry, modern agriculture, and modern science and culture. . . . To carry out our socialist construction at a high speed naturally requires constant readjustment to the relations of production and constant adaptation of the superstructure to the developing economic base. The fundamental thing, however, is to develop the productive forces rapidly. . . . The objectives are to abolish exploitation of man by man, and to build a classless society in which the difference between city and country-side, between mental and manual work will disappear and the ideal of "from each according to his ability, to each according to his needs," will become the order of the day.[5]

Within a short time, over 26,000 communes were organized. These contained around 5,000 households on the average, but the range was from 1,500 to 10,000. The former advanced APCs became 500,000 production brigades within the communes, and the former elementary APCs became 3 million production teams. The basis for the distribution of income was also changed, from distribution according to work and asset ownership, to distribution according to work only, to distribution according to work and needs; and, at the same time, the value of a peasant's workpoints was based on the work done by increasingly larger groups.

Some of these advances, however, were reversed during the downturn of economic acitivity in the early 1960s, when Maoist ideology waned. The number of communes was then increased greatly and thus the size of their populations reduced; decision-making authority was transferred to lower units; income distribution by need was de-emphasized; communal services were greatly reduced; and private incentives in several forms were restored.

The enlargement of rural units and the accompanying collectivization during the 1950s undoubtedly raised the standard of living of the peasant masses, but these policies probably did not increase the economic surplus from agriculture by much until the Great Leap Forward in 1958–1959. Collectivization had both positive and negative features, but I shall concentrate here only on its principal advantage for the economy, namely, the fuller and more efficient use of the rural labor force.

Throughout the 1950s, the percentage of the rural population comprised by the labor force tended to decline sharply owing to the rapid absorption of school age children by the educational system. However, since children did not work as long or as effectively as adults, this downward tendency had a smaller effect on actual output than on the sheer numbers of workers. In any case, the tendency was more than offset by the rapid growth in the number of women workers during the 1950s, as rural collectivization and communization proceeded.

The rural policies of the 1950s also induced increases in the total number of days worked each year by greatly raising the number of labor days for employed peasants in general and for women workers in particular. As can be seen in Table 5.3, an extremely large increase resulted from the increased employment of women and the greater number of days each employed person worked. In fact, under normal circumstances, total annual labor days would have risen by no more than 2–3 billion from 1950 to 1959. Instead, the rise was 29 billion. Furthermore, Peter Schran believes that even this figure may well understate the full impact of communization.

Increasing amounts of the additional labor were employed on large-scale water control projects, basic construction, and rural industrial efforts; and labor was used increasingly for communal services—administration, cultural activities, medical care, education, and the like. The data are in Table 5.4. Consequently, the mobilization of additional labor days served to increase not only agricultural input but also capital formation in the countryside and the communal services offered to the peasants. Instead of fiddling away their time individually during off-seasons, the peasants were mobilized into large units for community and area projects.

The gains in total labor days worked, however, did not result in commensurate increases in total output, since other inputs did not keep pace with labor inputs; the additional labor was sometimes employed inefficiently and at tasks with low returns; and during the years 1958–1959 there was some loss of the incentives to work hard. Nevertheless, total production in the rural areas did increase considerably throughout most of the 1950s, and capital formation made impressive gains toward the end of the period. A few indicators of rural activity during the 1950s are recorded in Table 5.5.

Table 5.3

Rural Population, Employment, and Labor Days: 1950, 1955, 1957, and 1959

	(1) Peasant population (in millions)	(2) Total employed peasants (in millions)	(3) Average annual labor days	(4) Total annual labor days (in billions)	(5) Index of col. 4 (1952 = 100)
1950	479.7	222.6	119.0	26.5	97.5
1955	523.8	243.3	121.0	29.4	108.4
1957	541.3	260.3	159.5	41.5	152.8
1959	539.6	309.1	189.0	58.4	215.0
Collectivization, 1955–1957	+17.5	+17.0	+38.5	+12.1	+44.4
Communization, 1957–1959	−1.7	+48.8*	+29.5	+16.9	+62.2

* Increase owing largely to the increased mobilization of women and the part-time employment of schoolchildren.

Source: Peter Schran, The Development of Chinese Agriculture, 1950–1959, (Urbana: University of Illinois Press, 1959), chap. 3.

Table 5.4
Indices of the Structure of Rural Employment by
Labor Days: 1950, 1955, 1957, and 1959
(Total labor days in 1952 = 100)

	Total labor days	Farm work	Subsidiary work*	Corvée, basic construction	Other†
1950	97.5	75.2	19.2	3.1	0
1955	108.4	83.0	21.0	3.9	0.4
1957	152.8	113.4	25.8	9.7	3.8
1959	215.0	151.7	29.5	12.3	21.4

* Includes gathering activities, domestic handicrafts, administration, professional services, and care of private plots and livestock.
† Includes collective affairs, communal services, and communal industry.

Source: Peter Schran, The Development of Chinese Agriculture: 1950–1959 (Urbana: University of Illinois Press, 1959), p. 75.

Table 5.5
Some Indicators of Rural Activity: 1952–1959

	Grain output (in millions of metric tons)	Area of irrigation (in millions of mou)	Gross value of agricultural output (in billions of yuan)	
1952	154	320	48.3†	
1953	157	330	49.9	
1954	161	350	51.6	
1955	175	370	55.5	
1956	183	480	58.3	
1957	186	520	60.4	53.7‡
1958	250 (200)*	1,000		67.1
1959	270 (170)*	1,070		78.3

* These are Western estimates, which are probably fairly accurate.
† The figures in this column are in 1952 prices.
‡ The figures in this column are in 1957 prices.

Source: Nai-Ruenn Chen, Chinese Economic Statistics (Chicago: Aldine, 1967), pp. 338–39, 289, 364.

Industrialization of the Rural Areas, 1960–1972

Adverse weather conditions which lasted for three years ("the worst in a century"), the pullout of the Soviet advisers, and peasant disincentives arising out of the extremes to which some Great Leap policies were pushed—all of these combined in 1959–1960, first to reduce agricultural output, including the commercial crops that fed light industry, then to hit heavy industry as the Soviet advisers withdrew with their blueprints and expertise. By late 1960 and early 1961, the economy had been damaged so severely that the Chinese leadership (probably no longer dominated by Mao), faced by a 20–25 percent decline in national output, altered its economic priorities to place agriculture first, light industry second, and heavy industry last. This officially changed the priorities established under Soviet-type planning during the 1950s, in which attention was centered on heavy industry and agriculture was relatively neglected so far as state investment funds were concerned.*

The change did not reflect any diminished interest in industrialization. Rather, it served notice that priority would go to industries that directly served agriculture, either by producing modern inputs for it or by processing outputs from it. Other industries would be emphasized to the extent that they directly served such industries. Increasingly, as the 1960s proceeded, the countryside was expected to establish not only small industries that directly served agriculture but also small basic industries, such as iron and steel making, cement making, and coal mining. Thus there was a redirection from the mobilization of traditional agricultural inputs (labor, natural fertilizers, draft animals, traditional tools) to the production of modern inputs, such as chemical fertilizers, insecticides and pesticides, small hydroelectric plants, electric motors, rice transplanters, tractors, trucks, and seed improvement stations. The agricultural task of the 1960s was, in short, to industrialize and modernize the rural areas. By the end of the decade, the economy was much better able to

---

* However, the agricultural sector generated a substantial amount of internal saving that was used for investment.

support agriculture, both with the output of large-scale urban industry and with tens of thousands of small, indigenous industries throughout the countryside.

Some results of these policies are recorded in Table 5.6, where it may be seen that chemical fertilizers, tractors, and other agricultural inputs rose very rapidly in the 1960s—in absolute amounts, though not necessarily in percentages, much faster than in the 1950s. The table also shows fairly good growth for a few of the available output series.

However, we do not have enough information to make a confident assessment regarding the impact of these increasing dosages of modern inputs on agricultural output. We do not have, for example, data on some kinds of inputs, such as threshers, harvesters, and trucks. Furthermore, we do not know the distribution of the various inputs among the various crops (wheat, rice, cotton, and so on), or the changes in the land area devoted to each crop during the period. Moreover, the grain output estimates for the beginning of this period are uncertain. Consequently, the most that can be said is that grain output rose fairly rapidly during the 1960s, apparently responding to modern inputs in this decade to about the same degree as it responded to traditional inputs in the previous decade.* It is probably true, however, that agricultural output would have fared much less well than it did if further institutional changes and dosages of traditional inputs had been heavily relied upon in the 1960s, as they were in the previous decade.

Somewhat more detail can be supplied for chemical fertilizers, which seem to have been the most important of the modern inputs during the 1960s. The Chinese leaders did not neglect chemical fertilizers during the 1950s, though after the downturn of 1959–1961 they placed much more emphasis on them. In the 1950s, the USSR constructed several complete fertilizer plants for China, and China imported machinery to modernize two

---

* The average annual grain output growth rates for several periods are as follows (in percent):

1952–1957	3.7	1959–1971	3.1
1952–1958	4.4	1961–1971	4.2
1952–1959	1.4	1965–1971	3.5

Table 5.6
Some Inputs and Outputs of China's Agriculture: 1952, 1959, 1965, 1970, 1971

	China's production of inputs				Other inputs		Some outputs		
	Chemical fertilizers (in million metric tons)	Tractors (in thousands of standard units)	Electric power in agriculture (in billion kilowatt hours)	Inventory of mechanical pumps (in million horsepower)	Area irrigated with mechanical pumps (in thousand hectares)	Imports of chemical fertilizers (in million metric tons)	Grain output (in million metric tons)	Sugar output (in million metric tons)	Cotton yield (kilograms per hectare)
1952	0.2	0	n.a.	n.a.	n.a.	0.1	154	0.45	232
1959	2.0	1.5	1.5*	3.4	646	1.0†	170§	1.1	285
1965	8.0	33.1	2.7	8.0†	1,520‡	2.3	200	1.5	333
1970	14.0	62.7	4.6			4.3	240	1.7	377
1971	18.0	73.4	5.5				250		381

n.a. = not available.
* 1962.   ‡ 1966.
† 1961.   § Western estimate.

Sources: Joint Economic Committee, *The People's Republic of China: An Economic Assessment* (Washington, D.C.: U.S. Gov't. Printing Office, 1972), pp. 83, 121, 124, 134, 138, 139, and 348; Kang Chao, *Agricultural Production in Communist China* (Madison, Wis.: University of Wisconsin Press, 1970), p. 151. A few of the figures for chemical fertilizers and grain output differ slightly from later estimates shown in Table 4.1.

plants inherited from the pre-1949 period. As Table 5.6 shows, chemical-fertilizer production increased from 1952 to 1959. In the 1960s, China purchased four complete nitrogenous-fertilizer plants from the Netherlands, Britain, and Italy, which were installed in 1966. It began building its own fertilizer plants in 1964, and around this time set a goal of one large-scale plant for each of the country's 180–190 special districts and one smaller plant for each of the more than two thousand counties. In fact, much of the increased production of chemical fertilizers in the 1960s came from the medium- and small-scale plants that were constructed throughout the countryside during the decade. Moreover, China began to import chemical fertilizers in increasingly larger volume, mostly from Japan and Western Europe. By 1970, the input of chemical fertilizers from both domestic and foreign sources had reached more than 18 million metric tons, or six times the 1959 level.

It is possible to relate only approximately the 15-million-ton increase in chemical fertilizers to the 70-million-ton increase in grain output during the period 1959–1970. From the available information, it may be roughly accurate to conclude that chemical fertilizers contributed between 40 percent and 55 percent of the increase in grain output.[6] During the 1960s, chemical fertilizers probably had a greater marginal impact on grain output than that of any other input. This impact, however, probably centered on the output of rice, which is grown in areas where water is generally available. The impact of chemical fertilizers on the output of wheat and cotton, grown mostly in the north, where water supplies are unreliable, was undoubtedly weaker.

As I noted previously, the countryside was industrialized to some extent during the 1960s by the establishment of thousands of small industries under local authority.[7] These industries produce and repair farm implements and machinery; produce fertilizers, consumer goods, insecticides, building materials, and rural transportation equipment; process agricultural products; and develop power sources. They have been encouraged by the central government to be as self-reliant as possible by developing new sources of raw materials from their own areas, using waste materials and older machinery from the larger central industries, and employing relatively labor-intensive, indigenous methods of production. In this way, more or less integrated industrial structures have been fashioned in each locality for the prime purpose of serving that locality's agricultural needs.

Local industries are said to have the following advantages: (1) They utilize dispersed deposits of material resources. (2) They lower average capital-output ratios and shorten the gestation periods. (3) They undertake repair, maintenance, and processing activities, freeing large-scale capacity for jobs which the modern sector alone can do. (4) They lower the costs of urbanization and social-overhead capital in general. (5) They create industrial consciousness among the peasantry. (6) They contribute to national defense. (7) They ameliorate the contradictions between the cities and the countryside.

Rural industrialization has certainly had some success in expanding employment opportunities in the countryside, in balancing production geographically, and in raising agricultural productivity.

Improvement in Agriculture's Terms of Trade

Living standards in the rural areas have also been raised by the change in the terms of trade between agricultural and industrial products in favor of the former. This improvement has been fairly constant throughout the Communist period, as shown in Table 5.7. By the end of the 1950s, a given amount of agricultural produce was purchasing about 35 percent more industrial goods than at the beginning of the decade. By the end of the 1960s, the increase was 67 percent.

Over the past two decades, the government has several times raised the price at which it purchases grain from the peasants. At present, this purchase price is above the level at which grain is sold by the state in urban areas and in rural areas devoted mostly to industrial crops. The difference in the prices is a subsidy from the state to the cultivators of grain. The prices paid by the government for other agricultural goods have also been raised.

Table 5.7
Terms of Trade Between China's Agriculture
and Industry, 1950–1970

	(1) Agricultural purchase price index	(2) Industrial retail prices in rural areas index	(3) Ratio of (1) to (2)
1950	100.0	100.0	100.0
1951	119.6	110.2	108.5
1952	121.6	109.7	110.8
1953	132.5	108.2	122.4
1954	136.7	110.3	123.9
1955	135.1	111.9	120.7
1956	139.2	110.8	125.6
1957	146.2	112.1	130.4
1958	149.5	111.2	134.4
1970	n.a.	n.a.	166.7

n.a. = not available.

Sources: Nai-Ruenn Chen, Chinese Economic Statistics (Chicago: Aldine, 1967), pp. 424–25, 409. The 1970 figure is based on information in China Reconstructs, November 1970, p. 4. For the same trends, see Audrey Donnithorne, China's Economic System (New York: Praeger, 1967), pp. 448–49.

On the other hand, the prices of industrial products bought by the peasants remained about the same from 1951 to the end of the decade, and in the last several years many of these prices have been reduced, some greatly. For example, the general price level of medicines is 80 percent lower now than it was in 1950, and most of this drop occurred in the last few years. "For the same amount of wheat, a peasant can get 70 percent more salt than at the time of the birth of the People's Republic, and for the same amount of cotton, he receives 2.4 times as much kerosene."[8] The prices of fertilizers, fuel, livestock feed, electricity, and various types of equipment have been lowered.

Rural Development in Tsunhua County

Some of the agricultural policies which I have discussed will perhaps have more meaning if they are shown in actual operation in a particular rural locality.

Tsunhua county is one of six counties within the special district of T'angshan, which is located in the northeastern part of Hopei province, about one hundred miles east and a bit north of Peking. The county is about 1,640 square kilometers in size and has a population of over half a million. It has only one town, Tsunhua. The land is mostly hilly, with three mountain ranges and two valleys or plains. The population's economic activities are largely agricultural—growing wheat, kaoliang, millet, and other grains as well as fruits, nuts, and vegetables—but the number of small industries has been increasing, and some people engage in various sideline occupations. Table 5.8 records some basic economic facts about the county.

The heart of the county's economy is agriculture, mostly food grains. Since 1949, the output of food grains per hectare has risen more than threefold, or at an average annual rate of 6 percent. Since 1958, however, the rate of increase has been only 2 percent; it was rather stagnant between 1958 and 1969 but substantial in 1970 and 1971. The Revolutionary Committee of the county attributed the stagnant period to the revisionist policies of Liu Shao-ch'i and his followers, who discouraged self-reliant policies, the building of small industries, and the full use of local resources. Since 1968 or 1969, however, the leaders of the county have "organized mass activities to change the backwardness of agriculture, make substantial use of local resources and rapidly develop local industry."[9]

The county has attempted to promote agricultural development by producing its own cement, chemical fertilizers, and iron and steel for the manufacture of agricultural machinery and implements, and it has supported these heavy industries, especially iron and steel, with profits from light industry and sideline activities. That is, the county has attempted to industrialize mainly by using its own initiative and its own resources to raise agricultural productivity and the living standards of the people.

Table 5.8
Some Economic Statistics of Tsunhua County, 1970-1971

Total area	164,000 hectares, or 1,640 square kilometers
Cultivated area	64,000 hectares
Irrigated area	18,700 hectares
Population	550,000
Households	116,000
Labor force	about 200,000
Communes	43 (average of 12,800 per commune)
Production brigades	691 (average of 800 per brigade)
Production teams	2,664 (average of 200 per team)
Grain production	3.8 tons per hectare
Value of grain production	about 50 million *yuan*
Value of industrial production	18 million *yuan*
Income from sideline occupations	22.7 million *yuan*

Sources: Jon Sigurdson, "Rural Industry—A Traveller's View," *The China Quarterly*, July-September, 1972; *Collective Notes* of economists visiting China during August 1972, mimeographed by Thomas Weisskopf, Department of Economics, University of Michigan.

In order to produce chemical fertilizers, cement, and iron and steel, the people of the county first had to locate the necessary ores and minerals. "Initially, we were aware only of the presence of gold and iron in the hills, but now local people have discovered 23 kinds of ore, helped by the geological team."[10] They then set up the iron and steel plant—first the small blast furnace, then a converter, after that a rolling mill. The iron and steel helped them to establish the cement factory, which was used largely to expand water conservation projects.

The iron and steel plant, however, ran at a loss. So light industry and sideline activities were developed which made more than enough profits to subsidize iron and steel. The county planted tens of thousands of fruit trees, for example, then constructed a small fruit-bottling factory with an annual capacity of 250 tons of bottled fruit—apples, apricots, pears, grapes, peaches, and other fruits. This factory required sugar, so some peasants began to grow sugar beets, turning out ten tons of sugar a year. The factory also needed glass for the bottles, and so a small glass-manufacturing plant was set up. The glass, of course, required pure soda, calling for the establishment of a 32-ton-per-year soda factory. And so on and on. The result is that the county is now able to produce crushers, threshers, oil presses, and other machinery for digging drainage and irrigation systems and developing agricultural and sideline activities.

Local industries are run not only by the county but also by the communes and the production brigades. At the county level, the aim of national policy is for every county to have the "five small industries"—iron and steel, cement, chemical fertilizer, energy (coal, electricity), and machinery. Such complete sets were established in one-half of China's 2,100 counties by 1971. Tsunhua was engaged in all these activities, except that its electricity was produced outside the county. In addition, the county runs a sulfuric acid plant, an electromechanical factory, a plastics factory, a papermaking plant and a textile mill; engages in mining operations; does major repairs on agricultural machinery; processes agricultural and sideline products—for example, flour milling and cotton ginning.

The communes and the production brigades are also involved in small industries. For example, there is a three-level agricultural-machinery repair and manufacturing network, which 90 percent of the counties, including Tsunhua, had established by 1971.

Three-level county, commune, and brigade agricultural scientific networks have been rapidly expanded all over the country in recent years. One important objective of this is to achieve a rapid seed-selection process which together with modern inputs to agriculture may quickly increase the yield per unit.[11]

In Tsunhua the county does the manufacturing and major repairs in 7 plants; the communes do lesser repairs and assembly in 37 plants; and the production brigades do minor repairs in their 407 shops. The three levels also process agricultural and sideline products. Households, brigades, and communes are engaged in sideline occupations, including such things as raising silkworms and bees, quarrying stones and mining ores, making mat bags, and growing fruit.

About 12,000–15,000 of the 200,000 in the labor force were employed in these enterprises in 1971. The 39 county-run industries employed 5,500; the 71 plants managed by the communes employed 2,500; the industrial units of the production brigades, 5,000.* In addition, many other workers are indirectly in the industrial sector. The proportion of the labor force engaged in industrial activities is not large, but the creation of employment opportunities is probably not the main purpose of rural industrialization. For given the increased school enrollment of children, the fact that older people no longer need to remain in the labor force, the large-scale water control and reforestation projects, the increasing numbers of people engaged in sideline occupations (cultural activities, medical services, education, and party work), the movement of millions of people to the northwest, the west, and other relatively virgin areas and the rising demands for just about every kind of agricultural product—given all these things, there would seem to be no significant surplus of labor in the rural areas, especially during the seasonal planting and harvesting peaks. The principal purpose of rural industrialization is to achieve mechanization in agriculture and hence greater agricultural productivity. It is also meant to narrow the differences between town and country, workers and peasants, and to widen the horizons and the abilities of the peasants.

---

* In these plants, there are permanent, temporary, and contract workers. The permanent workers are employed within the regular eight-grade wage system, earning from 28 *yuan* to about 100 *yuan* per month. The temporary workers rotate regularly between agriculture and industry, turn over half their wages to their production teams, then at the end of the year receive income from the teams based on their agricultural work. The contract workers are hired on a one-, two-, or three-year basis, and are in general treated in the same way as permanent workers; they are mostly from the city, not from production teams.

The Relevance for Other Countries of the Maoist Development Strategy

What relevance has China's attempts at rural economic development for other underdeveloped countries? To answer this, it is first necessary to describe the overall Maoist strategy for economic development, within which rural economic development is contained. Since this strategy is an evolving one and has already taken several twists and turns, one cannot be certain of getting it right. But at present the overall development strategy appears to consist of the following steps.

1. Destroy the landlord-bureaucrat class structure and redistribute land and other assets, income, and power to the peasants and the workers.

2. Establish socialist relations of production as soon as possible, and use the party to educate the peasants and workers in socialist values and ideals. That is, nationalize industry and bring about cooperativization in the countryside without waiting for agricultural mechanization. Begin to create a socialist superstructure.*

3. Establish a full planning mechanism to take the place of market price–determined resource allocation and income distribution, and go all out for industrialization, but emphasize industries having direct links to agriculture.

4. Achieve high rates of capital formation by encouraging savings at all levels and the use of the savings at each level for self-financed investment. Encourage rural areas, in particular, to meet their needs for capital goods by creating small-scale, indigenous industries, to finance their investments in those industries from their own savings, and to manage the industries themselves. Finance and manage at higher political levels capital goods that can be produced only by large-scale, modern methods.

---

* This is because if mechanization is introduced into an essentially individualistic, private-enterprise framework, the fruits of the new technology will be captured by only a few, leaving the majority resentful and ready to "break the machines." In addition, capitalist development creates capitalist people. Under certain circumstances, according to Mao, it is necessary to change the superstructure in order to release the productive forces of society. See point 5.

5. Develop and release human energy and creativity by promoting socialist values ("serve the people," selflessness, collective incentives) over bourgeois values (individualism, selfishness, materialism), by providing health-care facilities, by educating as many people as possible, by setting worthy goals that inspire people to work hard, and by encouraging basic decision-making at the lowest possible level.

6. Carry out a continuing revolution at all levels of society, and maintain the dictatorship of the proletariat.

It seems to me that the Maoist strategy, *as a whole*, probably has very little relevance for the governments of most underdeveloped countries today, since it involves breaking the power of ruling classes and their foreign supporters and opting for socialism and eventually communism over capitalism; for full-scale industrialization over trade, commerce, and agrarianism; and for continuing revolutionary activity over orderly procedures. Since most third world countries now play more or less subordinate and dependent roles in the international capitalist system, serving the wealthier countries of that system with raw materials, cheap labor, or additional markets, in order to follow China's path they would first have to break out of this global system and then take their chances on an all-out development effort with their own resources plus whatever aid could be obtained from socialist countries.* This program may be favored by some classes in these poor countries, but it is hardly a prescription that would appeal to their governments and propertied classes. Furthermore, such views are anathema to the United States, whose duty as the leader of global capitalism is to prevent such breakaways through some combination of economic aid, military aid, counterinsurgency, cultivation of domestic elites, and force. The alliance between the United States and the propertied classes and elites in the poor countries is a powerful one.

That is the overall picture. It stresses that one thing *does* depend on another in Maoist strategy, and indeed this is so in any

---

* This is also true for the ruling classes of the major oil-producing countries, who may gain some advantages over the industrial capitalist countries but who are so greatly dependent on international monopoly capital that they (or most of them) would not dream of breaking out of this global system.

development strategy. To make any substantial headway, the problem of underdevelopment often has to be tackled as a whole, not piecemeal. In the Chinese experience, for example, rural industrialization depended on the general acceptance of goals other than profits and efficiency. This acceptance was based in turn on the prior inculcation of socialist values throughout the society, which was reinforced by the prior establishment of socialist relations of production, including a full planning mechanism. These socialist relations of production could be developed only by the prior breakup of the old class structures of society. And so on.

I have emphasized the holistic view, the Maoist way. Now I wish to ask whether other underdeveloped countries can benefit, to some extent at least, from separate parts of China's total experience. Some socialist policies should be adaptable to capitalist developmental programs.

It should be recognized at the outset that many Chinese policies for development are universally known and in fact were acquired by China from the theoretical and practical work of bourgeois economists and other development experts, as well as from the experience of the Soviet Union. China has learned some things from others, and there are no reasons why other countries cannot take advantage of the same information. I refer to such policies as raising capital formation relative to consumption to attain higher growth rates; of encouraging saving for this purpose by such means as taxation and financial institutions; of using relative factor supplies to good advantage; of aiming for developmental government budgets and moderate growth rates of the money supply; of utilizing aid and trade efficiently. Much of China's overall performance can be explained "simply" in terms of the very high investment and saving ratios that were attained by 1953–1954 and more or less maintained thereafter. (Recall, however, that to attain *these* the old class structures were overthrown by revolution. That is what lies behind the word *simply*.) And the application of larger shares of this total capital formation to agriculture in the 1960s goes a long way toward explaining China's recent gains in rural development. Thus much of the story is standard fare, known to everyone.

But if China has learned much from others, it may also be able to teach a few things. First, China has demonstrated the importance of industrialization for economic development—that the large resources it devoted initially to iron and steel, machine building, nonferrous metals, oil, electric power, and chemicals were an indispensable basis for later advances in agriculture, transportation, consumer goods, and military weapons, and for freeing the economy from its dependence on foreign direction and influence. That initial stress on heavy industry, rather than on the infrastructure and consumer goods, was made possible only by socialist aid and trade. Despite the growing bitterness between the USSR and China, no other country has ever received so much help toward full-scale industrialization as China did during the 1950s. This is something of a lesson in itself.

Second, China has shown, especially during the 1960s, *how* to industrialize without generating social problems that threaten to blow a society sky-high. China has involved increasing numbers of people, especially in the rural areas, in industrial activities in order to break down the potentially antagonistic relations between city and country, between workers and peasants; to spread knowledge of industrial processes as widely as possible so as to promote talent, ingenuity, confidence, and the scientific attitude among masses of workers and peasants; and to transform rural areas into self-reliant agrarian-industrial-cultural local economies, which are attractive places to live in and can become, at least partly independent of higher political units, including the state. This is relevant for other poor countries because it demonstrates a pattern of industrialization that does not generate severe imbalances between urban and rural areas, between rich and poor, between employed and unemployed, or between one region and another. The lesson that many developing countries are learning from their own experience is that high rates of output growth are often the "good face" on an increasingly diseased body. Thus the last annual report of the World Bank, after noting the respectable growth rates of many underdeveloped countries, went on to say:

Statistics conceal the gravity of the underlying economic and social problems, which are typified by severely skewed income distribution, excessive levels of unemployment, high rates of infant mortality, low rates of literacy, serious malnutrition, and widespread ill-health.

The statistics also conceal growing urban problems, unmanageable foreign debts, social unrest, and other difficulties in many of these countries. Perhaps the most important message that China can send to other poor countries is that not one item in the above list applies to it.

The third lesson is the importance of raising work motivation and how to achieve this. Capitalist economists have concentrated far too much on how to reallocate economic resources to attain higher levels of national output and far too little on how to get people really interested in their work and so willing to exert great efforts to achieve their goals. I think that China has shown that the latter is much more important than the former; that people who really want to work completely eclipse the effects of nice adjustments toward more competitive markets and of fine calculations regarding factor inputs.

The Maoists believe that they have inspired and enabled people to work hard by altering their work environments, changing their incentives, and providing them with education, good health, and technical training. In capitalist development, it is necessary to raise output growth rates in such a way as to reinforce the existing class structures of society and the values which support these structures. The pursuit of higher growth rates, therefore, has generally reduced many human beings to unthinking, specialized, manipulated inputs in the production process, in which hierarchical structures of capitalists and workers, bosses and "hands," mental experts and manual workers, face each other in more or less antagonistic relationships. Such alienated work environments lower the general intelligence, initiative, and willingness to work hard of broad masses of workers. These are the obvious costs of pursuing growth in the context of sharp class alignments. The Maoists feel that developing people as full human beings in a warm, egalitarian, and cooperative working atmosphere leads to the rapid development of material output; that the former is possible only in the absence of feudal or capitalist class structures; and that the latter is desirable only within the context of the former.

Thus the Chinese lesson is that it is possible to achieve great increases in the overall productivity of peasants and workers by establishing less alienated work environments. In the absence of full-scale revolution, underdeveloped countries might benefit from China's experience by questioning their own organizations of rural and urban work and by experimenting with other forms. Are the existing organizations efficient from a factor productivity point of view, or are they mainly efficient in channeling part of the economic surplus to a landed aristocracy or a capitalist class? Do work organizations exist to maintain discipline and order— and, if so, why?—or do they promote energy and initiative? Are they designed to set off one group of workers against another to the benefit of the dominant class and to the detriment of factor productivity? On such matters, China may have much to teach the underdeveloped countries.

Work motivation in China has also risen, according to the Maoists, because of an increase in socialist consciousness among the masses of workers and peasants. This means that collective incentives—the willingness of increasingly larger groups of people to work hard without expectation of personal gain—have gained over individual incentives. The Maoists believe that people are inspired and can see real meaning in their lives only if they are working for goals worthy of human beings and not merely for their own selfish, material welfare. Indeed, people throughout China *do* seem inspired in this way, for whatever reason, and seem completely involved not only in their present accomplishments but in achieving collective goals for the future: "In two years, we'll have this and have a good start on that, and then . . ." Just about everyone talks like that.

Furthermore, with regard to work motivation, it is necessary to repeat that increasing numbers of people in China are able to work hard and more effectively because they have become more literate, are healthier and better nourished, and have been given more technical training.

Finally, the Chinese Communist Party has developed high

motivation among its own cadres to "serve the people" incorruptibly. The work motivation and collective incentives engendered within this large group have been of vital importance in effectuating policies at all levels in ways that do not dissipate the intentions of the policymakers. For several decades, the CCP has demonstrated the importance of having such cadres for the realization, rather than the mere verbalization, of national goals.

China offers other lessons, too, which there is space only to mention: how to adapt education to the needs of an industrializing society; how to achieve economic development without inviting foreign capital into a country; how to maintain stable prices over long periods of time; and so on.

China's principal lesson for underdeveloped countries, however, is the need to break out of all dependency relationships with advanced industrial countries and to pursue the course of self-reliance, at both the national and the local level.

Notes

1. R. H. Tawney, *Land and Labor in China* (1932; Boston: Beacon Press, 1966), pp. 72–73, 76–77.
2. Keith Buchanan, *The Transformation of the Chinese Earth* (New York: Praeger, 1970), p. 123.
3. Victor Lippit, *Land Reform and Economic Development in China* (White Plains, N.Y.: International Arts and Sciences Press, 1974).
4. See, for example, William Hinton, *Fanshen: A Documentary of Revolution in a Chinese Village* (New York: Monthly Review Press, 1966).
5. *Peking Review*, September 9, 1958.
6. This is based on Jung-Chao Liu, *China's Fertilizer Economy* (Chicago: Aldine, 1970), pp. 96, 106, 110–12; Kang Chao, *Agricultural Production in Communist China* (Madison: University of Wisconsin Press, 1970), pp. 150–51, 236; Leslie T. C. Kuo, *The Transformation of Agriculture in Communist China* (New York: Praeger, 1972), p. 102; and Joint Economic Committee, *The People's Republic of China: An Economic Assessment* (Washington, D.C.: U.S. Government Printing Office, 1972), pp. 140, 348.

7. See Carl Riskin, "Small Industry and the Chinese Model of Development," *The China Quarterly*, April–June 1971, pp. 245–73.

8. *China Reconstructs*, November 1970, p. 4. See also the issue for January 1973, p. 40.

9. *Collective Notes* of economists visiting China during August 1972, mimeographed by Thomas Weisskopf, Department of Economics, University of Michigan, p. 63.

10. Ibid.

11. Jon Sigurdson, "Rural Industry—A Traveller's View," *The China Quarterly*, July–September 1972.

6

Some Notes on the Financial System

I intend this essay to be no more than a modest survey of China's evolving financial system during the past several decades and a brief account of the several roles played by that system. In it, I hope to bring out a few important points about the functions of a financial system in a socialist economy.

The Roles of Financial Systems

A financial system is composed of financial institutions—usually a central bank, commercial banks, savings banks, insurance companies, and others—and of financial markets where securities are traded. Since financial institutions purchase primary securities (obligations of nonfinancial units) and issue claims against themselves (indirect debt), and since financial markets facilitate trading in primary securities, a financial system may be called a *debt-asset system*. This term distinguishes it from a fiscal system, which is mainly concerned with budget revenues and expenditures.

Financial systems—and, in particular, banking systems—have several economic functions. One is to provide an efficient payments mechanism that permits economic transactions to be made smoothly and at small cost in terms of real resources.

264

Another is, through control over the quantity of money, to establish a price level that is reasonably stable or at least reasonably predictable over long periods. In socialist countries, a third function of financial systems is to keep track of and control the key expenditures set by the national plan. Finally, financial institutions serve as intermediaries in the saving-investment process (in indirect finance), offering financial claims (currency, deposits, shares, certificates) on themselves to savers and purchasing primary securities (bonds, mortgages, equities, and other IOUs) from investors; and security markets facilitate direct finance between savers and investors, allowing the former to purchase primary securities directly from the latter.

So far as the first three functions are concerned, financial systems have no close substitutes; either they perform these functions well, or the functions are hardly performed at all. The saving-investment function, however, can be met in many alternative ways. The full list of alternative processes for placing saving at the service of selected investment is very long. However, the list may be compressed into two major classes: internal-finance processes and external-finance processes. In the former, the investor draws on his own savings; in the latter, he draws on the savings of others.

Internal finance comprises two principal techniques: self-finance and taxation. In self-finance, savings are put at the investors' disposal by adjustments in the relative prices on commodity, factor, and on foreign-exchange markets. These price adjustments permit, let us say, increases in business profits, which are then utilized by their owners for investment. The taxation technique employs taxes and other nonmarket alternatives to channel savings to the state for either governmental or private investment. With external finance, the debt-asset system is the technique for mobilizing domestic savings. In addition, foreign savings may be supplied by gift or loan, on the initiative of either private or governmental sources.

Thus, in the saving-investment process there are alternatives to the financial, or debt-asset, system. To the extent that saving is generated and allocated to investment by these alternative means, the financial system's role and size will be reduced—it will have smaller real amounts of assets and liabilities, and it will use fewer real resources in running and managing the system.

My principal purpose here is to assess the saving-investment role of the financial system of the People's Republic of China. After that, I shall analyze the way it has met its other functions. Before getting to these topics, however, it will be helpful to look briefly at the financial system inherited by the People's Republic—that is, at the financial system under the Kuomintang regime.

China's Financial System Before 1949

Under the Kuomintang, 1927–1949, there were three main types of banking institutions. There were, first of all, several hundred "native" banks which were located in commercial centers throughout the country. The capital and deposits of these banks came mostly from wealthy merchants, and their loans were to these and other businessmen, to government, and for speculation.

There were also dozens of highly influential foreign banks, established after the first Opium War of 1839–1842, all of which were located in treaty ports enjoying consular jurisdiction. These banks were mainly involved in the foreign-trade transactions of the foreigners and in their commercial and industrial pursuits within China.

Finally, by the 1930s there were a few hundred modern domestic banks in China's largest cities. These banks, organized after 1900, patterned their business methods on the foreign banks. Some of them were private commercial and savings institutions; others were government banks—central, provincial, and municipal.

Under the Kuomintang, there were four main (national) government banks: the Central Bank of China, the Bank of Communications, the Bank of China, and the Four Provinces Agricultural Bank. The Central Bank of China was originally organized in Canton in 1924 and was reorganized in 1928 after the country's "unification" by the Kuomintang. This bank never attained the status suggested by its name, for there was no strong monetary policy or control during the Kuomintang period. The Bank of Communications, with origins back to 1907, was reorganized in 1928 to develop industry and trade. It failed, however, to become an industrial-development bank, most of its loans going to the government and to existing (rather than new) private firms. The Bank of China, originally established in 1912–1913, immediately after the overthrow of the Ch'ing dynasty, was set up in 1928 as a special institution for foreign transactions. Finally, in 1933, the Kuomintang created the Four Provinces Agricultural Bank, mainly for the purpose of combating the Communists in the rural areas of Kiangsi, Hunan, Hupei, and Anhwei. In 1945, it was expanded into the Farmers Bank of China.[1]

Although there were over 150 modern Chinese banks in the mid-1930s, they were dominated by a small number of very large ones. "Through a total of thirteen banks [including the four government banks] the Kuomintang regime controlled 78 per cent of the combined resources of all modern banks in China,"[2] and these banks were controlled by a handful of powerful capitalists. In addition, Chinese and foreign banking was heavily concentrated in Shanghai, and only rudimentary credit and saving facilities existed in the rural areas where 85 per cent of the people lived. This and more is attested by Albert Feuerwerker in the following passage:

> It can, I think, be said in general that the Chinese banking system [from 1912 to 1949] failed lamentably to carry out the function of credit creation for the development of the economy as a whole. This is, of course, first to say that modern banking in China was underdeveloped. While 128 new banks were established from 1929 to 1937, and in 1937 China had 164 modern banks with 1,597 branches, these were overwhelmingly concentrated in the major cities of the coastal provinces (Shanghai alone had 58 head offices and 130 branch offices in 1936). Modern banking facilities were meager in the agricultural interior and never adapted themselves to the credit needs of a peasant economy. The cooperative societies which grew up in the 1920's and 1930's and which might have served as intermediaries between the banking system and the peasant farmer were in fact insignificant in number and tended to provide the bulk of their

credit to richer farmers who in any case could obtain loans at relatively low rates from other sources. The "native" banks . . . which survived and sometimes thrived into the 1930's tended to limit themselves to financing local trade. While the foreign banks in the treaty ports were amply supplied with funds, including large deposits by wealthy Chinese, their principal operations were the short-term financing of foreign trade and speculation in foreign exchange.[3]

What small progress in industrial development there was from 1912 to 1937 was based mostly on foreign saving (including Japanese saving applied to Manchuria); but this industrial development was confined to small areas and hardly touched the masses of Chinese. Domestic saving, especially private saving, part of it channeled through the financial system, contributed something to economic growth, but not very much. Most of the domestic saving was used up in ceremonial and luxury consumption, speculative accumulations of commodities, private acquisitions of foreign assets, military campaigns, government administration, and indemnity payments, interest, and profits to foreign imperialists. With all this, little or nothing was left for domestic capital formation.

After the outbreak of the Sino-Japanese War in 1937, the cause of economic development was lost in the fires of hyperinflation. The immediate sources of the inflation were the huge increases in government military expenditures and the grossly inadequate tax system. The feebleness of the latter was a consequence not only of the antiquated tax structure itself, of the loss of cities to the Japanese, and of the disorganization caused by warfare, but also of class conflict and of the corruption within the Kuomintang's ranks. The ever-expanding budget deficits were financed almost entirely by the creation of money—mainly by new issues of currency. Consequently, the nominal money supply rose rapidly after 1937, though it did not keep up with the steep ascent of prices, which rose 10–20 percent a month during the years 1941–1945, and then rose 2,500 times in the next three years. In the final months before the total collapse and the flight of Chiang to Taiwan, the price index also took off and disappeared into the Great Beyond.[4]

Thus, the pre-Communist Chinese financial system generated

much more inflation than it did saving for industrial and agricultural development. For a large part of the period from 1927 to 1949, however, it did provide a tolerable payments mechanism. Most transactions were made with a currency (banknotes and coins) that was issued by a variety of institutions, some of which failed. Each of the four main government banks issued currency, as did foreign banks in Hongkong and those with branches in China, provincial-government banks, other modern banks, native banks, cash-shops, and other financial institutions. Although this was a messy payments mechanism, it did a fair job for most of the Kuomintang period. Finally, through its control of the money supply, the banking system established a reasonable degree of price stability from 1928 to 1937, though the hyperinflation that finally enveloped China was one of the worst in history.

The Financial System of the People's Republic in the Saving-Investment Process

After the Communists came to power, the Central Bank of China was replaced by the People's Bank of China, which henceforth issued all of the country's currency and conducted ordinary banking business, making most of the short-term loans and having large amounts of deposit liabilities to nonfinancial units. Of the other three government banks under the Kuomintang, the Bank of China and the Bank of Communications became joint state-private institutions, subordinate to the People's Bank. The Bank of China specialized in foreign exchange and remittances to overseas Chinese. The Bank of Communications specialized in channeling investment grants from the Ministry of Finance to joint state-private enterprises. (In 1958, however, the Bank of Communications was transferred from the Ministry of Finance and placed under the People's Bank.) The functions of the fourth bank, the Farmers Bank of China, were assumed by rural credit cooperatives, the People's Bank, and the Agricultural Bank of China (which has had a checkered career, having been reorganized in 1963 but reduced to little or no importance by the early

1970s). In addition, in 1954 the Communists founded the People's Bank of Reconstruction, which directed funds from the budget to enterprises and institutions and made short-term investment loans. The private banks were transformed into joint state-private banks, completely under the direction of the People's Bank, and the foreign banks eventually disappeared. Several other new financial institutions have been created, and credit and saving facilities have been greatly extended, especially to the rural areas.

Essentially, the financial system now consists of the People's Bank, with its thousands of branch offices, which issues all banknotes and coins, accepts deposits, and makes loans mostly for medium- and short-term purposes; the People's Bank for Reconstruction, which manages capital construction and accordingly makes nonrepayable grants of budget revenues to state enterprises and other economic units for purposes of long-term capital formation; the Bank of China, which is the foreign-exchange bank that manages balance-of-payments transactions; and, in the rural communes, credit cooperatives and their branch offices in the brigades, which accept deposits from and make loans to commune members. The entire system is under the unified leadership of the People's Bank. The system's currency issues are highly centralized; most of its deposits are in the People's Bank; and it both loans funds and makes nonrepayable grants—thus serving both as a true monetary system and as a conduit between the state budget and those engaged in capital formation.

Most of the capital formation in China after 1949 was financed by government saving—by an excess of budget revenues over government consumption expenditures. This technique for channeling saving into investment did not employ the intermediary services of the financial system. That is, such saving did not take the form of claims on financial institutions, and investment was not financed by borrowing from financial institutions. Nor did this fiscal technique employ the services of security markets—through the issue of securities by investors and their direct purchase by savers. Instead, the principal saving-investment method used by the Communists imposed taxes on individuals, cooperatives (and later, communes), and firms; appropriated the profits of state enterprises; and made nonrepayable grants of these funds to those engaged in capital formation according to the Five-Year Plan. In this process, financial institutions performed only two functions: first, they kept track of the deposits transferred (or supplied the currency transferred), initially as tax or profit payments to the provincial and state budgets, later as investment grants to various economic units; second, they served as a conduit for investment grants, as was the case for the People's Reconstruction Bank. Neither of these functions involved the classic intermediary role of financial institutions.

During most of the 1950s a sizable proportion of saving came from foreign sources (mainly the USSR). In effect, this meant that China issued IOUs to the USSR for rubles to be spent on capital goods and other items in that country. Here again, the method of gaining saving and allocating it to investment did not involve China's financial system—its debt-asset system—as an intermediary between domestic savers and investors.

Finally, some investment was financed by saving of agricultural cooperatives. However, most of this activity dispensed with the financial system's intermediary role because the economic units doing the saving used most of it to meet their own investment needs; that is, they self-financed their own capital expenditures. The financial system did act as an intermediary for some investment—some saving of the cooperatives, in other words, took the form of financial assets acquired by savers, and this saving was then borrowed from the financial system by investors. However, this portion was quite small compared to the amounts financed by state enterprise profits, taxes, foreign saving, or retained earnings. Thus, during the 1950s China's financial system did not play the leading role in the saving-investment process and therefore, insofar as intermediary functions are concerned, did not contribute importantly to economic growth. Although the financial system's intermediary role has probably grown somewhat since the 1950s, it still represents, without any doubt, only a small portion of the total flows of saving and investment.

This suggests that China's financial assets have probably been small relative to its GNP or its national wealth. That is to say, the base of national wealth has been greatly expanded without the erection of a huge superstructure of financial assets. Most additions to real wealth have been financed in ways not involving the issuance of debt by investors or the accumulation of financial assets by savers.

The relative scarcity of financial assets in China is a hallmark of an economy in which socialist central planning is emphasized to boost saving and investment levels.[5] This saving-investment technique forgoes most of the division of labor in saving and investment on which relatively extensive financial structures are based. Saving and investment are generated principally within the state sector so that market transfers of savings at explicit rates of interest are unnecessary. The demand for financial assets in noninvestment sectors is depressed by constraints on personal income and wealth. It is also depressed because the state undertakes to supply various services for which people save in capitalist societies, because private bequests are minimized, and because reduced private risks imply reduced precautionary portfolios. Under the circumstances of demand and supply, there is little occasion for markets either in primary securities (issued by nonfinancial sectors) or in the indirect securities of financial institutions. Moreover, because of pressure for internal development, there has been no significant accumulation by socialist countries of foreign financial claims, and there has been no financial-intermediary industry to export its services.

The very process of socialist central planning reduces the dependence of economic units on a financial structure. Contact is made less through financial markets and financial institutions and more through planning bureaus and other central coordinating devices; the order of the day is internal finance and balanced budgets, not external finance and the issue of new securities. The theory and design of a socialist society are incompatible with a sophisticated financial-intermediary structure.

More specifically, China prohibits most commercial types of direct finance—borrowing by one economic unit from another—although individuals may borrow from and lend to each other under certain conditions, and other direct-finance transactions undoubtedly take place. The general prohibition of direct finance, however, has served to hold down primary debt.

Such debt is, of course, often purchased by financial intermediaries when investors borrow, but even in such indirect
finance the amounts are held down by budget grants for much
the same purposes.

Indirect financial assets are also relatively small. With some
exceptions, business enterprises, government organs, communes, and military units must deposit at the People's Bank all
currency in excess of three days' normal expenditures. Individuals are urged to deposit their excess currency holdings in the
People's Bank, credit cooperatives, or saving societies. These
practices have almost certainly held down currency in circulation. Moreover, not only is excess currency deposited, but currency transactions themselves are greatly restricted. Industrial
enterprises, communes, and other units draw upon their deposits
to obtain currency for wage payments, pensions, and other relatively minor expenditures—but most of the major outlays of such
units cannot be made with currency; much of the currency received by peasants and urban workers returns to the units which
made the wage and other payments and then is deposited in the
People's Bank as specified above. However, individuals may hold
on to currency or deposit it in savings accounts at the various
financial institutions. During the 1950s, they could also purchase
central government bonds. Restrictions on currency use have
been less rigid for agricultural production teams, but these too
have been coaxed or impelled to deposit excess currency in the
People's Bank or in credit cooperatives.[6]

In terms of value, most financial transactions in China are
made by deposit transfers at the People's Bank. Enterprises,
government organs, military units, and so on, have to use this
method to settle large transactions among themselves. These
transactions, however, can be made only if supporting documents show that the proposed expenditures are consonant with
the national plan. For this reason, bank deposits are not highly
liquid substitutes for the restricted currency holdings. The level
of liquidity in the economy is minimal: state enterprises hold little
currency and can make only limited use of their bank deposits;
communes, being cooperatives, are in a somewhat different position, but they too are probably only moderately liquid; and

households, whose consumption outlays approach their incomes, have had only small margins for saving in any form, though these have expanded in recent years. Government securities are also scarce because governmental units have consistently maintained close to balanced budgets, covering their expenditures with current revenues. Indeed, balanced budgets have been almost ubiquitous in China—which is still another way of saying that its capital accumulation has occurred without the accompaniment of large issues of debt and large accumulations of financial assets.[7]

Other Functions of China's Financial System

Although China's financial institutions and financial markets have not had to play a dominant role in the saving-investment process, its financial structure has, nevertheless, been of vital importance to the economy. For one thing, China's banking system has provided a smooth-working and highly efficient payments mechanism; for another, it has established a stable, predictable price level. Finally, the financial system has been an integral part of overall economic planning.

The Payments Mechanism

The quality of China's money supply and the efficiency with which payments can be made throughout the country are immeasurably higher today than at any time in the past. In the nineteenth century, China's money supply consisted of copper coins, silver coins (mostly foreign-minted), silver bullion (in the shape of "shoes"), paper money, and some current deposits. As this suggests, the currency system was bimetallic: copper and silver. The copper coins were "a mixture of old and contemporary, worn and new, heavy and light, legal and counterfeit, Chinese and foreign . . . . each coin [was] the potential subject of long and protracted debate."[8] Bar silver imported by banks was melted and molded into "shoes." "When a payment required tender of portions of these ingots, the correct amount would be cut off and weighed. Such a process would eventually leave broken silver."[9] Silver dollars, minted outside of China, also circulated, the principal ones being the Carolus dollar of Spain and the Mexican dollar. The issuance of bank notes was subject to varying restrictions, or none at all, and the bank notes of native banks usually had to be endorsed by the person passing them on, who then became responsible for payment if the bank failed.

This rather chaotic system persisted even after the downfall of the Ch'ing in 1911. Little progress toward eliminating it was made until the Kuomintang took over in 1928. Under the Kuomintang, the quality of the note issue was improved to some extent, but nothing like a uniform national currency was established. In late 1935, after the United States policy of purchasing at high prices had sharply reduced China's silver reserves, China left the silver bullion standard. A new managed system was established, and the nation's sole legal tender became the bank notes of the government banks. The notes of other banks were to be gradually retired, and eventually the Central Bank was to become the sole issuer of legal tender. In the meantime, the government coordinated the various bank note issues through the Currency Reserve Board. It also "introduced a new system of coinage, to substitute the subsidiary coins of dependable fixed value for the conglomeration of silver, copper, and paper subsidiary money of fluctuating value."[10]

The Kuomintang's attempt to establish a uniform national currency ultimately failed, of course, under the dual impact of the Sino-Japanese War, 1937–1945, and the subsequent continuation of the civil war. During the war and occupation years, all sorts of currencies circulated in China—Japanese currencies, currencies of the puppet government, currencies issued by the Communists in the regions they controlled, and various types of legal tender issued by the Kuomintang regime—the initial one being replaced by the gold *yuan* in August 1948, in a futile attempt to halt the runaway inflation, and the gold *yuan* being replaced in turn by the silver *yuan* in July 1949.

As the Communists entered one city after another in 1948 and

1949, they exchanged their own currency—the People's Currency (Jenminpi, or JMP)—for the various existing issues. By 1952, the JMP was the only currency in circulation (though local notes existed in Tibet until 1959), and all bank notes and coins were issued by the People's Bank of China. Since rapid inflation of prices and bank notes was not halted until the middle of 1950, the JMP circulated in very large denominations. To correct this, the Communists imposed a currency reform in March 1955, in which 10,000 *yuan* of old currency had to be exchanged for one *yuan* of new currency, and prices were reduced commensurately. Since that time, although there have been a few changes in the denominations of the bank notes issued, the currency system has been remarkably stable.[11]

There are two types of deposits: collective deposits (enterprises, government accounts, and so on) and individual (private) deposits. Use of the former is restricted by the detailed specifications of the national plan at the privincial and local levels. Unhampered withdrawals of the latter may be made by their owners. During 1972, the annual interest rate paid on the collective deposits was around 1.8 percent. The individual deposits carried a rate of about 2.2 percent on current (demand) deposits—on which checks cannot be written—and over 3.2 percent on fixed deposits of one year or more.

The present system is a managed-currency system, even though a gold stock held by the People's Bank backs the currency. The payments mechanism has been improved through the unification of currency and through the heightened use of deposit settlements to pay for goods and services. These payment methods appear to be highly efficient and uniform throughout the country.

The Price Level

China's monetary system has won its spurs by maintaining a stable price level. Until mid-1950 prices did rise sharply, but these spurts were the last gasp of the hyperinflation that had begun in the late 1930s. Since 1950, the overall price level has changed very little, though there appear to have been short-term inflationary pressures during the years 1953, 1956–1957, and 1960–1962. However, relative prices have changed. For example, the procurement prices of agricultural products have risen since 1950, while the retail prices of some industrial products sold in rural areas have fallen, so that rural terms of trade have improved substantially.

General prices have been stabilized within a context of fiscal and monetary controls of aggregate spending and long-run growth in the supply of output. Total wage payments to rural and urban workers are under the control of the central government—although this involves only general guidelines—as are the prices of major commodities. Consequently, real wages are established by the government. This largely determines total consumption expenditures, especially since, as previously explained, borrowing and lending activities are closely regulated and liquid assets are relatively small. Furthermore, the comparatively high commodity prices and the low nominal wages result in large profits to state enterprises and communes, most of which are appropriated or taxed by the central and provincial governments. These governments then allocate most of the funds for capital formation, making sure that their total expenditures, including those for administration, about equal their revenues. The surpluses retained by communes are about equal to their capital expenditures.

The fiscal system contains a built-in stabilizer in the form of very high marginal "tax" rates on state enterprise profits. That is, any increase in consumption or investment spending shows up largely as additional profits which are appropriated or taxed away. This stabilization feature, however, is eroded to the extent that government expenditures are increased as budget revenues rise.

China's monetary policy has been based largely on the doctrine of real bills—that is, bank loans are considered noninflationary as long as they involve, directly or indirectly, the production of commodities.[12] In capitalist systems, such a monetary policy has led to inflation because multiple borrowers bid for the same commodities—or for the same resources to produce commodities. In China, however, the real-bills doctrine has more validity, since a rather monolithic banking system is less likely to give firms competing loans to purchase factors of production and commodities, and since, even if excess money at existing prices is created, its use is tightly controlled.

Consequently, despite the potential instability of a fiscal system that tends to match expenditures with whatever revenues happen to be and of a monetary policy that follows the real-bills doctrine, the growth of China's economy and the general price level have in fact been fairly stable (except for the disasters of 1959–1961 and the adverse economic impacts of the Cultural Revolution, both of which came mainly from the supply side). The key has been the state's control over the price-wage equation, coupled with a low level of class conflict over shares of national income.

Economic Planning

During the First Five-Year Plan, 1953–1957, the economic-planning mechanism was highly centralized, patterned after the system in the Soviet Union at the time. "The emphasis was placed on overall control by the central government of the whole national economy."[13] In 1957–1958, however, China began to decentralize the planning system, reducing the central government's direct control over much economic activity, giving more scope for decision-making to local authorities, and emphasizing horizontal planning along territorial lines over vertical planning along industrial lines. The decrease in economic centralization, however, often meant an increase in party control at the local levels. Moreover, the central government still controlled aggregate investment in major products, total wages, exports and imports, the output levels of the most important industrial and agricultural commodities, receipts and payments of the national budget, and other key targets.

The financial institutions, and especially the People's Bank and its several thousand branches and sub-branches, are integral parts of China's economic-planning system. The national plan includes three major components: the plans for industrial output, for agricultural output, and for bank policy. The last includes the issuance of currency, the extension of loans, and other financial goals. In the making of the national plan, the People's Bank is equal to the other planning organs. It is also intimately involved in planning because most of the important purchases in the economy must be paid for by transfers of its bank deposits, and such transfers are watched by the banking authorities to see that they are made according to the Five-Year Plan. Either existing deposits or deposits newly created by loans are transferred, but in either case the People's Bank can supervise the settlements. Furthermore, many capital expenditures are financed through financial institutions by budgetary grants, and these too come under the scrutiny of bank officials.

> The banks are expected to take a major part in ensuring that production proceeds as planned. They have to see that plans for credit loans to enterprises accord closely with national economic plans. Banks are supposed to prevent the hoarding of raw materials by enterprises (which the banks should spot through the undue running down of the enterprises' bank balances) and they are charged with insisting that the distinction between working capital and long-term investment funds is maintained. The Construction Bank has responsibility for seeing that grants for investment and the use made of them, both tally with state plans.[14]

Three major kinds of economic units receive or borrow funds from the financial system: state-owned enterprises, collectively owned enterprises (handicraft cooperatives, supply and marketing cooperatives, and so on), and people's communes. These economic units need funds principally for capital construction, short-term purchases of raw materials, and inventories. In addition, state-owned enterprises periodically receive currency from the People's Bank for their wage payments. Some funds are granted; others are loaned. The chart ahead shows these distinctions, along with interest rates on some of the loans, as of the summer of 1972. Loans are for short-term purposes (maturity about one year), though occasional long-term loans are made to communes, with the interest rate dependent on the purpose of the borrowing. Capital-construction funds are supplied by state grants to enterprises. Since, unlike the enterprises, communes retain their own resources, they are expected to finance their

	State-owned enterprises	Collectively owned enterprises	People's communes
Capital-construction funds	Grants from the state through Bank for Reconstruction	Grants from the state through Bank for Reconstruction	Loans from People's Bank; some grants to poorer communes
Short-term funds	Loans from People's Bank (5% per year)	Loans from People's Bank (5% per year)	Loans from People's Bank (2.2-4.3% per year)
Circulating capital—wage payments	"Grants" from People's Bank out of enterprises' deposits		

capital needs internally, but grants are occasionally extended to the poorer communes.

It is not possible, however, for the banks to supervise adequately the use of all the funds they lend. Some loans for working capital, for example, may in fact be used for capital construction; and some loans for specific purposes may release funds that enterprises would have used for those purposes but now employ in other ways. Consequently, although the banks theoretically have control over all economic transactions other than currency and barter transactions, in fact that is probably not possible. In a broader and looser way, however, financial control is exerted by the banks, and so they do serve an indispensable role in the planning process.[15]

Conclusions

The financial system in Communist countries is often large and fairly sophisticated, not so much because it is a vital intermediary in the saving-investment process as because it is a necessary link in the economic-planning system. The financial system supervises loans and grants; oversees the transactions consummated with deposit transfers; assesses and recommends changes in enterprises' use of funds, even criticizing production methods and management techniques; and helps to train financial cadres in the communes and elsewhere.

China's financial system has been an integral part of the planning system and has developed an efficient method of making payments and maintained reasonably stable price levels. Its role in the saving-investment process has been modest, however, and that role is not likely to assume great importance in the immediate future.

Notes

1. Much more detail about these banks can be found in Frank M. Tamagna, *Banking and Finance in China* (New York: Institute of Pacific Relations, 1942).

2. Y. C. Wang, *Chinese Intellectuals and the West, 1872–1949* (Chapel Hill: University of North Carolina Press, 1966), pp. 485–86.

3. Albert Feuerwerker, *The Chinese Economy, 1912–1949* (Ann Arbor: Center for Chinese Studies, University of Michigan, 1968), p. 57.

4. For additional information on China's inflation, see Kia-ngau Chang, *The Inflationary Spiral: The Experience in China, 1939–1950* (New York: Technological Press of MIT and John Wiley & Sons, 1958); Shun-hsin Chou, *The Chinese Inflation, 1937–1949* (New York: Columbia University Press, 1963); Arthur N. Young, *China's Wartime Finance and Inflation, 1937–1945* (Cambridge, Mass.: Harvard University Press, 1965), all reviewed in Chapter 3 of this volume.

5. The analytical framework of this chapter, including the following paragraphs, is based on J. G. Gurley and E. S. Shaw, "Financial Structures and Economic Development," *Economic Development and Cultural Change*, April 1967.

6. Kao Hsiang, "The Function of State Banks during Socialist Construction," *Economic Research*, October 1962.

7. The above does not deny, however, that there has been a large percentage increase in savings deposits since 1950. Such deposits appear to have risen more than fiftyfold in the first decade, from negligible amounts to more than 8 billion *yuan*. Their rate of growth was highest in the earlier years because savings (and lending) outlets multiplied rapidly in response to the effects of land reform—that is, the decline of traditional moneylenders and the decentralization of decision-making greatly increased the supply of and the demand for loanable funds. Still, savings deposits represented only a small proportion of total investment (or saving) over these years, probably less than 5 percent. Furthermore, not all of the increase in savings deposits constituted additional saving, since some of the total must have been offset by the increased indebtedness of households (for example, to credit cooperatives).

The outstanding amounts of central-government bonds in the 1950s were never large, the highest amount having been just over 3 billion *yuan*, in 1958. After that these bonds were gradually retired down to zero by 1968. Currency in circulation may have risen about tenfold during the 1950s, reaching 8 or 9 billion *yuan* in 1959. There are few indications of the levels of current deposits. But if we assume that they were twice currency holdings, then total deposits of all types, currency, and government bonds may have been around 25 billion *yuan*, or about 25 percent of GNP, in 1957. Almost half of

this, it should be remembered, was in the rather illiquid current
deposits.

8. Frank H. H. King, *Money and Monetary Policy in China, 1845–1895*
   (Cambridge, Mass.: Harvard University Press, 1965), p. 53. King's
   book is discussed in Chapter 3 above.
9. Ibid., p. 72.
10. Arthur N. Young, *China's Wartime Finance and Inflation*, p. 132.
11. For a detailed account of the currency system, see Tadao Miyashita,
    The Currency and Financial System of Mainland China (Tokyo:
    Institute of Asian Economic Affairs, 1966).
12. Huang Ta, "Monetary Circulation and the Principle of Bank
    Credit," *Economic Research*, September 1962.
13. Audrey Donnithorne, *China's Economic System* (New York:
    Praeger, 1967), p. 498.
14. Ibid., p. 470.
15. Miyashita, *Currency and Financial System*, chaps. 4 and 8.

7

Economists, Prices, and Profits: Some Maoist Views

It is no secret that Mao has held the economists of China in low esteem. In his eyes, they were members of that community of city-bred or foreign-educated intellectuals who constantly aroused his suspicions and sometimes his wrath, and he has not been above making cutting remarks about them. With a touch of haughtiness, Mao characterized some of these intellectuals as "walking dictionaries," implying that their noses were always in books and that, for all their memorized knowledge, they were unable to explain, or sometimes even to recognize, problems in the real world around them.[1] To keep young students from growing up in the same way, Mao cautioned them against reading too much, even books by Marx. Too much reading, he insisted, would turn them into bookworms, dogmatists, and revisionists.[2] "The more you study [books]," Mao admonished, "the more stupid you become."[3] Mao told a group of educators that in the Ming dynasty there were only two good emperors, of whom one was completely illiterate and the other semi-illiterate. "Too much book learning," Mao concluded, "does not produce good emperors."[4]

Yet Mao himself has always been an avid reader. In his youth, he once spent every day for six months in a library. Later he carried books wherever he went, sometimes under the most trying conditions, and in recent years his temporary disappearances from public view have at times been for long sessions of solitary reading.[5]

So despite some exaggerated advice for the purpose of making a strong point, Mao is certainly not an anti-intellectual. What does concern him, though, is the danger that Chinese youth will become nothing but bookworms and thereby fail to develop into "intellectuals in the true sense."[6] True intellectuals not only read but also take part in practical work. Accordingly, Chinese youth should work in villages and factories, wherever there are peasants and workers. In this way, without always opening "big tomes or small pamphlets," they would gain some common sense.[7] The combination of theory and practice, of study and work, would produce, if not good emperors, good proletarians.

Correct ideas, according to Mao, do not drop from the skies, nor are they innate in the mind. They come from social practice, from man's activity in the struggle for production, in the class struggle, and in scientific and artistic pursuits. Mao was particularly incensed at the dogmatism of the Chinese students who had studied Marxism-Leninism in Moscow during the 1920s and returned to China with little conception of Chinese realities or of how to apply their theories to the Chinese revolution. "Chinese Communists," Mao warned,

> must fully and properly integrate the universal truth of Marxism with the concrete practice of the Chinese revolution, or in other words, the universal truth of Marxism must be combined with specific national characteristics and acquire a definite national form if it is to be useful, and in no circumstances can it be applied subjectively as a mere formula. Marxists who make a fetish of formulas are simply playing the fool with Marxism and the Chinese revolution, and there is no room for them in the ranks of the Chinese revolution.[8]

Mao has directed his barbs not only at intellectuals in general but at academic economists and other liberal-arts scholars in particular. Like many intellectuals, Mao observed, economists give all their attention to "eternal and immutable dogmas" and are therefore detached from reality. They have no contact with the current economic problems of the proletariat and are even ignorant of China's economic past. They are all theory and no practice. As early as May 1941, Mao went after the economists, singling them out as especially bad examples of intellectuals who did not have their feet on Chinese ground:

> Although we are studying Marxism, the way many of our people study it runs directly counter to Marxism. That is to say, they violate the fundamental principle earnestly enjoined on us by Marx, Engels, Lenin and Stalin, the unity of theory and practice. Having violated this principle, they invent an opposite principle of their own, the separation of theory from practice. . . . Professors of economics cannot explain the relationship between the Border Region currency and the Kuomintang currency, so naturally the students cannot explain it either. Thus a perverse mentality has been created among many students; instead of showing an interest in China's problems and taking the Party's directives seriously, they give all their hearts to the supposedly eternal and immutable dogmas learned from their teachers.[9]

Mao's disgust with economics professors who could not explain an exchange rate between two currencies carried over during the 1950s and 1960s to liberal-arts subjects in general and to the way they were taught. As Mao was preparing to launch the Cultural Revolution in 1964, he charged: "Liberal arts subjects are completely detached from reality. Students of history, philosophy, and economics have no concern with studying reality; they are the most ignorant things of this world." Mao then proceeded to recommend that economics and other faculties in universities should regard "the whole of society as their factory. Their teachers and students should make contact with the peasants and urban workers as well as with agriculture and industries. How else can their graduates be of any use?"[10] A short time later, Mao exhorted teachers to engage in manual labor. "It will not do to move only [your] lips and not [your] hands."[11]

In a famous 1965 talk in Hangchow, Mao guessed that young people, for sixteen to twenty years of their lives, "do not even have a chance to see rice, peas, wheat, cereals, and millet. They do not see how workers work, how peasants plough, and how business is done. Only their health is ruined." In that talk, Mao related how he told his children to go to the countryside and learn from the peasants. Before going to school, Mao claimed, a child has direct contact with the objective world, but once in school the child is cooped up and gradually loses all touch with reality. "It is really like murder."[12]

Mao inferred from this that, after graduating from a senior middle school, a student should do some practical work in villages, factories, and army units. After several years of work, he could be eligible to go on to higher studies, but "he need [have] no more than two more years of study." Furthermore, while in higher education, students should continue to work in industry, agriculture, and commerce. Their teachers, he said, should also do practical work. "They can work and teach at the same time. Can philosophy, literature, and history not be taught down below? Must they be taught in tall, foreign-style buildings?"[13]

Mao also indicted economists for conceiving of their subject in a narrow, technocratic way, separated from politics and ideology. Economists, whether they knew it or not, supported some social class; if they were not aware of their ideological role, they were simply bewildered scholars.

> To pay no attention to politics and to be fully occupied with business matters is to become a perplexed economist or technician. And that is dangerous. Ideological and political work is the guarantee for the accomplishment of our economic and technological work; it serves the economic base. Ideology and politics are the commanders, the soul. A slight relaxation in our ideological and political work will lead our economic and technological work astray.[14]

As early as 1942, Mao expressed the belief that, for all their "eternal truths," economists had hardly developed theories worthy of the name; their theories lagged far behind the rich content of revolutionary practice. "Just think," he asked, "how many of us have created theories worthy of the name on China's economics, politics, military affairs or culture, theories which can be regarded as scientific and comprehensive, and not crude and sketchy?" Mao observed that despite a century of Chinese capitalist development since the Opium War, there was not yet a single theoretical work which reflected that development and could be called genuinely scientific. "Can we say that in the study of China's economic problems . . . the theoretical level is already high? Can we say that our Party already has economic theorists worthy of the name? Certainly not."[15]

Mao also complained that the Chinese economists were virtually unreadable. Economists wrote in a deadly style, with vagueness and poor reasoning. Having specified these weaknesses, Mao suggested remedies:

> Essays and documents must be written precisely, clearly, and in a lively [manner]. . . . Most essays nowadays suffer from *a.* vague conceptualization, *b.* inadequate judgment, *c.* a lack of logic in the process of using concepts and judgment in reasoning, *d.* a lack of literary merit. [As a result], reading an essay becomes an ordeal, a gigantic waste of energy for very little reward. This bad tendency must be averted. Comrades engaged in economics work must pay attention not only to precision but also to clarity and liveliness when they are drafting [something. They] must not think [clarity and liveliness] are [only] for language and literature teachers, not for gentlemen like themselves.[16]

Since the late 1950s, Mao has attacked economists who were "taking the capitalist road" by emphasizing the primacy of productive forces in China's economic development, the importance of profits in allocating economic resources, and the usefulness of monetary and price relations for achieving more rational economic progress.

With regard to the first point, the Maoists have been quick to explain that economic development is not simply the development of "things" but also the development of social relations.

> Bourgeois economists always study social economy as a relationship between things, and use this to cover up the relations of capitalist exploitation. What Marxist political economy studies is not the relationship between things but the relationship between . . . one class and another.[17]

Bourgeois economists concentrate too much on the productive forces, on machinery and buildings, and they erroneously believe that the principal problem is how to get more output for a given input—how to raise labor productivity.

> The modern revisionists [say] . . . that in socialist society, there

is only the question of "rational organization of productive forces" and "how to obtain maximum economic results with minimum production expenses." . . . [They pay] attention only to grain, cotton and oil without distinguishing between the enemy, ourselves and friends. . . . [Their line] stresses only the material—machinery and mechanization—and goes in for material incentives. It opposes giving prominence to proletarian politics, ignores the class struggle and negates the dictatorship of the proletariat.[18]

The gist of the Maoists' complaint has been that the bourgeois economists regarded the struggle against nature as more important than the class struggle and that this belief led to capitalism, not socialism. What these economists were expressing was the "outright yapping of bourgeois lap-dogs."

Liu Shao-ch'i and the economists and others associated with him were also accused by the Maoists of desiring to elevate profits to a supreme role in the economy and to use the price mechanism to rationalize the structure of costs and revenues. The Maoists argued that these modern revisionists wanted to develop the economy by "economic methods" rather than "administrative methods," and that this meant "putting profits in command." It also amounted to "letting the capitalist law of value [production prices] reign supreme, developing free competition, undermining the socialist economy and restoring capitalism."[19] The Maoists preferred, for example, to decide through national planning ("administrative" rather than "economic") how much steel to produce; the revisionist economists, on the other hand, pressed for letting the quantity be determined by steel prices in a competitive market and by the resulting profits.

The Maoists have rejected the pursuit of profits—or moneymaking and material incentives in general—as life's major aim, mainly because this would restore power to the bourgeoisie. They have further asserted that putting profits in command would lower the workers' productivity and thus retard economic growth. They have objected to using profits as a guide to efficient allocation because there were simply too many externalities involved and because this would create severe imbalances in the economy. They have rejected the distribution of profits as private incomes because, as part of surplus value, profits were unearned and because their private distribution would lead to undesirable disparities in family incomes. Finally, they have denounced the pursuit of profits as a prime goal because it would "corrupt the soul." Each of these charges is worth a few comments.

The Maoists have maintained that ubiquitous profitmaking would restore the bourgeoisie to power by reinforcing all the values by which bourgeois society operates. It would emphasize the struggle between man and nature and thus veil the fundamental struggle between the bourgeoisie and the proletariat. Such an emphasis would suggest that all societies, capitalist and socialist, have essentially the same problems. This point was well made in a *Peking Review* attack on a prominent economist during the Cultural Revolution:

> Sun Yeh-fang [former director, Economics Institute, Chinese Academy of Sciences, and reputedly economic adviser to Liu Shao-ch'i] advocated that the main task was to raise the ratio of output to man-hours. Maoists say that the main task is to defeat the bourgeoisie; if they are not defeated, then even if the aim of Sun is achieved the benefits will not go to the workers. . . . Using the customary tricks of the bourgeoisie and the revisionists, Sun Yeh-fang tried to negate class contradictions and deny class struggle with the so-called contradiction between man and matter. He did his utmost to publicize that the "contradiction between man and matter" is "the deepest common root source" of all economic contradictions. [20]

The Maoists have also urged that, contrary to the conventional economic wisdom, generalized moneymaking would lower the workers' productivity. This, they contend, is because workers do not have sufficiently worthy and stimulating goals under the profit motive and the material incentives and individualism that accompany it. Making private gain life's ranking purpose cannot be a lasting inspiration for working hard and doing one's best. "We must never work like capitalists who work exclusively for profits, work hard when there is a big profit, work less hard when there is little profit and do not work at all when there is no profit." Workers are deeply and enduringly motivated, the Maoists believe, by cooperative efforts and by the selfless goals of helping others and building up their country. The private-profit motive fragments all such cooperative endeavors into self-seeking, personal efforts which in the end degenerate into complacency, corruption and other unproductive and criminal attitudes and activities. The Maoists have also claimed that moneymaking as a prime aim breeds a selfishness that leads workers to withhold knowledge and help from others; it even leads the strong to knock out the weak and the disadvantaged rather than come to their aid.

The Maoists also contend that the ascendancy of private profits would preclude the production of many essential goods because resources would not be allocated to socially profitable goods if it were privately unprofitable to do so. Their point, in effect, is that social profitability differs so markedly from private profitability that it is highly inefficient to start from the latter and try to reach the former via price or tax adjustments of one kind or another. They consider it wiser to strive directly, through national planning, to achieve what is *socially* profitable and desirable. According to the Maoist argument, it is socially profitable to assure everyone enough food, decent housing and clothing, and adequate medical care and schooling,[21] and private profitmaking, whatever else can be said for it, is not capable of attaining those socially profitable goals.

The Maoists have also pointed, with some exaggeration, to still other deficiencies of the private-profit motive:

> [If we follow the profit motive], it is impossible for unprofitable national-defense industries to develop; it is impossible to establish heavy and inland industries; it is impossible for regions, provinces, and municipalities to build industrial systems under different conditions proceeding from the viewpoint of war preparedness; it is impossible for the support of agriculture to develop those industries of low productivity value that make little profit in the short run; it is impossible for the state to run and develop certain categories of daily necessities that must be subsidized within a certain period of time; and, in accordance with the proletarian spirit of internationalism, it is impossible to produce products needed for the struggle of the revolutionary people of the world.[22]

Continuing their case, the Maoists insist that profitmaking would eventually lead to at least de facto private ownership of the means of production and hence to the distribution of large amounts of unearned income to private individuals simply because they owned or controlled material forces of production. This in turn would culminate in unwelcome disparities in the distribution of income and, consequently, to an intensification of class differences and antagonisms.

Finally, the Maoists argue that the pursuit of money as a prime goal of life corrupts the soul. It leads to individualistic, selfish, grasping behavior, and these unadmirable bourgeois traits do not bring people close together in mutual respect and cooperative endeavors. They are, in fact, just the opposite of the traits sought by the Maoists: selflessness, serving the people, honesty, and motivation by collective and moral incentives rather than individual and material incentives. Material incentives say the Maoists, "corrode our working class with bourgeois 'egoism' and disgrace our working class with money, fame, material comfort, and other bourgeois garbage." For the Maoists, the task of enterprises is not only to develop production but also to "prepare both the material and spiritual conditions for the future communist society." If enterprises devoted themselves solely to production and profits, "everything would be turned into a cold, capitalist relationship of monetary transactions"; warm, human relationships would be sacrificed.

The Maoists picture moneymaking as the sole happiness in bourgeois society. They quote Engels as having said,

> It is the bourgeois viewpoint that there is not a single thing on earth that does not exist for the sake of money, including the bourgeoisie themselves, because they live for the purpose of making money. Aside from a quick fortune, they are unaware of any other kind of happiness.

But one cannot make money, the Maoists warn, without exploiting and plundering others, and even launching aggressive wars. With profits in command, speculators, swindlers, embezzlers, and other sinister types would all run wild.[23]

To demonstrate how the moral decline of a society sets in after moneymaking is given free rein, the Maoists drew on a letter of a Russian woman to the periodical *Literaturnaya Gazeta*:

Rubles, rubles, money, and business . . . this is all you read in the newspapers and hear on the radio nowadays. For fifty years we have been taught to deal with people and functionaries in an unselfish and human manner, refusing to soil our hands with cash, and now suddenly people can think of saying: "I've all the respect in the world for you, as long as you can bring me profit." . . . In our place, profit and material incentives are beginning to push the high standards set by one's moral integrity into the background.[24]

And this society now hopelessly addicted to moneymaking and personal possessions, say the Maoists—and you can see them throwing up their hands in despair—was once on the road to socialism! Such is happiness in revisionist countries!

In capitalist economies, the social benefits of private profitmaking are supposed to be enhanced by flexible prices which move sensitively with demand and supply conditions. If demand rises for some commodity, more of it will be produced as its price rises to stimulate the profit motive of private producers. Contrariwise, the profit motive would induce less production of a commodity whose price is declining from lack of demand. Bourgeois economists claimed that these supply responses are "efficient," in that they facilitate the utilization of resources up to the point at which the marginal costs of producing commodities equal the marginal benefits to their buyers. Hence, they argue, a competitive, flexible price system promotes economic efficiency and therefore economic growth.

Though it is difficult for bourgeois economists to understand how anyone could oppose these arguments, the Maoists have done exactly that. Mao himself has repeatedly stated that China's policy is to stabilize prices,[25] and by that he has meant not only that the overall price level should be stabilized but that individual prices, especially the key ones, should not rise or fall frequently or markedly with changes in demand and supply conditions. More radically, China's long-run policy, as it moves into the stage of communism, is to gradually reduce the role of money and prices in the spheres of production and distribution.

In China, commodities are priced according to their average costs plus a tax and a "profit" per unit. The average costs include production costs and the expenses of administration in wholesaling and retailing. However, for basic daily necessities, such as cotton cloth, grain, and edible oils, prices are set on the low side, usually accompanied by rationing. The aim is a fair distribution of basic items to everyone. For non-necessities, prices are set relatively high, yielding larger profits, most of which go to state and provincial budgets. The State Council and the State Planning Commission fix the prices of the most important commodities; the Ministry of Commerce sets other important prices; the provinces establish all other prices, except those determined by demand and supply (subject to ceilings) in rural markets. But no matter how prices are arrived at, they are meant to remain fairly stable over long periods.[26]

The Maoists reject free competition and flexible prices for some of the same reasons that they reject private profit-making.[27] For instance, they insist that stable prices prevent or, at any rate, discourage the proliferation of speculation, underhanded deals, bribery, and corruption. With fluctuating prices, some people would spend much of their lives betting on the ups and downs, trying to make killings, and in the process would become increasingly tempted to bribe and corrupt others to influence the outcome. Another Maoist contention is that no price is sacrosanct, even one that equates supply and demand. Additional benefits and costs of a social nature are so pervasive and complex that no price can be proved to be *the* socially correct one. Competitive prices reflect relative scarcities only from the standpoint of private interests; they do not reflect the extra benefits to society of using a commodity or the extra costs to society of producing it. However, it is virtually impossible to allow for such social externalities with anything approaching accuracy. Hence, it is best to establish prices administratively, through national planning, at levels that will achieve the most important social goals, such as providing everyone with adequate supplies of the basic necessities.

Furthermore, the Maoists argue, stable prices themselves help to achieve the national plan. If prices, especially the major ones, could change at any time, enterprises might respond to them in ways that would either reduce the supplies needed by other enterprises or leave surplus goods to accumulate unused. In either case, the national plan would be upset.

The Maoists have also said that excess demands (which tend to raise prices) and excess supplies (which tend to lower prices) are often only temporary. They consider it a waste of time and resources to change prices in response to such temporary imbalances, for very shortly the next prices would have to be shifted back to more or less their original levels. Consequently, it is best to maintain stable prices that average out these transitory fluctuations.

It should also be taken into account, the Maoists say, that a rise in the price of an essential commodity would eliminate some worthy potential buyers. The correct policy, they believe, is to hold the price relatively low for such a commodity and, considering the excess demand for it, to ration it equitably. Moreover, the maintenance of prices in the face of growing excess demand for a commodity puts pressure where it should be—on the suppliers to increase its production. This pressure would be exerted, not by the incentives of private gain, but by the moral and collective incentives associated with the achievement of the national plan. It is better to encourage greater supplies in this way than to discourage buyers by pricing them out of the market. The pressure on suppliers will lead to greater production efforts, which, as Mao has never tired of saying, are the key to solving most economic and financial problems.

Finally, the Maoists favor stable prices because they enhance class alliances, especially the alliance between the peasants and the urban workers, which Mao considers the basis of China's socialist society. If the prices of the goods purchased by the peasants rise relative to the prices of the goods they sell, their real income is reduced. If the reverse is true, their real income of course rises. Price movements, therefore, especially those of the most important commodities, can enhance the living standards of one class at the expense of the other's. This would threaten the alliance of the two classes, as the burden of investment and growth (which is essentially a lower consumption level) falls more heavily on one class than on the other. For this reason, the

Maoists have declared that rising real incomes for both classes can best be attained on the basis of stable prices.

In fact, however, absolutely stable prices have not been achieved in China, for the Maoists, who use the term *stable* rather loosely, have not really sought that goal. Their target, instead, has been to control prices so as to minimize short-run fluctuations and to establish levels at which social goals can be met. This has required changes in many individual prices at one time or another, for example, lowering the prices of some manufactured goods purchased by the peasants for the purpose of raising living standards in the countryside. Consequently, while for over a quarter of a century prices have displayed more stability in China than almost anywhere else, *stable* has meant for the Maoists purposeful control rather than rigidity.

The Maoist case against many of China's economists has rested on the contention that they have been too production-minded and have not allowed sufficiently for the intensity of the class struggle that continues even in a socialist society. Production can be increased in many ways, but if bourgeois methods are used, the fruits of rising output will not be widely enjoyed by the proletariat, and the values and incentives associated with those methods will enhance the position of the bourgeoisie and corrupt the working classes. According to the Maoists, the theory that the productive forces need to be increased above everything else and the advocacy of profitmaking and flexible prices are nothing but bourgeois strategies for defeating the proletariat in the struggle between the two classes. That is why the Maoists have combated some economic theories and policies that appear to be verities to bourgeois economists.

Notes

1. "Talk at the Reception of Secretaries of Big Regions and Members of the Central Cultural Revolution Team" (July 22, 1966), in Jerome Ch'en, ed., *Mao Papers* (London: Oxford University Press, 1970), p. 33.

2. "Spring Festival Day on Education" (February 13, 1964), ibid., p. 96.
3. "Educational System," ibid., p. 131.
4. "Spring Festival Day on Education," ibid., pp. 93–94.
5. Edgar Snow, *The Other Side of the River* (New York: Random House, 1962), p. 156.
6. Mao Tse-tung, *Selected Works of Mao Tse-tung* (Peking: Foreign Languages Press, 1965), 3: 40–41.
7. "A Talk in Hangchow," in Jerome Ch'en, *Mao* (Englewood Cliffs, N.J.: Prentice-Hall, 1969), p. 105.
8. "On New Democracy," in *S.W.*, 2: 380–81.
9. "Reform Our Study," in *S.W.*, 3: 20.
10. "On Education—Conversation with the Nepalese Delegation of Educationists," in Ch'en, *Mao Papers*, pp. 21–23.
11. A Mao Instruction during the Cultural Revolution, ibid., p. 84.
12. "A Talk in Hangchow," in Ch'en, *Mao*, pp. 105–7.
13. Ibid.
14. A Mao Instruction during the Cultural Revolution, in Ch'en, *Mao Papers*, p. 82.
15. "Rectify the Party's Style of Work," in *S.W.*, 3: 37.
16. "Sixty Points on Working Methods," in Ch'en, *Mao Papers* , p. 72.
17. "Study Some Political Economy," *Hung-ch'i*, July 1, 1972.
18. Ibid.
19. "Criticizing and Repudiating China's Khrushchev: Two Diametrically Opposed Lines in Building the Economy," *Wenhui Pao* (Shanghai), August 23, 1967; in David Milton, Nancy Milton, and Franz Schurmann, *People's China* (New York: Vintage Books, 1974), pp. 318–20.
20. In *Peking Review* during the Cultural Revolution.
21. Mao has recently referred to the basic necessities as food, clothing, shelter, *and books*!
22. In *Peking Review* during the Cultural Revolution.
23. The above quotations are from various issues of the *Peking Review* during the Cultural Revolution.
24. In *Peking Review* during the Cultural Revolution.
25. "On the Ten Great Relationships," in Ch'en, *Mao*, p. 74.
26. The Chinese Communists fear inflation of the general price level because they saw how damaging it was to the Nationalist government under Chiang Kai-shek. The hyperinflation that then developed greatly reduced the economic efficiency of that government and tore apart whatever fragile social cohesion had existed previously. During the Anti-Japanese War the Communists themselves suf-

fered from inflation within their own areas. After gaining power, they quickly put an end to the rapidly rising price level, and since mid-1950 there has been general price stability most of the time. The Maoists favor such stability because it facilitates national planning and promotes alliances among various classes and groups of the society. These and other arguments for price stability are discussed below.

27. The following arguments for stable prices have been collected from discussions of visitors to China with officials of the Ministry of Commerce and the People's Bank, and from various Chinese publications. This presentation of the Chinese case for stable prices is couched mostly in their own expressed terms but is also in part my extension of those terms into contemporary bourgeois economic language.

8

Is the Chinese
Model Diffusible?

This question has been raised by some economists who believe that the postwar economic-development policies of many poor countries, however much they may have contributed to their growth rates, have failed to come to grips with the many problems associated with mass poverty, hunger, unemployment, and discontent. These economists have also observed that in China development has occurred without large disparities in family incomes or high rates of unemployment and with much dedication to the task. Cannot the Chinese model or elements of the Chinese model, they have asked, be used by other underdeveloped countries to establish growth with equity and high employment in those countries?

This is not an easy question to answer. From one point of view, it might seem plausible to assume that the various parts of an economic system are all so closely interrelated that no single element could be profitably removed and used by another country—either all elements must be used or none at all. However, this "plausible assumption" appears to be invalidated by the many examples of countries which have imported foreign technologies, religions, and almost everything else, and almost always piece by piece. Consider, for example, the Japanese after the Meiji Restoration, Turkey under Atatürk, or Russia under Peter the Great. In fact, if one thinks about it, cultural diffusion appears to be the rule, so that, from this point of view, the

Chinese system, or at least parts of it, would seem to be accessible to all comers. Is this really true? If so, which parts? And to what effect within a different culture?

In working toward answers to these questions, I shall first attempt to develop elements of a theory of cultural diffusion in order to provide a framework for analyzing the particular case of China. My next step will be to ask about the composition of the Chinese model itself—exactly what is this system of economic development? Finally, I shall tackle the key questions: What in China's economic processes is importable, and which countries might benefit from such imports?

Elements of a Theory of Cultural Diffusion

Can any economic model by exported? "Yes" is a good initial answer to this question: the diffusion of economic processes—or at least some of them—is entirely feasible. But before settling for that quick answer, it would be best to investigate exactly what is meant by the question.

Economic systems are components of what anthropologists call "cultures." One anthropologist has recently defined a culture as "the artifacts, institutions, ideologies, and the total range of customary behaviors with which a society is equipped for the exploitation of the energy potentials of its particular habitat."[1] This is similar to the Marxian conception of a social formation, which also includes productive forces ("artifacts"), institutions, and ideologies. In the Marxian scheme, however, the productive forces, the relations of production, and the superstructure are the major categories—the first two comprising the society's economic base and the last the ideology and institutions supporting its class structure. The productive forces encompass the material means of production that people fashion and use to gain a livelihood from their natural environment, as well as the people themselves—their knowledge, talents, aspirations, and needs. As people change their world, they develop capabilities and desires to change it still further. People thus make their living and themselves simultaneously. Human activity is, therefore, an integral part of the productive forces, which cannot be reduced to "artifacts." The relations of production are the institutions and practices most closely associated with the way goods are produced and exchanged. These institutions and practices include property relations; the manner in which labor is recruited, organized, and compensated; markets and other means for exchanging the products of labor; and the methods the ruling class uses to acquire and utilize the surplus product. Social relations are, in effect, the class structure of a society that is revealed in its work processes. Finally, the superstructure embodies the ruling ideas and systems of authority (political, legal, military, and so on) which support the dominant position of the ruling class, along with the ideas and institutions that reflect the needs of the society's subordinate classes.

Cultural adaptation, as many anthropologists view it, is the process by which people within a given natural environment use their productive forces effectively. It occurs through the medium of cultural evolution, which has largely replaced the adaptive mechanisms of natural selection and genetic mutation.[2] Cultural evolution, or the progress of a social formation, is determined principally by internal forces, but it can also be significantly shaped by the importation of institutions, values, and techniques from other cultures—that is, by cultural diffusion.

Cultural diffusion is the transfer of cultural information from one group to another, much as hybridization, its genetic counterpart, is the transfer of genetic information from one species to another. The former, however, has been of prime importance in sociocultural evolution, while the latter has been rather unimportant in organic evolution. In Marxian terms, cultural diffusion includes the transmission of elements of the productive forces, the relations of production, and the superstructure. Anything from machinery to art, from scientific knowledge to superstitious beliefs, from work institutions to political organizations, can be transmitted from one social formation to another.

These definitions allow us to advance several propositions about cultural diffusion. Whenever feasible, I will illustrate the propositions with historical examples.

First, cultural diffusion has been prevalent throughout human history. To appreciate this, one has only to think of the spread of cereal cultivation, industrial techniques, ancient Greek and Roman culture, Islamic ideas and institutions, the values of Western capitalism and so on. Cohen states:

> Every major technological advance in the course of cultural evolution—cultivation by means of a digging stick or hoe, plowing, terracing, large-scale centralized irrigation, domestication of large herds of animals, machines driven by steam or electricity—was discovered independently in a few places, but spread from its center of development to neighboring groups. This spread of technology continued until it was halted by a natural barrier.

He then surmises that "80 percent or more of the elements of any culture may have been borrowed from others."[3] Childe has recorded the rapid diffusion of the Neolithic (cereal) revolution and of the later urban (commerce and industry) revolution. Of the latter, he stated that

> once the new economy had been established in . . . [Egypt, Sumer, and India], it spread thence to secondary centers, much like Western capitalism spread to colonies and economic dependencies. First on the borders of Egypt, Babylonia, and the Indus valley—in Crete and the Greek Islands, Syria, Assyria, Iran, and Baluchistan—then further afield, on the Greek mainland, the Anatolian plateau, South Russia, we see villages converted into cities and self-sufficing food-producers turning to industrial specialization and external trade. And the process is repeated in ever-widening circles around each secondary and tertiary center.[4]

In the modern era, Peter the Great imported Western European technology as well as some of its culture into Russia. His "Grand Embassy" to Western Europe in 1697–1698 was undertaken for the purpose of learning that area's modern ways, and he later sent many Russian students to Western Europe to gather further information. Within a short time, Russia had imported not only industrial technology (in textiles, leather, glass, and so on) and agricultural novelties (for example, potatoes) but also new principles of military organization, Western dress (including the shaving of beards), Western European chronology, ideas about the more equal treatment of women, modern medical schools, newspapers, universities, museums, libraries, and much more.

Over a century later, continental Europe was busy "stealing" technical knowledge from England, which had initiated an industrial revolution in the latter half of the eighteenth century. The Continent imported textile and other technology, as well as British entrepreneurs, managers, and skilled workmen, even though for many years Britain erected barriers to prevent the overseas diffusion of much of its advanced technological knowledge.

In the latter half of the nineteenth century, Japan began to modernize along Western lines. The country imported technicians—but temporarily and warily—to build railroads, construct new plants, operate ships, and train local labor in industrial operations, such as in textiles, crude metallurgy, and shipbuilding. Thousands of Japanese students were sent abroad for study, and technical books and manuals by the hundreds were translated into Japanese. Eventually, Japan acquired not only a modern industrial structure but some of the West's relations of production and superstructural ingredients as well—in short, much of the capitalist mode of production.

However, most of these diffusions occurred over long periods of time—from several decades to several centuries. If sufficient time is allowed, a great deal can be diffused. Nevertheless, despite the dramatic examples cited above, much does not get diffused, even after a great deal of time. Western democracy, for example has not been widely accepted, nor has the Hindu cow cult. So while the above observations are interesting and useful in alerting us to the possibilities of cultural diffusion, they do not enable us to distinguish between those cultural elements that march around the world and those that stay at home.

Second, elements of culture have been disseminated throughout history by military conquest, commerce, population movements, missionary activity, and other forms of societal contacts. In this century, cultural diffusion has also occurred through the revolutionary victories of oppressed classes against their ruling classes, the former then introducing new cultural elements into their country. Recent examples include Cuba, Vietnam, Cambodia, Mozambique, and Ethiopia.

Third, the extent of a culture's diffusion depends mainly on the strength of its productive forces and, within these, of its military power. Such strength leads not only to military conquests but also to superior products and technology, as well as to population movements to and from the dominated areas. For example, the spread of United States culture around much of the world in recent decades emanates from the nuclear-military strength of the country, which is itself based on its powerful productive forces. One anthropologist has surmised that "a British gunboat on the Yangtze was often a far more potent ambassador or germinator of ideas than a visiting lecturer from Oxford."[5] Gerhard Lenski has generalized this thought by stating that

> while conscious choice is an important and distinctive feature of sociocultural selection . . . the fate of specific cultural patterns as well as entire cultural systems often depends on power struggles rather than on rational decision making. When this happens, it is military, political, or financial power that determines the outcome.[6]

He adds, however, that the basic determinant of intersocietal selection has been military power.[7] Raymond Firth has made the same point: "War is a great solvent of refractory social phenomena. Conquest thus paves the way for the spread of culture by the removal of the possibilities of active opposition to cultural change." However, Firth goes on to say:

> It must not be forgotten, though, that many passive forces of resistance still remain. . . . Only when [a new trait] can be adapted to the sum total of custom, belief, technique, and material apparatus by which people regulate their lives is it received and utilised by them as their own.[8]

Examples of cultural diffusion by military force are too well known to be more than mentioned. Consider, for example, imperial Rome's penetration of Europe and the eastern Mediterranean, the diffusion of Han and T'ang China's culture to the country's west and south, the spread of Muslim culture across north Africa and into Spain, Western Europe's colonial conquests around the world, and tsarist Russia's sweep to the Pacific.

The sword established the Alhambra in Granada, Roman roads in Britain, Confucian thought in Annam, and the English language in India.

Fourth, a primitive society (that is, a largely classless society with crude productive forces) threatened or invaded by a superior (stronger) foreign culture often responds by importing elements of that culture selectively and sequentially. In his study of the Europeanization of the New Zealand Maori, Raymond Firth concluded that elements of European culture were transfused over time in separate stages. In the first stage, the Maori accepted material goods—potatoes, steel tools, blankets, guns, flour. At the next stage, they acquired technical processes, including some material productive forces, which enabled them to produce some of the goods previously imported or, at least, to repair such goods. The third stage comprised the diffusion of forms of organization—modifications in the communal system of industry and in other social relations of production and exchange. In the final stage, the Maori accepted beliefs, values, and other institutions—that is, certain elements of the superstructure. Thus, material goods preceded technical processes, which preceded new organizational forms, and foreign values were the most difficult to assimilate. This sequence would seem to be the general rule in such cases.[9]

Fifth, if an advanced society (that is, one with a definite class structure) is encroached upon by an even more advanced society (with, say, superior productive forces and weapons), the former's oppressed classes (or intellectuals acting in their name) are more likely to import the ideology of the aggressor, while its ruling classes are more likely to absorb elements of the productive forces and perhaps some institutional reforms. That is to say, the initial reaction of the ruling classes is to import the stronger culture's weapons and related productive forces in order to defend their social, political, and economic privileges and the values and institutions on which these privileges depend. On the other hand, the ideology of a superior foreign culture is often used by the threatened country's lower classes or rebel groups in attempts to overthrow the ruling classes. While machinery and other productive forces may be welcomed by the ruling classes, they are sometimes smashed or otherwise sabotaged by the working class-es; on the other hand, foreign ideology is often shunned by the ruling classes and adopted by the lower classes. However, while these class reactions are typical, they are not invariable—for example, peasants are often extremely hostile to a foreign reli-gion. This is understandable, since peasants retain the values and ideology of their ruling classes until they can develop a rev-olutionary consciousness of their own.

The history of the impact of Europe on China demonstrates the manner in which the cultural diffusion of material objects and ideas can occur. The Jesuits' influence on China, which dates from the late 1500s, was technological rather than ideological; they influenced China's science more than its religion. While the Jesuits did, of course, introduce Western ideas into China—elements of mathematics, astronomy, religion, certain manufac-turing knowledge—they interested the Chinese upper classes primarily in material objects: military weapons, clocks, organs, telescopes, eyeglasses, maps, the calendar. "The early Jesuits introduced some ideas about labor-saving machines but they failed to rouse any general interest"—of a long list of newly imported goods only eyeglasses were actually imitated by Chinese artisans. European mechanics were brought into China, an in-termediate step between importing goods and manufacturing them locally.

> European mechanics [under Ch'ien-lung] were still employed to assemble and repair the clockworks and other devices brought from Europe, and several Jesuit missionaries served as architects of the buildings and landscape garden in Italian style which formed a part of the Old Summer Palace.[10]

From the 1840s to the end of the nineteenth century, a small group of Ch'ing officials set out to defend Chinese civilization through the selective adoption of Western devices and technol-ogy. In the 1840s, China began to translate books about Western countries, and over the next several decades it attempted to copy the West's cannon, gunboats, other military appurtenances, and paddle wheel ships. In the 1860s, the so-called self-strengthening movement began in earnest. It was broadened in the 1880s to include the adoption not only of Western technology but of many Western institutions. The movement's aim was to preserve the values of Chinese society by strengthening other elements. In the meantime, Chinese students were sent abroad to study the West. These efforts culminated in the Reform Movement of 1895–1898, in which a handful of bourgeois reformers sought to bring about revolutionary changes in Chinese political and economic institutions "from above." This group believed that China could become prosperous and strong only by adopting the science and technology of the West and by changing the political system into a constitutional monarchy. Many conservatives criticized the proposed reforms on the ground that Chinese learning and values could not be preserved in the face of a wholesale technological transformation. Techniques, it was said, affect values; means determine ends. The conservatives sought changes within the framework of Confucian values and the class structure associated with Ch'ing dynastic power. But the reformers, too, had no desire to see class structures upset; they simply believed that more drastic means were necessary to preserve them.

Many rebellious Chinese peasants have utilized foreign ideas as weapons against the ruling classes. Buddhism, Christianity, nationalism, and Marxism have been readily sinicized by the lower classes but scorned by their social superiors. Once the Chinese Communists gained victory with Marxist ideology, the way was cleared for the introduction of many other elements of foreign cultures, including new relations of production and foreign technology.

Sixth, if a militarily stronger culture, which is inferior in other respects, overruns another, the former is likely to accept many of the cultural elements of the latter. It was in this sense that the Chinese absorbed their conquerors, the Mongols and the Manchus. In the same way, the northern "barbarians" absorbed much of ancient Rome, and the crusaders much of the East.

Seventh, other things the same, cultural elements are more likely to be diffused the closer different cultures are to each other geographically. Thus, the Han Chinese greatly influenced their immediate neighbors but had virtually no influence around the Mediterranean. Even at the present time, the United States has a greater impact on Canada and Mexico than on Argentina or Greenland. The differential effect of proximity is largely owing to population movements between neighboring countries. Modern communications modify this principle but do not invalidate it.

Eighth, the incorporation of one element of a foreign culture is likely to affect other elements of the indigenous culture, which may weaken those elements and thereby force the importing country into further cultural borrowings. Firth stressed how each foreign import influenced other aspects of the Maori's culture:

> From consideration of the most outstanding changes in Maori economic life—the adoption of the potato and the pig, iron tools, clothing, and the musket—it has been proved that with the introduction of each of these objects was correlated far-reaching changes in tradition, technique, magical belief, social authority, and economic institutions.[11]

In the same way, the attempts of missionaries to abolish Maori slavery led to a decline in the chief's power and social standing (as his slaves disappeared), which caused a partial breakdown in authority structures and slovenliness in work. New technology reduced the need for magic, which diminished the status of a priestly group and so altered the economic organization of Maori society.

Finally, the degree to which imported elements of another culture are effective depends mainly on the degree of similarity between the two cultures' modes of production. That is to say, cultural diffusion between two dissimilar modes of production— say, socialist and feudal—is unlikely to be effective. It is easier for cultural diffusion to occur, other things the same, when the two modes are alike, as are those of China and Cuba or of the United States and Brazil. While most cultural elements die when transplanted to an alien environment and many survive transplantation to more hospitable environments, the latter are nevertheless reshaped by their new soil. For example, Japanese capitalism is not exactly anybody else's capitalism, and Chinese Marxism is not at all the same as Russian or European Marxism.

To summarize the highlights. Cultural diffusion is certainly possible, but it has often occurred by virtue of the exporting country's powerful productive forces and, within these, of its military might. Even when supported by these, many cultural elements are not widely disseminated. Diffusion is more likely to occur between cultures having similar modes of production, but in cases of dissimilarity the different classes in the absorbing culture will frequently import different elements of the foreign culture. In any event, the acceptance by a society of one component of a foreign culture is likely to affect other areas of its own culture, and each cultural transplant tends to be reshaped by its new soil.

The Chinese Model of Economic Development

What is China's style of economic development? The answer is complex because China's system of economic development has undergone almost constant change since 1949 and is still changing. For much of the 1950s, it was akin to the Stalinist model, which stressed heavy industry over light industry, industry over agriculture, investment over consumption, urban areas over rural areas, the primacy of material productive forces, and the advantages of tight centralized planning. Mao and his followers began to depart from this model as early as 1955; the Great Leap Forward (1958–1959) was their emphatic assertion of independence from it. Although the Great Leap ended in near disaster, China did not return to its previous model, but instead, under pressure, adopted something in between the Stalinist-Soviet and Maoist versions of development. On the Maoist side (though also on the side of necessity), policies of the early 1960s emphasized more than formerly the agricultural and consumer sectors—food crops, rural industry to serve agriculture, and light industry to serve consumers. On the Stalinist-Soviet side, policies crept into the development program that favored individual incentives over collective incentives, economic concerns over political concerns, gradual processes over "leap" processes (the former approved not by Stalin but by his successors), and experts and technicians over the politicized masses. One immediate effect of the offensive launched by the Maoists during the Cultural Revolution (1966–1969) was to reverse to some extent the direction taken by Stalinist-Soviet policies and to deepen and extend the Maoist policies. However, the 1970s have witnessed a partial retreat by the Maoists from their most advanced positions, attained shortly after the Cultural Revolution.

Consequently, *the* Chinese system of economic development is difficult to identify, not only because it has changed so radically over time, but also because it prevails today as an amalgam of an ongoing struggle between at least two opposing forces—those favoring the Maoist program and those opposing it, in whole or in part. China presents us, therefore, with past and present amalgamated models, a purer Maoist model, a purer Stalinist-Soviet model, and a potential model that may transcend the present one and can perhaps be discerned in it. Which of these models is the most relevant for possible diffusion to other underdeveloped countries? The answer is uncertain because different people see China through different eyes and are impressed by different things. However, the set of development policies actually carried out in China since the Cultural Revolution has drawn much commendation from the third world. It is this set of policies that I shall take as the Chinese model.

What is this model? It should first be noted that the relations of production in China are socialist, which means that the proletariat has political power (the Communist Party acting as the vanguard of the proletariat) and that the major means of production are owned collectively by various segments of the proletariat, extending from the nation down to production brigades and teams—that is, from fully socialist forms down to small cooperatives. Furthermore, in keeping with the tenets of socialism, the current Chinese system includes a heavy measure of economic planning, in which major decisions are made by planning authorities (national and local) rather than by the market outcomes of many individual actions. Within this socialist framework, the Chinese have achieved in the past several years high levels of employment, reasonably good rates of output growth, and little inflationary pressure. These accomplishments, in view of recent economic downturns elsewhere in the world, have raised the prestige of the Chinese system.

In addition, China has had above-average success in population planning. Birthrates have apparently fallen markedly owing to the success of continuing programs—themselves based on mass movements—urging postponement of marriage for several years, making contraceptives available throughout the country, providing free abortions, and endorsing sterilization. The Chinese have also carried out a health-care program that has attracted much attention. The most notable achievement here in recent years has been in the countryside, where tens of thousands of barefoot doctors, midwives, and health workers provide environmental sanitation, health education, immunizations, first aid, and the treatment of the most prevalent diseases and injuries. In the cities, "Red Medical Workers" and "worker doctors" provide similar services.

A widely noted facet of China's development effort is the extent to which economic equality among the nation's families has been attained. This has resulted principally from the fact that the major means of production are no longer privately owned; incomes from the private ownership of property are neither substantial nor highly concentrated. In addition, most families have access to the essential goods and services, including food, clothing, housing, primary education, medical care, and cultural and recreational facilities. Furthermore, in the countryside some income is distributed according to basic needs rather than work done. Retired workers receive pensions totaling 70 percent of their previous pay. Although wage rate differentials prevail, and are occasionally substantial, they are modest in the rural areas where most people live and for the large majority of workers in urban industries.

Individual (or family) and material incentives still dominate the workplace, but the Maoists have been persistent in encouraging collective endeavors that return benefits to the group generally and in promoting hard work partly through "revolutionary fervor" rather than entirely through promises of material gains. Since 1969, the Chinese have energetically advanced rural industrialization, which ordinarily features small-scale firms using labor-intensive methods, local supplies of raw materials, and local labor. To a significant extent, China's efforts have focused on rural communes and especially counties as basic economic units for the development of agriculture, industry, education, medical care, and culture and recreation. These units have been called upon to develop self-reliance—that is, to keep the initiative in their own hands and to do as much as possible on the basis of their own resources.

China's economic model is not only Marxist-socialist but Chinese as well. It is Chinese in the sense that many of its features reflect the distinctive cultural traditions of the Chinese people—for example, the high value placed on education and literacy, a dialectical outlook on life derived from Buddhism and Taoism, kinship and communal loyalties, and a drive to achieve.[12] It is also Chinese in the sense that China is an unusual country: it is much larger than the average, possesses ample natural resources, and has the largest population of any nation in the world. Thus, China is a country with distinctive (nonreproducible) cultural, demographic, and geographic features.

These, then, are the characteristics of what may be called the *general* Chinese model of economic development—the features of China's actual development efforts since the Cultural Revolution.

This general model shares several key elements with the Stalinist-Soviet model: nationalization of industry, central planning, large-scale cooperative agriculture, and reliance on the internal generation of saving for domestic capital formation. In addition, both China and the Soviet Union are large in area and population, and both possess rich natural resources—characteristics that may make them less suitable as models for the smaller, poorly endowed nations.

There are features, however, that distinguish the Chinese model from that of the Soviet Union. While these features have already been included in the discussion of the general Chinese model, it will be useful to gather them together here in what we may call the *distinctive* Chinese model. Compared to the Stalinist-Soviet model, this model includes: (1) a greater emphasis on the economic development of rural areas, in which communes, small industries, and high priorities for agriculture figure prominently; (2) a greater encouragement of decentralized development and planning carried out within the context of local self-reliance; (3) a more egalitarian outlook that seeks to reduce economic and social differentials throughout the society; (4) a greater emphasis on moral, nonmaterial, and collective work incentives—on politics over economics; (5) a greater reliance on politicized mass movements, which help to formulate and implement policies—the mass line; and (6) a strategy of economic development through struggle, dialectical movement, and leaps rather than through gradual, orderly, straight-line, planned methods.

China's Model and Developing Countries

Can any elements of China's model, especially the distinctive ones, be effectively transmitted to other countries? The earlier part of this paper proposed that, while international diffusions are common, they are more readily made between cultures with similar modes of production, unless force is employed. Specifically, components of China's model are most likely to be diffused effectively only to countries with socialist modes of production. This would seem to limit the potential use of that model to a narrow group of countries. The widespread diffusion of the techniques of Maoist economic development apparently awaits sweeping socialist victories around the world. But many, if not most, of these revolutionary movements might be inspired by Maoist ideology.

According to this view, the Chinese model's major impact on much of the world over the near term is likely to be in the reshaping of the ideology of workers and peasants. As one author recently expressed this: "If China cannot be taken as a model for development by the peasant societies of the underdeveloped world, then it is the more likely that she will be taken as a model for revolution."[13] Indeed, Mao has made the point that guerrilla warfare is not only necessary for the seizure of political power but is also essential training for the later carrying out of socialist economic development. In sum, this view is that, so far as many poor countries are concerned, the most relevant and immediate Chinese model is that of revolutionary tactics and strategy by peasants and workers rather than that of economic development.

But is a socialist revolution really necessary before a developing country can utilize the Chinese economic model? Can poor countries with feudal, dependent-capitalist, or other modes of production effectively utilize some elements of the model? I think that the answer is a highly qualified yes (or a lightly qualified no). It is best, I believe, to begin with the qualifications—that is, with the difficulties of transplanting socialist components into alien environments.

It is often thought that the persistence of poverty stems from the inability of national leaders to solve unusually difficult problems, from their lack of technical knowledge or perhaps from their obstinacy in the face of good advice.[14] The problem is certainly not viewed as their lack of desire for economic development and the elimination of poverty. However, this approach does not take adequate account of the class structures of societies, the often conflicting aims that exist among the various classes, and the class nature of "success" and "failure." When poverty is looked at from the standpoint of ruling classes, it may not be a failure at all but rather a prerequisite for their accumulation of wealth, their privileges, and their social, political, and economic domination.

This is partly because poverty is often the carcass left from the acquisition of wealth or, at best, the stagnant backwaters of society, as yet untouched by a development process that stresses private profitmaking and hence efficiency and "building on the best." But poverty also persists because it is closely associated with peasant characteristics which are highly supportive of the privileges and wealth of the existing upper classes. I refer to the peasants' illiteracy, passivity, obedience, fatalism; to their lack of awareness of the world at large and, therefore, their propensity to blame themselves for misfortunes or to turn to mythical and spiritual explanations of social hardships and disasters; to their lack of organization, their willingness to work hard for very little; to their being setups for all sorts of manipulation.

A widespread, thoroughgoing program of economic development, which reaches deeply into the structure of society, endangers the ruling classes, for it tends to eliminate the very qualities of the masses of people that nourish the wealthy and powerful. Such a program awakens people, and for the ruling classes it is often best that they doze; it mobilizes people for immense economic efforts, and such organization can be turned to political subversion; it sweeps away people's illusions and thus may open their eyes to the causes of their oppression.

Furthermore, any serious economic-development program that involves industrialization within an agrarian and commercial society threatens existing class structures by creating new economic bases from which new social classes arise, weakening the economic foundations that support the present dominant classes. Economic development stirs up a society, fashioning new classes that compete with the old order, socially, politically, and economically.

There is often, therefore, an almost complete lack of interest by ruling classes and foreign investors in pressing for an economic-development effort that would so strengthen the poor as to threaten a society's class structures. Peasants remain poor not only because of the inherent difficulties of eliminating poverty but also because poverty serves a purpose—or, at least, it does not interfere with the wealthier classes' extraction of economic surpluses from the countryside. Consequently, a major difficulty of transplanting elements of China's economic model to some underdeveloped countries is that, despite the lip service paid to development, there is no serious purpose behind the flow of words.

There are other difficulties as well. A few elements severed from the model as a whole may wither and die in hostile surroundings. For example, the proliferation of small rural industries in China depended on the general acceptance of goals other than mere profits and efficiency (among them, the goal of building diversified and pleasant rural communities). This acceptance, in turn, was based on the prior inculcation of socialist (Maoist) values throughout the society, values which were reinforced by the previous establishment of socialist institutions, including rural communes. These socialist institutions could be created only after the destruction of the old class structures, and that required a revolution. It is therefore likely that a rural-industrialization program in an underdeveloped country that lives and works by other, incongruent values would be limited (though not eliminated) by short-term profit considerations and by the program's potentially adverse effects on the migration of cheap rural labor into urban-industrial centers, its threat to the landlords' labor supply, and its unfavorable effects on the profits of foreign manufacturers ensconced in the larger industrial centers.

In the same way, a "Chinese program" aimed at stimulating work motivation requires, as a prior condition, that people, by virtue of literacy, health and nutrition, and training, be able to work hard and long. It also requires a leadership of cadres who set a good example for the masses. It should, in addition, establish goals that people consider inspiring, worthy of their best efforts. And it should mobilize people to realize those goals. But all of this presupposes a peasantry that is not exploited to the point of ignorance and resignation. On the contrary a Chinese program postulates rural institutions, such as cooperatives and schools, that stimulate and reinforce the rational behavior of peasants and all efforts to enhance the quality of their lives. These institutional prerequisites may conflict with the interests of the privileged.

Similarly, the success that Communist China has had in designing a development program that equitably distributes the burdens and the rewards of growth could not easily be duplicated within a dissimilar social formation. An equitable distribution of burdens necessitates the absence of exploitative social relations. An equitable distribution of income, of the fruits of economic growth, presupposes that the ownership of urban and rural wealth is not narrowly concentrated in private hands, that wage and salary differentials are not distended, that unemployment and underemployment are not grave problems, that large economic differences do not exist between rural and urban areas, and that the basic services of health care, education, and retirement are distributed generously among the population. But few if any of these conditions have been met in many underdeveloped countries—and not simply because they are too expensive or too difficult to obtain, but rather because they would interfere with the ruling classes' extraction of surplus value from the system. Thus, if industrial profits depend on continuing supplies of cheap labor from rural areas; if the franchises of the upper classes rest on large income flows from private holdings; if the values of society require private monetary payments for harder and longer work (and, hence, broad wage differentials); if welfare programs dampen work incentives because such incentives are overwhelmingly pecuniary; if unemployment and underemployment provide bargaining advantages and production flexibility to a propertied class—then inequalities will serve positive functions in a society. In such a milieu, the Chinese program would not have much of a chance.

I think that the same reasoning applies to programs to achieve high levels of employment in the Chinese manner. Although China continues to have some, perhaps substantial, *under*employment, it has managed in the last decade to provide employment of some type for just about everyone, including a growing proportion of women and young people. In this respect, China has become a paragon among the developing countries, almost all of which suffer from serious labor idleness. China has in the main solved these problems by operating the economy at near-maximum levels; by providing rural employment for tens of millions of potentially unemployed city youth; by increasing job opportunities in rural industries, education, health care, cultural activities, administration, and large-scale public works (water control projects, reforestation, road building, and so on); by designing labor-intensive methods of production wherever feasible; by using millions of people to develop frontier territories and virgin lands; and by establishing a social and economic environment that allows comfortable retirement and reduces the need to engage in parasitic activities—vagrancy, begging, gambling, stealing, extorting.

Could these programs be undertaken successfully in a developing country with propertied classes and profit-oriented goals? Much of the previous reasoning about the function of cheap labor applies here as well. In addition, the accumulation process in capitalist countries is subject to wide swings of optimism and pessimism, and hence to wide variations in employment levels. Furthermore, private profitmaking often avoids labor-intensive methods, if only because large labor forces, when in antagonistic relationships with employers and managers, are less reliable, less predictable, and more volatile than machines. Also, in a private-enterprise economy, in which much of the total product goes to a few property owners, the amount per worker of what is left over is often very low, and labor's marginal product is even lower, often below minimum subsistence. Thus any subsistence wage would find many workers unemployed. Such unemployment is the necessary by-product of the concentrated private appropriation of surplus value plus the payment of a wage rate that is at minimum subsistence for the workers.[15] Again, some of China's programs (for example, moving millions of people from cities to rural areas) require a widespread acceptance of Maoist ideology, including the party's goals and methods, and the values and behavior patterns it wishes society to approve. These programs could be copied only with the greatest difficulty in societies with intense class struggles or with ignorant masses who are only barely conscious of their society's potentials.

China's successes in many other areas, too, come from sources deeply embedded in its Chinese-socialist society. For example, the programs to reduce population growth have depended on a transformation of peasant attitudes, which itself was the result of radical changes in the country's socioeconomic conditions. The family planning efforts have also enlisted the Communists' mass-line campaigns, in which, as Leo Orleans recently said, "everyone is expected to be involved in the new ideology and habit of 'practicing birth control for the revolution.'"[16] The Chinese have been particularly imaginative in the areas of motivation and education, but, as Orleans added, "it is difficult to imagine China's saturation approach to family planning attempted in any other society." Orleans does not believe that

China's experience in this area is transferable: "As for the value of China's model for developing countries, the answer in every field of development has become almost a cliché and holds true for family planning as well: China's experience is not transferable— but there is much to be learned from it." [17] I would clarify this by saying that the ruling classes in many countries of the third world could not, and would not, utilize China's experience but that the oppressed classes in many Third World countries have much to learn from it.

Similarly in the area of health care. The health of the Chinese people has improved markedly since 1949—so much so that two experts in social medicine have recently stated that "a case can be made for China's having made more rapid progress in health than any other society in a comparable period of time." [18] This, they say, has been accomplished "through a combination of improvements in nutrition, in living conditions, in sanitation, in preventive medicine, in health education, and in medical care" [19]—but these changes required a party and government dedicated to the welfare of workers and peasants, which in turn necessitated an upheaval in the structure of political control, which itself had roots in at least a quarter-century of revolutionary peasant movements. Moreover, success has depended on the Communists' methods of mass participation, decentralization, deprofessionalization (barefoot doctors, worker doctors, and Red Medical Workers), and ruralization.

Thus it would seem that many, perhaps most, of the important elements of China's economic model could not be easily integrated into dissimilar social formations. This is also the opinion of Lloyd Reynolds, who recently stated:

> It would be overly facile, however, to conclude that Chinese experience provides lessons readily transferable to other LDCs [less-developed countries]. Economic policies cannot be wrenched out of the political and social context from which they have emerged. China did, after all, have a full-scale revolution. The willingness of the population to accept sustained hard work plus austerity in consumption, while it may in part be traditionally Chinese, depends also on a quasi-religious devotion to Maoist doctrine. [20]

Donald Keesing has also recently noted many of the unique or distinctive features of China's development efforts, summarizing his findings as follows:

> The [economic lessons from China] . . . would not be easy to apply elsewhere. A majority of these lessons appear transplantable only to socialist countries with goals and values somewhat like China's. . . . Thus, there may be little scope for borrowing from China without wholesale reforms of institutions and revisions of priorities in controversial directions. Even under favorable conditions it is risky to assume that what works in China would work when transplanted to another country. China is unique in many ways—traditions, size, ideology, the regime's political assets, and so on—so that some features appear impossible to duplicate elsewhere.[21]

However, Keesing then proceeds in a more positive way to determine the extent to which China's economic lessons are in fact diffusible. He believes that elements of China's model are exportable to nations whose cultures subordinate individualism to group interests; that China's relatively narrow income differentials supplemented by moral incentives can be widely imitated; that its method of group decision-making "should not prove hard to transfer to other countries because it is not uniquely Chinese in the first place"; that China's policies of stable prices without heavy excess demands can certainly be transferred to other socialist countries; that most developing countries can give the highest priority to agriculture, as the Chinese have; and that China's emphasis on small rural industries can be applied, though perhaps with difficulty, by other countries.[22]

Except for a few references to Cuba, an oblique mention of Yugoslavia, and a sweeping allusion to Asian and African countries in general, Keesing does not specify which countries of the world would be most receptive to components of the Chinese model. Without this perspective, many elements of the model seem readily diffusible; with this perspective, as we shall now see, the matter is not so clear.

Leaving China aside, at present around twenty countries, with 13 percent of the world's population (1970), can be called Marxist-socialist. (See Table 8.1 for these and the following data.)

Table 8.1
Some Characteristics of the World's Countries

Number of countries	Percentage of the world's 1970 population		Characteristics
1 (China)	21%		Marxist-socialist
20+	12		Marxist-socialist*
24	19		Industrial-capitalist†
120	48		Non-Marxist developing
7		27	Over 45 million population‡
10		8	20–45 million population§
100+		13	Under 20 million population‖
33	29		Industrial
130+	71		Agrarian

* Marxist-socialist: China, USSR, Eastern Europe (8), Indochina (3), Mongolia, Cuba, North Korea, Angola, Mozambique, Guinea-Bissau, Somalia, People's Republic of Benin, Cape Verde, People's Democratic Republic of Yemen.
† Industrial-capitalist: United States, Canada, Australia, New Zealand, Japan, Western Europe (14), Puerto Rico, Hong Kong, Singapore, Israel, South Africa.
‡ 7 developing: India, Pakistan, Bangladesh, Indonesia, Nigeria, Brazil, Mexico.
§ 10 developing: Egypt, South Korea, Philippines, Thailand, Turkey, Argentina, Burma, Colombia, Ethiopia, Iran.
‖ 100+ developing: the remaining countries of Asia, Africa, Latin America, and other areas.

One such country is the USSR, which is not likely to go the Chinese way in the near future; aside from the USSR, only 6 percent of the world's population is left in this category, and many of these people are in Eastern European countries under Soviet hegemony. Of the other Marxist-socialist countries, several are heavily influenced by the USSR and hence not in a position to accept distinctively Chinese methods. The Marxist-socialist countries which either have been or might be favorably influenced by the Chinese model—Albania, Laos, Cambodia, Vietnam, and perhaps North Korea—have no more than 2 percent of the world's population. (Cuba, although under Soviet sway, has responded to certain of China's charms.) But perhaps only one or two of these countries are certain soldiers in the Chinese camp.

Another twenty-five countries or so, with 19 percent of the world's population, are industrial-capitalist nations. Although a few of these have strong Communist parties (Japan, France, and Italy), and two others (the city-states of Hongkong and Singapore) have heavy Chinese populations, it is most unlikely that much, if anything, of the distinctive Chinese model is diffusible into such alien industrial territory. Italy would seem to be the only industrial-capitalist nation that might (and this is only a slim possibility), in the near future, be hospitable to certain parts of China's development design. But it is a better bet that the Soviet Union will become the dominant force there, and indeed may come to have a broader influence if the Latin European countries of France, Italy, Portugal, and Spain all turn to communism. China is too remote culturally and geographically from this region to be able to exert controlling influence.

Approximately 120 countries may be described as the non-Marxist underdeveloped countries; these have 48 percent of the world's population. Seven of them have large populations (over 45 million), ten have medium populations (20–45 million), and more than one hundred have small populations (under 20 million). Of the seven large countries, India, Pakistan, Bangladesh, and Indonesia could accept some elements of the general Chinese model (for example, economic planning, nationalization of industry, and some aspects of family planning and health care), but in view of their class structures and their dependent relationships to one or another of the superpowers, they are hardly in a position to import the distinctive Chinese model. Still, these countries, and especially India, have often been considered the countries "ripest" for the Chinese model. This is largely because—like China—they are Asian, poor, and large. But the characteristics they share with China are not sufficient to make these lands congenial to the Chinese way. "Ripest" has sometimes been used to mean "closest to a Chinese-type revolution." This, of course, would be another matter, and it has little bearing on the present issue. Brazil, Mexico, and Nigeria are even less plausible candidates, owing to their distance from China, their markedly different cultures, their exploitative class structures, and their close relationship to international capital. These characteristics need not, of course, prevent them from importing a few elements of the Chinese model, but, as I have argued, a Chinese element or two might not survive such alien environments. Consequently, although the potential of the Chinese model might be large within this group of countries, it seems farfetched to expect them to do more than reform some of their programs in the light of China's successes.

Among the ten medium-sized countries, the Asian nations of Burma, Thailand, South Korea, and the Philippines would certainly be more receptive to China's model than the others, with the possible near-future exception of Ethiopia. However, none of these nations is in the position of, say, Cambodia to follow the Chinese path of development; Burma, it would seem, comes closest. Only a handful of the one hundred or so small countries are capable of being significantly influenced by China's economic experience: Tanzania, Zambia, Sri Lanka, and perhaps in the near future (though this is doubtful), Peru, Algeria, Iraq, and Uganda. But even some of these are more under Soviet than Chinese influence.

Thus I would guess that, under present conditions, no more than twelve to fifteen countries might be hospitable to the Chinese model of development or to a large number of its components. Most of these countries, naturally enough, are in Asia, and some of them are already Marxist-socialist countries. All in all, I do not think there is much immediate global scope for the diffusion of what is distinctly Maoist in the Chinese model, given the strength and dominance of the two superpowers throughout most of the world and the absence of Chinese military power outside China. As I have noted, any rife diffusion of the Chinese model would probably have to come in the wake of sweeping revolutionary movements, which, however, might be heartened by Maoist ideology.

So I close on the Marxian theme that has guided me throughout these chapters: not criticism but revolution is the driving force of history.

Notes

1. Yehudi Cohen, "Culture as Adaptation," in Cohen, ed., *Man in Adaptation: The Cultural Present* (Chicago: Aldine, 1974), p. 46.
2. Ibid., p. 45.
3. Ibid., p. 50.
4. V. Gordon Childe, *Man Makes Himself* (New York: New American Library, 1951), p. 136.
5. Francis L. K. Hsu, *Americans and Chinese* (Garden City, N.Y.: Natural History Press, 1970), p. 388.
6. Gerhard Lenski, *Human Societies* (New York: McGraw-Hill, 1970), p. 68.
7. Ibid., p. 91.
8. Raymond Firth, *Economics of the New Zealand Maori* (Wellington, New Zealand: R. E. Owen, Government Printer, 1959), pp. 433–34.
9. For a short discussion of Firth's findings, see Bert F. Hoselitz, "Advanced and Underdeveloped Countries: A Study in Development Contrasts," in William B. Hamilton, ed., *The Transfer of Institutions* (Durham, N.C.: Duke University Press, 1964), pp. 28–29.
10. Ssu-yü Teng and J. K. Fairbank, *China's Response to the West* (Cambridge, Mass.: Harvard University Press, 1954), p. 18.
11. Firth, *New Zealand Maori*, p. 490.
12. For a discussion of most of these features, see Dwight H. Perkins, "Introduction: The Persistence of the Past," in Perkins, ed., *China's Modern Economy in Historical Perspective* (Stanford, Calif.: Stanford University Press, 1975), pp. 1–18. I have refrained from developing this topic at any greater length, though it is a very important one. For more, see Donald J. Munro, *The Concept of Man in Early China* (Stanford, Calif.: Stanford University Press, 1969), and Wei-ming Tu, "The Neo-Confucian Concept of Man," *Philosophy East & West*, January 1971.
13. Neville Maxwell, introduction to "China's Road to Development," in *World Development*, July-August 1975, p. 454.
14. The following five paragraphs are based on my "Rural Development in China, 1949–1972, and the Lessons to Be Learned from It," *World Development*, July-August 1975, pp. 456–57. That article also appears in Edgar O. Edwards, ed., *Employment in Developing Nations* (New York: Columbia University Press, 1974) and as Chapter 5 of this volume.

15. This is a point made by Donald B. Keesing, "Economic Lessons From China," mimeographed, pp. 7–8.
16. Leo A. Orleans, "China's Experience in Population Control: The Elusive Model," *World Development*, July-August 1975, p. 517.
17. Ibid., p. 525.
18. Victor W. Sidel and Ruth Sidel, "The Development of Health Care Services in the People's Republic of China," *World Development*, July-August 1975, p. 539.
19. Ibid., p. 549.
20. Lloyd Reynolds, "China as a Less Developed Economy," *American Economic Review*, June 1975, p. 247.
21. Keesing, "Economic Lessons," pp. 1–2.
22. Ibid., pp. 10, 19, 29, 38, 42, 49–50.